The Media Society:
Basic Issues
and
Controversies

by

ROSS A. EAMAN, Ph. D.

.Butterworths
Toronto and Vancouver

The Media Society: Basic Issues and Controversies

Printed and bound in Canada.

The Butterworth Group of Companies

Canada:
Butterworths, Toronto and Vancouver
United Kingdom:
Butterworth & Co. (Publishers) Ltd., London and Edinburgh
Australia:
Butterworths Pty Ltd., Sydney, Melbourne, Brisbane, Adelaide and Perth
New Zealand:
Butterworths (New Zealand) Ltd., Wellington and Auckland
Singapore:
Butterworth & Co. (Asia) Pte. Ltd., Singapore
South Africa:
Butterworth Publishers (SA) (Pty) Ltd., Durban and Pretoria
United States:
Butterworth Legal Publishers, Boston, Seattle, Austin and St. Paul
D & S Publishers, Clearwater

Canadian Cataloguing in Publication Data

Eaman, Ross Allan, 1945-
  The media society

Includes bibliographical references and index.
ISBN 0-409-81034-7

1. Mass media. 2. Mass media policy.   I. Title.

P90.E25 1987   302.2'34   C87-093239-X

Quotations on p. 11 reproduced from *The Human Use of Human Beings* by Norbert Wiener. Copyright 1950, 1954 by Norbert Wiener. Copyright © renewed 1977 by Margaret Wiener. Reprinted by permission of Houghton Mifflin Company.

Executive Editor (P. & A.): Lebby Hines
Sponsoring Editor: Janet Turner
Managing Editor: Linda Kee
Supervisory Editor: Marie Graham
Editor: Priscilla Darrell
Cover Design: Patrick Ng
Production: Jill Thomson
Typesetting & assembly: Computer Composition of Canada, Inc.

For Pat and T.

Foreword

Several years ago I attended a convocation at Carleton University at which Dr. Albert Trueman, formerly the President of the University of New Brunswick and by then a retired professor of English, received an honourary degree. In his remarks, Dr. Trueman drew attention to the differences between the peasant of medieval Europe and the citizen of the modern world. He suggested that the mind of the peasant was radically limited in its perception of both space and time. Lacking printed publications such as books and newspapers as well as means of transportation such as motorized vehicles, he could only learn what was communicated to him directly and could only travel as far as his limbs or a horse could convey him. Dr. Trueman asked his audience to imagine what life would be like without books or, by implication, the telecommunications systems which now envelope the globe. He asked us to consider the differences in our psychological composition, our culture, and the nature and content of the information and knowledge with which we conduct our lives. In short, he reminded us that we tend to take for granted advances in communication which have been centuries in the making.

As a result of these advances, we now live in what might be called a media society; that is, a society in which the institutions and processes of mass communication are a defining characteristic. What this means in the first instance is that there has been a tremendous increase in the scope and magnitude of media activities. For example, five million Canadians watched the first part of "Anne of Green Gables", aired by the CBC in December of 1985. (Adilman, 1985: B1) More than 12 million Canadians watched the second game of the 1972 hockey series between Canada and the Soviet Union. (Scanlon, 1976: 104) In the summer of 1985, over 1.5 billion people watched the "Aid for Africa" concert performed on stages in London and Philadelphia. (Goldberg, 1985: 24) At such times, there does indeed seem to be what Marshall McLuhan called the global village.

More revealing statistics for an initial portrait of the media society consist of the domestic circulations of newspapers and the aggregate audiences for radio and television. In 1983 Canada's 112 daily newspapers had an aggregate weekly circulation of 31,564,458. (Editor and Publisher, 1984: 5) (Sunday and weekend papers had an additional circulation of 4,803,562.) According to the 1981 Royal Commission on Newspapers, adult Canadians devote an average of 53 minutes per day to newspapers during the week and 66 minutes on the weekend. (Canada, 1981: 34-5) In 1983 there were 117 originating television stations and 755 AM and 673 FM radio stations in Canada. (Southam, 1984: 9) About 99 per cent of Canadian households are equipped with radios and 98 per cent with television sets. (CRTC, 1984: 5, 14) Each Canadian listens to an average of 18.4 hours of radio and watches 24 hours of television each week. (CRTC, 1984: 5)

Comparable media penetration has occurred in other Western countries. For example, in Britain there were 120 daily and Sunday newspapers and another thousand weeklies serving its population of 65 million in 1983. The 10 major national newspapers had an aggregate daily circulation of 14.8 million; the circulation of the regional dailies was about seven million and that of the Sunday papers 17.7 million. It is estimated that three out of four persons over the age of 15 read a national morning paper every day. (Central Office of Information, 1984: 360-2) About 99 per cent of British homes have at least one television set. In 1983 the average viewing time per week per capita was 20 hours, 22 minutes for television and 10 hours, 3 minutes for radio. (Central Office of Information, 1984: 368, 370; British Broadcasting Corporation, 1984: 4, 44)

In the United States, there were 1,701 daily newspapers with an aggregate daily circulation of 62,644,603 in 1983. (Editor and Publisher, 1984: 5) There were 831 commercial and 283 educational television stations. (Newspaper Enterprise Association, 1985: 428) At least 99 per cent of American homes had at least one television set, and over 80 per cent of these sets were in colour. Sets were found to be turned on for almost 51 hours a week or more than seven hours a day. (Quigley, 1985: 10a) There were also 9,320 radio stations and 470 million radios in the United States in 1983. (CRTC, 1984: 14; Broadcasting Publications, 1984: A2)

These figures illustrate the physical presence of the mass media in our daily lives. However, they do not tell us what it means to live in a media society. This was implicitly what Dr. Trueman invited us to consider. To understand the media society in which we live, we need much more than a description of technologies of communication from the printing press to satellites and the audiences which have grown in their wake. We also need an analysis of the political, economic, and social factors that govern the operation of these technologies, as well as an account of their effects on human behaviour, culture, and politics. For example, it is essential that we know the extent to which the news media determine the results of elections, the effects on children of dramatized violence on television, the role the state ought to play in fostering national culture, and so forth.

As we probe into these things, it becomes clear that the mass media are a basic element of the social system. Like education or the state, they are a primary institution in modern society. In the final analysis, this is what is meant by the term media society. The media are a fundamental component of modern society in that they are in the foreground of human experience and actively shape our patterns of behaviour. This does not necessarily entail that other institutions such as the family and religion are less important now than they once were (although some theorists have made this claim). Nor does it follow that these institutions are less worthy of sustained study. But what it does entail is that the study of the media is essential for understanding modern society.

Once we move beyond empirical descriptions of media technologies and audiences, it becomes apparent that there is no single account of the nature and dynamics of the media society upon which scholars are agreed. Rather, there are numerous and often conflicting theories and interpretations of how the media operate and with what effects. In many cases, these have been inspired and influenced by concrete developments involving the mass media. For example, concern about the propaganda techniques used by the Axis and Allied powers during the First and Second World Wars motivated a number of social scientists to study mass communication in the 1930s and 1940s. (Schramm, 1983: 6, 7) In the 1950s, further interest in the mass media was stimulated by the exploitation of the press by the American Senator Joseph McCarthy in his campaign against communism at the height of the Cold War. Of even greater importance was the advent of television, which led to a fundamental change in "the common symbolic environment involving directly, constantly, and systematically, though not of course uniformly, all who grew up in the new culture." (Gerbner, 1983: 360) Television not only added a new layer to the media society but turned the investigation of it into a recognized field of enquiry.

Canadian contributions to this field have been partly inspired by a preoccupation with the development and integrity of the nation. For Canada is largely an achievement in communication. From the building of the CPR to the creation of the English and French networks of the CBC, Canadians have engineered some of the world's largest communications systems. From the pioneering studies of Harold Innis to the present day, Canadian scholars have sought to understand the communications requirements for maintaining an independent Canada in the face of the massive message-making technologies south of the border.

The fact that there is not a single intellectual vision governing media studies, in Canada or elsewhere, will become clear to readers of *The Media Society*. It demonstrates the extent to which debate and controversy permeate the field. What do we mean by the term communication? What are we actually exposed to when we read, listen to, or watch the news? To what extent should the state control the information and ideas that are circulated by the media? On these and other fundamental issues there is not a consensus, even within societies sharing democratic values. But this should not be a cause for cynicism or dismay. The media society is complex and it resists easy explanation.

G. Stuart Adam
September, 1986

References

Adilman, S.
    1985 "Green Gables Movie Delighted 4,908,000 Viewers."
        The Toronto Star (December 18): B1.
British Broadcasting Corporation
    1984 *BBC Annual Report and Handbook 1984*. London: BBC.
Broadcasting Publications
    1984 *Broadcasting/Cablecasting Yearbook 1984*.
        Washington: Broadcasting Publications.
Canada
    1981 *Royal Commission on Newspapers, Report*.
        Hull: Ministry of Supply and Services.
Central Office of Information
    1984 *Britain 1984*. London: Her Majesty's Stationary Office.
Canadian Radio-television and Telecommunications Commission
    1984 *CRTC Facts Digest*. Ottawa: CRTC.
Editor and Publisher
    1984 *International Yearbook 1984*. New York: Editor and Publisher.
Gerbner, George
    1983 "The Importance of Being Critical – in One's Own Fashion."
        Journal of Communication 33 (no. 1): 355-62.

Goldberg, Michael
  1985 "The Day the World Rocked." *Rolling Stone*
         (August 15): 23-24.
Independent Broadcasting Authority
  1984 *Television and Radio 1985*. London: IBA.
McLuhan, Marshall
  1964 *Understanding Media*. New York: McGraw-Hill.
Newspaper Enterprise Association
  1985 *The World Almanac and Book of Facts*.
         New York: Newspaper Enterprise Association
Quigley Publishing
  1985 *1985 International Television Almanac*. New York: Quigley.
Scanlon, T. Joseph
  1976 "The Not So Mass Media: The Role of Individuals in Mass
         Communication." In G. Stuart Adam (ed.), *Journalism, Com-
         munication and the Law*. Scarborough: Prentice-Hall.
Schramm, Wilbur
  1983 "The Unique Perspective of Communication: A Retrospective
         View." *Journal of Communication* 33 (no. 3).
Southam Communications
  1984 *Corpus Almanac and Canadian Sourcebook*. Vol. 1, Don Mills:
         Southam Communications Ltd.

Preface

Canadian students have long suffered from the lack of a Canadian textbook on the mass media. While there are now several good collections of media-related articles by Canadians and a growing number of Canadian studies on specific media topics and themes, there is still no general introduction to mass communication or media studies written primarily for Canadians. This book constitutes an attempt to fill this void in part, but it does so in a rather unconventional way. It does not endeavour to provide its readers with a detailed and comprehensive description of media institutions and practices in Canada today, nor to survey all or even most of the questions that currently engage Canadian media scholars and researchers. Instead, it simply tries to examine some of the fundamental and thus enduring issues in the field of media studies, to place these issues in an appropriate historical context, and above all to make clear the extent to which thought about them is polarized between different points of view.

As with most general works written by a university teacher, this one is indebted to both students on whom preliminary versions were tested and colleagues who provided many helpful suggestions for improvement. While the former are far too numerous to mention by name, I would like to express my appreciation to my colleagues G.S. Adam, R. Bird, P. Bruck, W. Kesterton, E. Saunders, T.J. Scanlon, A. Westell, and J. Weston for both their encouragement and their constructive critiques. They are not, of course, in any way responsible for whatever errors of fact or judgment still remain. Finally, I would like to thank those among the staff of Butterworths with whom I have worked for the patience and care which they have exercised at all stages in the preparation of this book.

R.A.E.
September 1986

Table of Contents

Introduction

For several years now, I have inflicted upon my first year students in mass communication a quotation from Charles Darwin["How odd it is," [Darwin once said, "that anyone should not see that all observation must be for or against some view if it is to be of any service." (McCombs, 1972: 4) I like this quotation because it suggests two things that I think should be kept in mind at all levels of enquiry.

[First of all, it implies that in virtually any area of investigation there will be conflicting theories, interpretations, and points of view. This means that what students should be trying to learn, in the first instance, is not what is universally accepted as true, but rather what different groups of scholars consider to be closest to the truth. The academic world does, of course, have its share of dogmatists, who regard any deviation from their own particular viewpoint as a step towards error and unreason. But for the most part academics recognize that they themselves have often revised their thinking and will no doubt continue to do so in the future. The most that one can say, therefore, is that one position currently has more to recommend it than another; that it can for the moment accommodate the available evidence more adequately, not that it is right and all other views are wrong. Becoming educated thus consists in part of learning about various debates over the relative adequacy of conflicting intellectual positions.

To be truly educated, however, one must also enter into such debates, which brings us to Darwin's main point. There is little value in making random observations of the world or haphazardly collecting the observations of others. The process of observation must be linked to the development of more adequate ways of understanding the world. More specifically, we should always observe reality with a view to finding additional support for or evidence against a specific point of view. This means that most of the "facts" with which we are bombarded are seldom of great significance in and of themselves. Rather they are important because they provide a partial basis upon which to assess different intellectual positions. They are not the only consideration involved in the assessment of a particular viewpoint. Requirements of logic must also be considered. But no matter how logically tight an intellectual construction may be, it must ultimately meet the test of accommodating our observations of reality.

Entering into current intellectual debates is a demanding task. It is easier simply to learn what others have thought, rather than challenge,

1

defend, and even devise positions ourselves. It would be helpful, therefore, to have a pedagogical approach that satisfies two requirements. First, it should make the different positions on any given issue more readily apparent and easier to understand. Secondly, it should do so in a way that helps to organize and direct the observations gathered by students.

During the last few years, I have experimented with a number of devices in an attempt to meet these requirements. One device was simply to imagine a spectrum of positions in relation to a given either/or proposition. I would then sketch these positions in a little diagram as follows:

thesis   Position P   Q   R   antithesis

X — — — — — — — — Y

Figure I

Use of this device helped to explain some debates by showing how positions were polarized between the extremes of X and Y. However, it was too primitive a tool to do justice to most of the debates with which I was concerned. It simplified things, but also tended to oversimplify them.

Some of the other schematic devices I tried had the opposite effect. They complicated things to the point of obfuscation, so that the diagrams I sketched were more of a barrier than an aid to understanding and organization. Recently, however, I discovered a device which strikes me as providing a reasonable compromise between the demands of clarity and insight. I call this the "double polarity" and must admit that it still occasions looks of amusement on the faces of my students whenever I employ it. I continue to use it, however, for a number of rather pragmatic reasons. It has greatly facilitated the organization of large amounts of lecture material; it has produced better answers on examination papers; and it seems to have stimulated livelier exchanges in discussion groups. I have, therefore, decided to make use of this teaching device in each of the chapters of this introduction to media studies and hope that others will find it as useful as I do.

The "double polarity" simply consists of superimposing two separate spectrums of opinion so as to yield four distinct intellectual positions as shown in Figure II on p. 3.

By allowing us to consider two either/or situations simultaneously, this schema reveals partial agreements as well as disagreements between different intellectual positions. For example, while A and B differ with regard to X/Y, they agree in terms of P/Q. Similarly, B and C agree about X/Y, while disagreeing about P/Q. And so on around the diagram. The only complete disagreements from the standpoint of the polarities under examination are between A and C and between B and D. This more

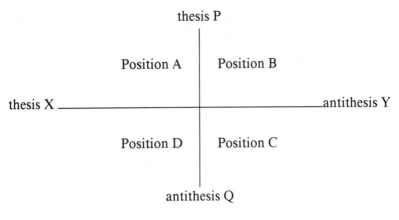

thesis P

Position A | Position B

thesis X ——————————————————— antithesis Y

Position D | Position C

antithesis Q

Figure II

accurately reflects the kind of situation that usually exists in scholarly debates.

This device should, of course, be used with a good deal of flexibility. Intellectual issues and controversies can seldom be reduced to only two aspects. Certainly, for each of the issues examined in the following chapters, other polarities could easily be introduced. At the same time, moreover, the positions that result from any particular double polarity are essentially archetypes or representative constructions which do not necessarily coincide exactly with the thinking of any particular individual. The result is that individual scholars will often straddle two or more of the positions represented on a particular schema. However, recognizing this can increase our understanding of their positions.

In presenting some 28 positions related to seven different issues, I have sought to accomplish three things. First, I have tried to introduce students to a substantial body of literature on communication in the humanities and social sciences. I hope that my capsule accounts of a wide range of books and articles will encourage readers to consult some of these items for themselves. Secondly, I have tried to place most of the issues treated into a broad historical context. I think that in the long run this will make their exploration more interesting and rewarding. Thirdly, I have tried to make clear the importance of continually refining the concepts through which we interpret the world. Concepts are the building blocks of theories; if they are poorly made, any structure using them will be weakened. Moreover, the way in which they are understood determines the nature of what we study and even how we proceed to study it. Humpty Dumpty once said of some of his more remarkable words: "I pay them extra, and make them do what I want." That no doubt exaggerates the flexibility of language, but to understand most theories, we need to begin by grasping their conceptual base.

I have endeavoured, therefore, to provide students with an appropriate starting point for media studies. While some of the discussions in this book may be of interest to students in more advanced courses, they are written primarily with the needs of first year students in mind. It is hoped that as a result of these discussions, students will have a better idea of the issues that confront us in the rapidly changing communications environment in which we live.

Chapter 1

What is Communication?

Communication has been treated by many thinkers as if it were an unproblematic concept. Definitions of the term have been set forth confidently with often only a token analysis of their implications for research and scholarship. One is given the impression that there is more or less general agreement about the fundamental nature of communication and the concerns to which it should give rise. When we look more closely at what has been written about communication, however, we discover that there are a number of quite different conceptions of what it involves. There is, in fact, considerable disagreement about its essential nature. This is one of the reasons why the field of communication studies contains within it a number of very different bodies of literature.

The divergent conceptions of communication that currently exist emerge more clearly when two questions are raised. First, is communication essentially a process of some kind? Or is it the result or product of one or more processes? Is it an actual sequence of events? Or is it a particular state or condition that sometimes arises from certain chains of action? It would seem safe to say that communication involves the sending and receiving of messages. But is it equivalent to message making as such? Or is it the outcome of certain kinds of message making under certain special conditions? Those who have written about communication are by no means agreed as to whether, in the final analysis, it is a process or a product.

Secondly, is communication a one-way or a two-way "affair"? (This terminology is awkward, but we cannot use the word 'process' at this point without prejudicing the first issue.) In other words, is communication inherently interactive? Is it a dialogue or merely a monologue? Is feedback not only desirable but necessary by definition for genuine communication? As with the first issue, there is a division of opinion about whether the receivers of messages must also participate to some degree as senders for communication to occur.

These are not the only questions that could be raised about the basic nature of communication. But they provide a useful basis for distinguishing between four main conceptions of communication in the field of media studies today. See Figure 1:

5

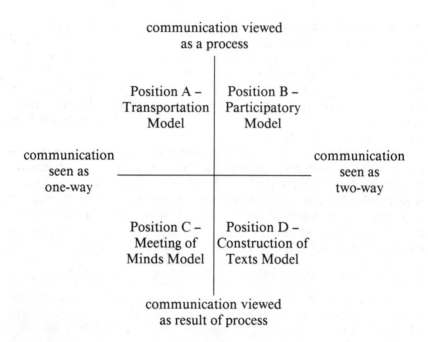

communication viewed
as a process

Position A –
Transportation
Model

Position B –
Participatory
Model

communication
seen as
one-way

communication
seen as
two-way

Position C –
Meeting of
Minds Model

Position D –
Construction of
Texts Model

communication viewed
as result of process

Figure 1

Position A, which regards communication simply as the sending and receiving of messages, has been adhered to by most North American researchers until quite recently. In large measure it stems from a concern with the efficient and effective transmission of information. It has provided the basis for hundreds of studies on the uses and effects of the mass media, enabling us to understand better the conditions of successful persuasion. But it also suffers from serious limitations, including its inadequacy for studying media institutions and its weakness as a basis for communications policy.

Position B, which holds that communication requires a direct exchange of messages, has had less support from academic researchers. Its appeal is greatest in developing countries, where it underlies the campaign for a New World Information Order with a more balanced flow of information. In this regard, it also has relevance for Canada, which is likewise threatened by a massive influx of messages from a neighbouring power. Taken to its extreme, however, it would severely restrict the field of communication studies, since it suggests that mass communication does not really exist. For with the possible exception of cases such as phone-in programs and letters to the editor, the masses do not participate directly in the sending of messages.

Position C has received the least attention to date. It can be found in certain Christian discussions of communication, but does not have to be interpreted within a religious context. In essence, it restricts communication to cases where the receiver comes to know better what the sender is actually thinking or feeling. Thus, it makes a basic distinction between communication and deception. Because this forces one to probe into human intentions, it makes certain kinds of scientific research difficult. At the same time, however, it throws new light on the role of journalism in modern society and provides a more critical perspective from which to assess communications policy.

Position D conceives of communication in terms of shared meanings that emerge at both the interpersonal and the social level of message making. It was first embraced by European scholars, but is now gaining acceptance in North America as well. Its major strength lies in the way that it ties together communication and culture. Its weakness lies in its tendency to indulge in rather abstract theorizing and its concomitant lack of awareness of, or at least concern about, media history.

Position A — Communication as the Movement of Messages

Position A is the least complex view of the nature of communication. It has been called the transportation model (Carey, 1975: 177), because it relies heavily on the metaphor of something being carried from one point to another. Put most simply, communication is the process by which messages are conveyed from a sender to a receiver by means of some medium of transmission. This coincides with the way that we usually use the term in ordinary language. There are, however, certain aspects of this relatively simple way of looking at communication that are not entirely obvious. The transportation metaphor brings to mind the movement of messages between persons separated by space. It implies that the greater the number of messages that are sent, the more communication that takes place. It also suggests that once a message is received, it has a direct effect upon the person receiving it. But over the years, various adherants to the transportation model have shown that each of these ideas is an oversimplification of the situation. In so doing, they have refined the transportation metaphor into a workable model for certain kinds of empirical research.

Communication involves the movement of messages not only across space but also through time. One of the first persons to draw attention to the temporal dimension of communication was the early American sociologist, Charles Cooley. A critic of the social Darwinism of Herbert Spencer, Cooley believed that advances in communications technology were leading to an unprecedented degree of social unity. In works such as *Social Organization* (1909) and *Social Process* (1918), he defined communication as "the mechanism through which human relations exist and develop — all the symbols of the mind, together with the means of conveying them through space and preserving them in time." Progress in the means of conveyance, he argued, had made possible a truly democratic community in America. In particular, it had created a communications environment distinguished by four factors: "Expressiveness, or the range of ideas and feeling it is competent to carry. Permanence of record, or the overcoming of time. Swiftness, or the overcoming of space. Diffusion, or access to all classes of men." (Czitrom, 1982: 98-99)

The idea that communication involves the movement of ideas over both space and time has received its fullest treatment by the Canadian scholar, Harold Adams Innis (1894-1952). Innis is still best known for his work in the field of Canadian political economy, especially the "staples thesis" which he developed in studies such as *The Fur Trade in Canada* (1930) and *The Cod Fisheries* (1940). But during the 1930s, he began to perceive a connection between communication and the workings of the price system in which he was interested. At the same time, he also became concerned about the course of Western civilization, particularly after the fall of France in 1940. When, therefore, he began to search for the causes of the chaos around him, the thought arose that changes in communication might provide a partial explanation. This idea took hold, and by the time Innis was finished with it, he had worked out the basis for a new philosophy of civilization. This was presented in various lectures and articles, which were drawn from a thousand-page manuscript entitled "A History of Communication" and later published in three volumes: *Empire and Communications* (1950), *The Bias of Communication* (1951), and *Changing Concepts of Time* (1952).

Innis undertook to explain the evolution and impact of communications technology from the civilizations of ancient Egypt and Mesopotamia to the present day. He did so on the basis of two fundamental assumptions. First, media of communication differ in terms of their ability to disseminate ideas across space and preserve them over time. On the one hand, media that are light and easily transportable (*e.g.* papyrus, paper) facilitate the rapid transmission of messages over a large area; they have, therefore, what Innis called a bias towards space. On the other hand, media that are heavier and more durable (*e.g.* stone, clay, parchment) are better suited to retaining messages over long periods of time; in other words, they have a bias towards time.

Secondly, according to Innis, the particular mixture of media possessed by a society exerts a powerful influence on its institutions and values. "Materials that emphasize time favour decentralization and hierarchical types of institutions, while those that emphasize space favour centralization and systems of government less hierarchical in character." (Innis, 1972: 7) Ideally, a civilization would have media enabling it to control extensive territory and at the same time keep its customs and values relatively intact. This was the case, Innis believed, in classical Greece, Renaissance Italy, and Elizabethan England. But at most other times, the dominance of either space-biased or time-biased media had produced a general imbalance within civilizations which eventually led to their downfall. The decline of Western civilization in the twentieth century was thought by Innis to stem in large measure from its predominantly space-biased media system. Newspapers, film, and radio enabled ideas to spread further and faster than ever before. But they also eroded society's interest in, and respect for, the beliefs and ideals of its past.

Though now recognized as a major contribution to the field, Innis's writings on communication were largely neglected during his lifetime. His Canadian colleagues were bewildered by his strange ideas and they could not understand how he could abandon the secure haven of economic history for the largely uncharted waters of the history of communication. Tied to their traditional academic disciplines, they were not yet ready to appreciate the importance of studying communication. Nor did they share Innis's concern about the threat of American media imperialism to Canadian culture. In the United States, the study of communication was rapidly developing into a separate field of study. But its practitioners were concentrating on the short-term effects of the media on behaviour. American researchers assumed, like Innis, that communication consists of the movement of messages over space and time. But they suffered from what Innis would have called a spatial bias. That is, they were generally uninterested in the historical development of human communication.

During the 1940s and 1950s, the predominant influence on communications research was exerted not by Innis or Cooley, both of whom sought to understand the entire process of social change, but by two other social scientists with a much narrower range of concerns. The first of these was Harold Lasswell (1902-1978), an American political scientist whose interest in communication was stimulated initially by the propaganda of the First World War. In *Propaganda Techniques in the World War* (1927) and *World Politics and Personal Insecurity* (1935), Lasswell tried to find a theoretical explanation for the effective operation of propaganda campaigns in democracies as well as dictatorships. His search led to the formulation of what came to be known as the "hypodermic needle" theory of communication. Drawing upon Freudian psychology, Lasswell suggested that the power of the propagandist lies in his special ability to translate the nonrational urges within his own subconscious into concrete symbols that appeal directly to the subconscious of his audience. In this way, the propagandist is able to inject his message directly into the mind of the masses like serum from a hypodermic needle. (Davis *et al.,* 1981: 25-6)

Thus, what interested Lasswell primarily was not the mere transmission of messages, but rather the conditions of successful persuasion. He wanted to know why some messages are accepted while others are rejected. There was a hint of this concern in the famous formula that he later devised to describe the communication process. "A convenient way to describe an act of communication," he wrote, "is to answer the following questions: Who Says What In Which Channel To Whom With What Effect?" (Lasswell, 1960: 117) But to understand fully what Lasswell had in mind by this formula, we need to recall the context in which it was enunciated.

The origins of Lasswell's formula have been traced to a memorandum that he and a few other scholars drew up in 1940. Entitled "Research in Mass Communication," the memorandum sought to outline the means of maintaining a consensus among Americans in the face of the German threat to the democracies of the West. It argued that research into the effects of mass communication could provide the government with better means of influencing public opinion. "Techniques for the study of communication," it stated, "have long since been developed and applied in the fields of market research, advertising, propaganda, publicity, and public relations. Studies using these techniques produce facts of great importance for *private* policy. The techniques themselves are transferable and should be used to support *public* policy." (Czitrom, 1982: 131).

Not unexpectedly, American government officials readily embraced this suggestion and made funds available for research on the mass media. As Lucien Pye later observed, "the prime thrust behind the development of modern communications studies [in the United States] was the challenge of Nazi propaganda and the need for a major effort in psychological warfare in support of democracies during the Second World War. In response to that national crisis, social scientists soon learned that they could make significant contributions to the field of public affairs." (Pye, 1963: 13) After the war, additional support for research on the formation of public opinion came from the corporate sector, which was intent on stimulating demand for new consumer goods. Communications research became closely tied to the needs and interests of the capitalist system. At the same time, however, the transportation model of communication underlying this research was reinforced by a number of non-commercial factors. These included work being done in cybernetics and information theory and the predisposition towards behaviourism among American social scientists.

Cybernetics (from the Greek word *kubernetes* meaning steersman) was founded in the 1940s by Norbert Wiener, a professor of mathematics at the Massachusetts Institute of Technology. It was essentially the science of maintaining order in any system of interrelated elements and survives today as general systems theory. As developed by Wiener, it took as its starting point the second law of thermodynamics, according to which a closed system has a natural tendency to reach a state of complete uniformity or disorder in the sense of lacking any pattern or structure. For example, a perfectly sealed room that initially has separate areas of hot and cold air would tend to move towards a state of uniform temperature throughout. Entropy is the formal expression for this statistical tendency for ordered structures, including the universe as a whole, to disintegrate or run down.

It was the threatening implication of this idea for man and society that led Wiener to write *Cybernetics,* which was published in 1948 and subtitled "Control and Communication in the Animal and Machine." He subsequently dealt with the same problem in less technical terms in *The Human Use of Human Beings: Cybernetics and Society* (1950). In both works, Wiener accepted the idea that entropy is on the increase in the universe as a whole. But he also argued that there are local pockets or islands of decreasing entropy, such as living organisms, which run counter to the general trend. "In the world with which we are immediately concerned," he wrote, "there are stages which, though they occupy an insignificant fraction of eternity, are of great significance for our purposes, for in them entropy does not increase and organization and its correlative, information, are being built up." (Wiener, 1967: 45) Wiener conceived of cybernetics as the study of how to preserve these organized, differentiated, less probable stages.

For students of communication, the most interesting idea set forth by Wiener was that information is the main antagonist of entropy. "Just as entropy is a measure of disorganization," he stated, "the information carried by a set of messages is a measure of organization. In fact, it is possible to interpret the information carried by a message as essentially the negative of its entropy, and the negative logarithm of its probability. That is, the more probable the message, the less information it gives." (Wiener, 1967: 31) The most important mechanism for maintaining a differentiated state, therefore, is feedback or "the method of controlling a system by reinserting into it the results of its past performance." (Wiener, 1967: 84)

Like Cooley and Innis, Wiener believed that social scientists had failed to grasp the full significance of communication in their studies of society. They did not, to his way of thinking, appreciate the degree to which the very existence of society depends upon communication networks. In this regard, however, it is questionable whether Wiener's own work served as a needed corrective. As a matter of necessity, his systems approach reduced communication to the movement of information. *The Human Use of Human Beings* eliminated any thought about such human qualities as honesty, trust, and tolerance, which may be equally important ingredients of communication. It ignored the fact that societies need not only the means to live, but also the will to live, which comes less from information and feedback than from identification with a common purpose.

Wiener's general approach to communication underlay the more specialized work being done about the same time in information theory, which was essentially a component of cybernetics or one of several sets of ideas within it. However, the concept of entropy underwent a rather strange transformation in the hands of information theorists such as Claude Shannon, a mathematical engineer who worked at the Bell Telephone Laboratories before joining the staff at MIT. In July and October of 1948, Shannon published two papers in the *Bell System Technical Journal* in which he too examined information in terms of entropy. Although Shannon had earlier been a student of Wiener's, his so-called "mathematical theory of communication" was developed independently and probably in advance of Wiener's work on cybernetics. (Campbell, 1982: 20-1)

In any event, Shannon was mainly concerned with the technical engineering problem of how to transmit the largest amount of data possible with the least amount of interference. One of the main points made by Shannon was that any interference or "noise" disrupting the transmission of a signal could be counteracted by means of redundancy; that is, by building into the original message an appropriate amount of repetition so that it could still be reconstructed from the portion of the signal received. While Shannon's concern was with what he called technical noise (*e.g.* static on the radio, snow on a television set), he also introduced the idea of semantic noise (*e.g.* thinking about last night's date while reading this chapter). The implication was that the effective, efficient transmission of ideas depends on building in just the right amount of redundancy for the intended audience. If there is too little redundancy, the audience will miss part of the message. But if there is too much redundancy, this will lead to boredom, which is itself a form of noise.

Applied in this context, the concept of entropy took on a very different meaning than in cybernetics. Instead of regarding information as a means of counteracting entropy, information became almost the equivalent of entropy. That is, an entropic message was considered to be one containing a high degree of information, as opposed to a redundant message which contains very little. An interesting attempt to extend these concepts to the study of mass communication was made by Wilbur Schramm in "Information Theory and Mass Communication" (1955). But Schramm more or less exhausted the possibilities in this regard and in so doing inadvertently made clear the limitations of Shannon's mathematical model for the study of the mass media.

Even after the shortcomings of the mathematical model became evident, however, American social scientists remained committed to the basic idea of communication on which it was based. The major reason for this was their desire to build a science of communication. This was no doubt a laudable objective, but again it is important to keep in mind the manner in which it was understood. When American social scientists thought of science, they thought first and foremost of the natural sciences. They regarded science not simply as any form of rigorous enquiry, but as research aided by the tool of mathematics. To be scientific one had to test for probabilistic relationships between quantifiable variables by statistical means. What this meant, moreover, was that one had to restrict oneself to the study of overt behaviour (behaviourism) and ignore such unquantifiable phenomena as human motives and intentions. This requirement has not been adhered to without exception. But the extent to which behaviourist principles have dominated communication research in the United States is illustrated by the fact that one researcher still felt it necessary recently to point out that "to think of communication as prompted by intentions, motives, cognitions, and so on, is to employ a different conceptual base." (Fisher, 1982: 198)

The Lasswellian formula "who, says what, in which channel, to whom, with what effect" was an inherently behaviourist approach to communication. For it avoided any need to examine the motives or intentions of the sender; it said "*with* what effect," not "*for* what effect." At the same time, it also meant that advertising, public relations, and even propaganda could be regarded as forms of communication. It allowed that deliberate misrepresentation or even outright lying is as much an act of communication as an honest attempt to convey one's true beliefs or feelings. Thus, it seemed to legitimize the acceptance of funds from private commercial agencies for "scientific" research on techniques of mass persuasion.

A further rationalization of the relationship between academic researchers and the commercial sector was offered by Paul F. Lazarsfeld, an Austrian psychologist, who first settled in the United States in the mid-1930s. Among those who signed Lasswell's memorandum in 1940, Lazarsfeld eventually came to be known as the father of mass communication studies in America. Before emigrating to America, he had set up the Vienna Research Institute to undertake various projects, including marketing studies subsidized by funds from private businesses. He admitted that these market surveys were designed to enable businessmen to forecast and control consumer behaviour, but he argued that the raw data accumulated would also aid the development of communication theory.

In 1937, Lazarsfeld established the Office of Radio Research at Princeton University with the aid of a grant from the Rockefeller foundation and funds from radio networks, publishers, and various marketing firms. A few years later, he moved this research unit to Columbia University in New York and renamed it the Bureau of Applied Social Research. Along with Frank Stanton, a young researcher at CBS, he carried out pioneering studies of radio content and comparative demographic studies of radio and print audiences. It would be unfair, perhaps, to suggest that Lazarsfeld sold his academic soul for commercial contracts. He believed that his quantitative studies were laying a scientific foundation for the field of communication research. He also thought that his own primarily "administrative" research could exist in harmony with "critical" studies addressing questions of aesthetics and social control. (Lazarsfeld, 1941) But the fact remains that his research offered broadcasters and advertisers the means to deal with their overriding problem of how to get a message through to, and accepted by, a mass audience.

There was an underlying irony to the use that was made of the narrowly based studies of media effects conducted by Lazarsfeld and his colleagues. On the one hand, media practitioners found in them ways of increasing their power over mass audiences. But on the other hand, media observers thought that they showed that the media's influence on behaviour had been greatly exaggerated. In particular, they were believed to have discredited the so-called mass society theory which had dominated early thinking about mass communication.

The mass society theory postulated that society had once consisted of integrated, organic communities and groups such as the church and family, which served to anchor the individual in society. But the growth of industry and the city supposedly broke down these forms of association and left the individual rootless and alone. Society became simply the aggregate of its members, an undifferentiated mass of atomized and isolated individuals. The American sociologist, David Riesman, encapsulated the basic idea in the title of his book *The Lonely Crowd* (1950). The implication was that the modern individual had few defences against media manipulation; he was a *tabula rasa* or blank slate on which the media could write whatever they wished. This pliability seemed confirmed by the widespread panic in the United States caused by Orsen Welles' famous radio dramatization of H. G. Wells' *The War of the Worlds.*

In the opening chapter of *The End of Ideology* (1960), American sociologist Daniel Bell directly challenged this view of the media, calling the mass society theory a "slippery" phenomenon which, "like the shadows in Plato's cave, generally never gives us more than a silhouette." (Bell, 1962: 22) He said it was really more of an "ideology of romantic protest against contemporary life" than an accurate "description of Western society." (Bell, 1962: 38) He insisted that "individuals are not *tabula rasa.* They bring varying social conceptions to the same experience and go away with dissimilar responses." (Bell, 1962: 26) He took issue specifically with the idea that America had suffered from a weakening of communal activities.

Bell did not actually provide a very strong counter-argument against the mass society thesis. But, by that time other researchers had conducted a number of studies showing that the masses are not an undifferentiated aggregate that responds more or less uniformly to media messages. These were summarized by Joseph T. Klapper in *The Effects of Mass Communication* (1960). Klapper noted that:

> [L]ay critics, social observers, and occasional social scientists have been asserting for over a decade that movie viewing, radio listening, and especially TV viewing are passive occupations which may wither the critical acumen and creative abilities of the audience. The more alarmist have forseen a

populace reduced to lethargic acquiescence and a nation in which active democracy has atrophied. (Klapper, 1960: 247)

But he found that "virtually none of these writers has offered any documentation in substantiation of these fears."

On the contrary, what the "scientific" evidence was thought to show was that the individual has a number of defence mechanisms against media manipulation. People expose themselves to media messages selectively; they filter out many messages that go against their pre-conceived way of looking at things; and they tend to forget disruptive messages that might make it through their initial filter. It was thought, moreover, that the media exert their influence less directly than had earlier been assumed. This idea, which was first developed by Lazarsfeld in *The People's Choice* (1944), came to be referred to as the "two-step flow" hypothesis. The suggestion was that media messages are first received by the "opinion leaders" in society; they are then passed on in a somewhat altered form to the "opinion followers," who are thus influenced by the media only indirectly.

Since Klapper's day, most of these hypotheses have undergone substantial modification. It is now realized that they greatly over-simplified the relationship between the individual and the mass media. (Tan, 1985: 179-209) More refined approaches to the analysis of media effects have been developed. In *Does Mass Communication Change Public Opinion After All?* (1981), for example, James B. Lemert has presented evidence that public opinion is not an inherently lethargic force. On the contrary, it can lead to politically effective action against perceived grievances in cases where journalists provide the public with adequate "mobilizing information" (the names and locations of persons or organizations who might take action if contacted by members of the public). Too often, journalists merely provide information designed to change public opinion without including the means for the public to act upon its new attitude.

To their credit, the early adherants to the transportation model of communication did lay the foundation for a significant body of empirical research on media effects. But their work was based upon a conception of communication that was too narrow from one angle and too broad from another. It was too narrow because it was restricted largely to those aspects of communication that can be quantified. It was also too broad because it made no distinction among the different kinds of message making in which the media are engaged. In so doing, it overlooked a number of important political, economic, and social questions that arise when communication is seen as a special kind of message-making activity.

Position B — Communication as the Mutual Exchange of Messages

Advocates of Position A usually make a distinction between interpersonal and mass communication. The basis for this distinction is taken to be the nature of the receiver involved in the process of communication. In interpersonal communication, the receiver consists of no more than a few persons who are in direct contact with each other as well as with the sender. In mass communication, the receiver consists of a large audience whose members are not in direct contact with each other or with the sender. One adherant to this distinction has written that "in a functional sense, one speaks of mass communication in terms of media which are capable of reaching a vast number of people simultaneously." (Steinberg, 1970: 13) But it is not simply the size of the audience that makes mass communication. It is also the fact that its members are anonymous; they are not really aware of themselves as an audience.

For Position A, this does not necessarily mean that the "masses" in mass communication are always on the receiving end of the messages being sent. Mass communication is not simply communication from the few to the many. There is also a sense in which the masses send messages back to the original senders. As Steinberg put it, "the receiving audience also has a point of view which is occasionally expressed harshly and overtly, but is also present in many subtle ways — the selection of one movie over another, the tuning out of a given program, the cancellation of a subscription to a particular magazine." (Steinberg, 1970: 14) In other words, Position A acknowledges the existence of a degree of feedback in the process of mass communication. It is this kind of concession, however, that marks the point of departure for Position B. For to call audience reactions of this kind "communication" is, from its standpoint, to misuse the term. Indeed, for Position B, even the original process by which messages are sent from the few to the many is not actually communication.

The crux of Position B is that the masses must participate as message makers in a genuine and meaningful way for there to be mass communication. An anticipation of this thesis can be found in R. Birdwhistell's *Introduction to Kinesics* (1952). "An individual," Birdwhistell wrote,

> does not communicate; he engages in or becomes part of communication. He may move, or make noises . . . but he does not communicate. In a parallel fashion, he may see, he may hear, smell, taste, or feel — but he does not communicate. In other words, he does not originate communication; he participates in it. Communication as a system, then, is not to be understood as a simple model of reaction and reaction, however complexly stated. (Fisher, 1982: 202)

Birdwhistell's point was that communication must be seen as a two-way process. That is, it involves a mutual exchange of messages so that those who enter into it participate as both senders and receivers.

While adherants to the orthodox transportation model of communication allow that a certain amount of feedback is usually involved in communication, they would not agree that such feedback is essential for communication to occur. It is not built into the very meaning of communication. This, however, is precisely the claim of Position B. Communication is regarded as the process of *exchanging* messages; it is considered to be an inherently reciprocal process. "In short," writes one advocate, "communication requires sharing, interaction, participation or feedback of more than a token kind that is not controlled by the sender or message-maker." (Beattie, 1981: 36)

The author of this definition is led to the rather startling conclusion that mass communication does not really exist to any significant degree. Journalists, he argues, do not communicate; nor do broadcasters or other media professionals. What they are engaged in are monologues, whereas communication must by definition be a dialogue. "The vehicles of mass media — print or electronic — are not carriers of *communication* but one-way delivery systems for messages." (Beattie, 1981: 34) They may inform immense audiences, but they do not communicate, since dispensing information for a price is not communication. Only if meaningful feedback loops were installed would mass communication become a reality.

In response to this analysis, those who subscribe to Position A (or, as we shall see, Position C) might counter that Position B is based upon a serious misunderstanding. For it seems to assume that for the masses to enter into the communication process, they must literally get into print or on the airwaves. That is, they must send messages themselves in the same way that journalists and other mass media persons presumably do. The assumption is that those whose by-line appears in print or whose voice is heard on radio or television are the real senders of messages. But by way of criticism of this position, it could be argued that journalists are, in many cases, merely a vehicle through which other individuals and groups are able to communicate with society. That is, they are as much the "medium" of communication as the technology of message transmission.

A couple of examples may help to clarify this point. In *The Ottawa Citizen* for October 22, 1984 (p. D1), there appeared a lengthy story by staff writer Sherri Barron entitled "Where can the mentally ill go?" In a trivial sense, it could be said that Ms. Barron was the person sending a message to the public by means of this story. But in a more profound sense, the message being conveyed was coming from those persons who were being forced out of mental institutions into communities ill-prepared to receive them. They were, in effect, acquiring a voice through the efforts of Barron. In some cases, they were able to speak directly about their plight. As one said of a mission in which he stayed for a time: "It was so cold there in the winter, some days I used to stay in bed all day just to keep warm. They only gave you one blanket and a sheet." Even when they were being quoted directly, however, the persons in this story were essentially archetypes or representatives of the group as a whole.

Another story using the archetypal method was prepared by staff writer Pat Bell for publication in the *Citizen* on February 23, 1985 (p. F1). Entitled "Visiting rights, but no visits," it gave a voice to divorced or separated fathers who, despite court orders allowing them to visit their children, have been unable to do so. Their general frustration with a situation not generally known by the public was expressed clearly by one father: "If I don't pay, I can be put in jail. But I don't get anything in return." While it could be argued that this is just one individual speaking, that is not the effect for the reader. The identity of the individual quoted is soon forgotten; what remains is an impression of what such persons generally are thinking and feeling.

There has been much more of this kind of journalism in recent years than media scholarship would suggest. The conventional wisdom is that groups need some kind of formal organization to gain access to the media. But this is simply not the case. Conscientious journalism provides a voice for many groups without formal organization, ranging from the homeless and destitute (*e.g.* "The Homeless: From 20,000 to 40,000 Canadians live on the streets," *The Ottawa Citizen,* March 22, 1986: B1) to abused women and children (*e.g.* "New focus on battered women," *The Toronto Star,* September 19, 1986: B1). Moreover, the technique of having a few carefully chosen individuals represent a larger group is by no means confined to the print media. On the contrary, it is even better suited to the broadcast media, where it is used not only in news and public affairs programming but also in dramatic productions and even comedy shows. It underlies panel discussions, forums, and phone-in programs.

In each case, the masses (or even a sizeable segment thereof) do not directly acquire access to the airwaves. But they do so indirectly and more effectively than if they did have actual access. This suggests that mass communication does, to some extent, consist of communication *among* and not merely *to* the masses. It points to the fact that mass communication is not only vertical and elitist but also horizontal and collective. Moreover, it could conceivably become even more democratic in the years ahead. But if this were to happen, it would not be primarily by increasing the kind of feedback that Position B has in mind. This could actually impede mass communication. Rather it would be through the greater and more diverse use of archetypal media presentations.

However, it is not difficult to see why many people would find Position B's approach appealing. For developing countries suffering from media imperialism, it is rhetorically effective to say that one-way information flows are not communication. Participatory communication seems to be what is required. Certainly, the participatory model transcends the transportation model by placing more stress on the *interaction* that communication often involves. Despite this emphasis, however, it still assumes that communication consists of the sending and receiving of messages. It is precisely this assumption that is challenged by the next two positions to be considered. Both insist that it is more useful to think of communication as a particular product of various message-making processes, rather than as equivalent to those processes as such. What they disagree with each other about is the nature of the product in question.

Position C — Communication as a Meeting of Minds

The third position to be examined rejects both of the main assumptions of the participatory conception of communication. First, it disagrees with the assumption that communication must *necessarily* be interactive. (Otherwise, the author of this book could not be said to be communicating with his readers or with those, at least, who do not reply with a nasty review.) It agrees, as did the first position, that feedback or interaction is often a tremendous aid to communication. But it does not conclude from this that it is part of the very meaning of communication. Secondly, it disagrees with the assumption that communication is essentially a message-making process of some kind. In this respect, it is at odds with both the first and second positions. It acknowledges that certain message-making processes must take place before communication can occur. But it suggests that communication can be understood better by seeing it as a product of these processes, rather than by identifying it with such processes *per se.*

It has frequently been pointed out that the word 'communication' comes from the Latin word *communis,* meaning common. But the question, of course, is to what does this "commonality" apply? According to the conventional conception of communication, it applies to the *message* involved in the process of communication. (We shall see later that position D basically agrees with this point, although it would say that it applies to the *text* involved in an *act* of communication.) In other words, communication occurs whenever an idea or feeling is expressed by one person or group and perceived and understood by another. It is acknowledged that the message received will never be exactly the same as the message sent. But provided that there is a reasonable degree of correspondence between what is expressed by the sender and what is interpreted by the receiver, then communication is thought to have occurred. In other words, there is communication as long as the message received has something in common with the message sent.

The point that needs to be stressed about this conception of communication is that it does not matter whether the message being sent actually reflects what the sender is thinking or feeling. It makes no difference whether the sender says one thing while believing another, or conveys one emotion while really feeling something else. According to the orthodox approach, communication does not depend upon whether the sender reveals, or even attempts to reveal, the true state of his or her mind. As long as there is some understanding of the message being sent, then there is communication, regardless of whether the receiver has been misled or deceived. In other words, the intention of the sender is considered to be irrelevant.

For Position C, however, the intention of the sender is a vital consideration. The thesis of this position is that communication occurs if, and only if, one person or group comes to understand better the actual thoughts, beliefs, or feelings of another person or group. The fact that the sender makes a genuine attempt to convey what he is thinking or feeling does not guarantee that communication will result. Messages sent with the intention of informing might still become garbled during their transmission or be completely misinterpreted. But an honest attempt on the part of the sender to reveal the true state of his mind is nonetheless a *sine qua non* of communication. There is no communication, according to Position C, where the receiver ends up with *less* insight into the mind of the sender, which is what happens, of course, in cases of deception.

In other words, communication, when it occurs, consists of a sort of "meeting of minds." This does not mean that the sender and receiver must be in agreement. On the contrary, the receiver might disagree completely with the thoughts expressed by the sender. But what it does mean is that the thoughts attributed to the sender by the receiver must, in fact, be a reasonably close reflection of what the sender is actually thinking. Insofar as the sender deceives the receiver, there is no communication. Communication is thus relative; it occurs to the extent that one mind comes to a better understanding of another mind. It depends less on the amount of message making than on the degree of honesty involved. This is why we sometimes feel that a breakdown of communication has occurred, even though messages continue to be exchanged and understood.

This conception of communication has been hinted at recently by three American academics. "At base," they write, "we see communication as originating in the attempt to *make publicly available some private state* and the organization of behavior toward that end." (Delia *et al.,* 1982: 159; emphasis added) Making a private state publicly available is not, of course, simply the same as making public statements. It is easy to make statements in public while at the same time keeping one's true thoughts and feelings hidden. Unfortunately, the authors do not develop this idea nor point out its implications for conventional views of communication.

A less oblique statement of the notion of communication as a meeting of minds can be found, however, in the writings of Jürgen Habermas, a member of the Frankfurt school of communication. In an essay entitled "What is Universal Pragmatics?", first published in German in 1976,

Habermas says that communication consists of coming to a reciprocal understanding with another person. Moreover, he states that anyone communicating by means of speech must, among other things, "have the intention of communicating a true proposition (or a propositional content, the existential presuppositions of which are satisfied) so that the hearer can share the knowledge of the speaker. The speaker *must want to express his intention truthfully* so that the hearer can believe the utterance of the speaker (can trust him)." (Habermas, 1979: 2-3; emphasis added)

The idea that communication consists of a "meeting of minds" is an essentially humanistic one. It sees communication as a positive human value, though one that is by no means easy to attain. The German sociologist, Niklas Luhman, has suggested that communications researchers should start:

> . . . from the premise that communication is improbable, despite the fact that we experience and practise it every day of our lives and would not exist without it. This improbability of which we have become unaware must first be understood, and to do so requires what might be described as a contra-phenomenological effort, viewing communication not as a phenomenon but as a problem; thus, instead of looking for the most appropriate concept to cover the facts, we must first ask how communication is possible at all. (Luhman, 1981: 123)

He then listed three things that would appear to make communication improbable: namely, that each individual has a different way of looking at the world; that individuals engaged in communication are often separated in both space and time; and that they may be unwilling to accept a message as a basis of their own behaviour even when its meaning is understood.

This is a potentially fruitful line of enquiry. But if Position C is accepted, Luhman's analysis goes too far in one direction and not far enough in another. On the one hand, acceptance of a message to the point of behaviour modification is not necessary for communication. If John tells Mary something that she already knows, there may be communication (*i.e.,* if John actually believes it), but it will probably not affect Mary's behaviour. In many cases, even if John tells Mary something that she does not know, it may not affect her behaviour. On the other hand, what is necessary for communication is that John attempt to convey his actual thoughts or feelings to Mary. This, moreover, is what also makes communication so problematic. For although it would be unduly cynical to suggest that communication in this sense never occurs, it would also be naive to assume that communication results from all instances of message making. Deception may not be the norm in human encounters, but it is certainly not a rare occurrence.

A major implication of Position C is that social communication is fundamentally different from propaganda. Indeed, communication is the opposite of propaganda. This point depends, of course, on how we define propaganda. In the original sense of the term, propaganda was not necessarily incompatible with communication. But its meaning has changed fundamentally over the centuries. As Helmut Heiber relates:

> The word originated in connection with the work of the Catholic missions, the Sacra Congregatio de Propaganda de Fide, where it meant merely "propagation." However, in the nineteenth century the word had acquired a negative connotation, which seemed to be confirmed when in World War I the nature of such work became evident to a broad public in the war propaganda of both sides. By the time the stridently conducted propaganda duel had ended, the word had become almost a synonym for lying. (Heiber 1972: 118)

Since then there has been a further evolution in its meaning. One of the factors behind this has been a classic study by the French social philosopher Jacques Ellul. The book in question was first published in 1962 with the title *Propagandes,* because its author wanted to stress that there are various forms of propaganda. Ellul himself actually refrained from defining propaganda. Moreover, he was a prolific writer whose thought evolved over time. It is thus difficult to pinpoint his conception of propaganda without a certain amount of distortion. Nonetheless, in *Propagandes* at least, he considered propaganda to be essentially *any deliberate and organized attempt to distort reality, as it is perceived to exist, in order to influence, modify, or control the behaviour of some group.* The implication of this definition is that propaganda combines five elements, each of which is necessary for it to exist in the full sense of the term.

First, modern propaganda is engaged in quite *deliberately;* it is a conscious, purposeful activity. Some authors have suggested that propaganda is largely unconscious and thus unintended, but this is quite misleading. There can be no doubt that political propagandists like Joseph Goebbels knew exactly what they were doing; the same is true of those who conduct an advertising or public relations campaign. As Ellul pointed out, the modern propagandist often consciously develops techniques based on research conducted in psychology and sociology (and, we can now add, mass communication). (Ellul, 1973: 4) This would hardly be the case if propaganda was an unconscious activity. It is true, of course, that journalists and other media persons may unwittingly serve the cause of the propagandist. In such cases, the propaganda that results might be said to be unintended. But the manipulation of the journalist by the original agents of propaganda is still quite deliberate.

Secondly, propaganda is an *organized* activity. On this point, Ellul is quite insistent. "Organization is an intrinsic part of propaganda," he declares. "It is illusory to think that one can separate them." (Ellul, 1973: 29) There are, of course, countless instances of isolated individuals using a particular mass medium to mislead people. But these do not constitute propaganda except in a very loose sense of the term. Since it needs to make use of various mass media in combination to be successful, propaganda requires tremendous resources. It is not something that can be engaged in by individuals, but only by governments, corporations, religious movements, lobbying groups, and so forth.

Thirdly, propaganda involves the *distortion* of reality, but not its complete falsification. As Ellul emphasized, the modern propagandist does not tell blatant lies; on the contrary, he subtley weaves into his images of reality many verifiable facts in order to maintain credibility. These facts do not comprise the truth, however, because the propagandist interprets them out of context while ignoring other facts. Joseph Goebbels, who served as Hitler's Minister of Propaganda, stressed that to be successful propaganda must be as accurate as possible in terms of particular details, which is why, in part, it is a conscious activity. The distorted view of reality presented by the propagandist is a carefully contrived product.

Fourthly, however, it is not the distortion of reality *per se* that makes certain images of reality propaganda; it is the fact that the images in question are a distortion of what the propagandist actually believes to be the case. In other words, if the disseminators of a particular view of reality believe it to be accurate, then they are not propagandists no matter how far-fetched their beliefs may be. Propaganda is grounded in an intention to deceive; where there is no deliberate deception, there is no propaganda. What this means, therefore, is that something that starts out as propaganda may not continue to be so, even though the message may remain the same. That is, the propagandist may gradually come to believe his own misrepresentation. This is perhaps what led Ellul to see propaganda as endemic to modern social systems. However, it might be better to say that what starts out as propaganda sometimes turns into ideology or a value-laden image of reality with widespread acceptance.

Finally, the propagandist engages in deception for a definite purpose; namely, to alter (or, in some instances, reinforce) the behaviour of some group. This does not mean, however, that every attempt to influence behaviour is propaganda. It is only propaganda if it involves a conscious attempt to distort what is perceived to be reality. A teacher, politician, or religious leader who tries to convince others to see the world as he sees it is not a propagandist if he does so honestly and openly. He is only a propagandist if he says one thing while believing something else.

In distinguishing between honest message making and propaganda, Position C does not propose that communications research somehow confine itself to the former and have nothing to do with the latter. This would obviously be impractical, since communication and propaganda are, in the present sense, often so closely interwoven to make it difficult to tell where one leaves off and the other begins. For Position C, nonetheless, it is vital to make a distinction between them. Otherwise, we cannot even begin to consider what kind of message-making environment contributes to genuine communication and discourages propaganda. We cannot compare different institutional structures, economic arrangements, and technological strategies to see whether some are more likely to promote communication than others. We cannot, therefore, use communications research to help create a basis for better human relations.

Position D — Communication as the Social Construction of Texts

Position D is probably the most difficult conception of communication to understand. Its theoretical underpinnings can be traced to the American philosopher, Charles S. Peirce. During the late nineteenth and early twentieth centuries, Peirce wrote a series of papers in which he worked out a new philosophy called pragmatism. He also developed a foundation for what has come to be known as semiotics or semiology, which consists of the study of the signs and codes by means of which messages are constructed and interpreted. A sign, in this context, refers to anything that is used to signify something other than itself; a code is a system or set of signs together with the rules governing their use.

It was not until the publication of Peirce's *Collected Papers* (1931-58) that his work on semiotics began to receive wider circulation. In the meantime, a few other scholars probed into this uncharted territory. In 1915 the Swiss linguist, Ferdinand de Saussure, issued his brilliant *Course in General Linguists*; while in 1923, two other Americans, C. Ogden and I. Richards, published *The Meaning of Meaning*. It is only since the end of the Second World War, however, that semiotics has become a major area of research, engaging the scholarly talents of Roland Barthes and Umberto Eco among others.

Because some of the concepts developed by these scholars have been borrowed by orthodox communications theorists such as Wilbur Schramm to create more elaborate process models, it is difficult at first to see the extent to which semiotics gives rise to new conception of communication. But while this conception has certain elements in common with the first three, it differs quite radically from each. It agrees with Position C that communication is less a process than a product of various processes, but it does not conceptualize this product in terms of one mind coming to understand the actual thoughts or feelings of another. It agrees with Position B that communication is interactive, but it does not take this necessarily to mean the mutual exchange of messages. Finally, it agrees with Position A that messages are, in some sense, sent and received in any act of communication, but it analyzes such message making in an entirely different way.

Position D conceives of communication in terms of shared meanings or common understandings that emerge not only between individuals but also within cultures and sub-cultures. These shared meanings are thought to arise by means of what are usually referred to as "texts". A text may be defined as any artefact that possesses meaning by virtue of the way in which it has arranged certain symbols or signs in accordance with certain rules or codes. In this sense of the term, a text could refer to not only a string of words (or letters) placed on a page using a certain form of grammar, but also a film, a radio or television program, a concert, an opera, a work of art, and so forth. Moreover, texts include the products of popular culture as well as high culture. Billboards, rock music, comic books, and advertisements are also texts.

Both the production (encoding) and interpretation (decoding) of texts are considered to be social processes. Those who produce a newscast or comedy show, for example, do so on the basis of various conditions and practices of production. They work within a particular social setting and are governed by specific institutional constraints, organizational policies, and professional conventions. Similarly, audiences "read" or make sense of different texts on the basis of their own social background and culture. They interpret any given text within a certain historical context. It is for this reason in part that the term 'text' is generally used rather than 'message'. Each text invariably contains more than one potential message. There is, of course, the message intended by the person or group involved in the initial encoding. But there are also the messages that are actually decoded by those who receive the text. The two are seldom the same.

The question naturally arises as to how much autonomy various audiences actually have in the interpretation of texts. As J. Corner has observed, "one of the most important developments in recent media research has been the attempt to investigate the extent to which audiences do, at different levels, produce variations of meaning and significance from the same media text according to the socially situated logics of meaning-production through reading." (Corner, 1983: 267) Theories of textual openness downplay the determining power of texts, while theories of textual closure accord the audience little autonomy in the process of interpretation. In an attempt to reconcile these extremes, a number of recent scholars have developed the idea of a "preferred meaning" within any given text. That is, texts "never deliver *one* meaning; they are rather the site of a plurality of meanings, in which *one* is preferred and offered . . . over the others, as most appropriate." (Hall *et al.,* 1976: 53) The extent to which the preferred meaning is the one actually derived from a text presumably depends on the corresondence between the codes of those encoding and decoding the text. (Morley, 1983: 110)

It is clear that these processes, while still a matter of considerable debate, are "certainly not to be thought of (following early 'communications theory') as 'sending' and 'receiving' linked by the straight conveyance of a 'message' which is the exclusive vehicle of meaning." (Corner, 1983:

268) However, to take position D to its logical conclusion, we need to go one step further. That is, we need to see communication between individuals and among groups as consisting of the set of shared meanings that emerge from the encoding and decoding of texts. Communication is the collectivity of common images of reality that exist within any particular public sphere; indeed, communication is what defines the public sphere. In other words, it is more a product than a process; and insofar as it results from certain message-making processes, these are far more complex and numerous than conventional process models ever imagined.

A simple example may help to illustrate these points. In the late1960s, long hair on males came to stand for an attitude of rebellion against political authority ("the establishment") and many social norms. It would be impossible to trace the complex process by which this meaning came to be shared by entire societies. Certain rock groups no doubt made a contribution to the process. But the meaning in question was in any event a social "text" in that it was conveyed by any male who wore his hair long regardless of his intentions. Actually, there were different meanings involved, depending upon who was doing the decoding. For most youths, long hair meant a desirable disregard for out-dated social conventions; for many of their parents, it meant an irresponsible rebellion against proven social values. At present, of course, long hair on males no longer conveys such meanings. Somehow, by another imperceptible process, the commonly shared meaning of long hair on males was socially "deconstructed."

Those who are interested in the "social construction of texts" are obviously concerned with more significant cases than this. One scholar has shown how capitalist society has developed a view of the economy as something which transcends particular political or sectional interests. "The economy, in short, appears to be on no one's side. In this way unpopular political decisions can be taken and justified whilst avoiding the charge of class or self-interest. The nation's economy is apparently more important than its citizens." (Emmison, 1983: 154) Another scholar has tried to show that "the image of the world embedded in the vocabulary of the socialist press is decidedly different from the image of the world in the vocabulary of the capitalist press. If work, followed by organization, nation, and plan, prevails in the socialist image of the world, then money, followed by government, joint stock company and market, dominates the capitalist image." (Pisarek, 1983: 163)

The major weakness to date of studies based on the social texts conception of communication is their ahistorical bias. They tend to consist of models and generalizations that apply to a timeless present and cannot, therefore, be supported or refuted by historical facts. There is, however, no reason why this should remain the case. Since the early 1950s, a number of intellectual historians have been tracing the development of what are, in effect, social texts, though they have never identified their subject in such terms.

An important pioneer in this regard was the American historian Henry Nash Smith, author of *Virgin Land: The American West as Symbol and Myth*. In using the terms 'symbol' and 'myth', Smith had in mind "larger or smaller units of the same kind of thing, namely, an intellectual construction that fuses concept and emotion into an image." Moreover, the symbols and myths with which he dealt were "collective representations rather than the work of a single mind." (Smith, 1950: v) Though Smith was not alone in being interested in such representations, he played an important role in helping to shift the focus of American intellectual history away from individual thinkers and their ideas towards conceptions of reality shared by society as a whole. Among those who soon followed in his footsteps were John William Ward, Merrill Peterson, and one of his own students, Leo Marx.

Smith and his successors have built a rich literature on the origins, nature, and practical influence of the mental constructs that Americans have shared over the years. They have also had a significant impact on Canadian historiography. In some respects, however, their work could benefit from a more theoretically sophisticated conception of the process by which shared meanings develop within a society. They could profit, in other words, from exposure to some of the current work in semiotics and cultural studies. By the same token, students of communication interested in the social construction of texts might find their enquiries more rewarding if they anchored them more firmly in historical waters.

References

Barron, Sherri
   1984 "Where can the mentally ill go?"*The Ottawa Citizen* (October 22): D1.
Beattie, Earle
   1981 "Confused Terminology in the Field of Communication, Information and Mass Media: Brillig But Mimsy." *Canadian Journal of Communication* 8 (no. 1): 32-55.
Bell, Daniel
   1962 *The End of Ideology: On the Exhaustion of Political Ideas in the Fifties.* Rev. ed., New York: Macmillan.
Bell, Pat
   1985 "Visiting rights, but no visits." *The Ottawa Citizen* (February 23): F1.
Bennett, Tony
   1982 "Theories of the Media, Theories of Society." In Michael Gurevitch, Tony Bennett, James Curran, and Janet Woollacott (eds.), *Culture, Society and the Media.* London: Methuen.
Bruck, Peter A.
   1981 "The Social Production of Texts: On the Relation Production/ Product in the News Media." McGill University Graduate Communications Program Working Paper Series.
Campbell, Jeremy
   1982 *Grammatical Man: Information, Entropy, Language, and Life.* New York: Simon and Schuster.
Carey, James W.
   1975 "Communication and Culture." *Communication Research* 2 (no. 2): 177-78.
Corner, J.
   1983 "Textuality, Communication and Media Power." In Howard Davis and Paul Walton (eds.), *Language, Image, Media.* Oxford: Basil Blackwell.
Czitrom, Daniel J.
   1982 *Media and the American Mind: From Morse to McLuhan.* Chapel Hill: University of North Carolina Press.
Dance, Frank E. X.
   1982 "A Speech Theory of Communication." In F. E. X. Dance (ed.), *Human Communication Theory: Comparative Essays.* New York: Harper and Row.

Davis, Dennis K. and Stanley J. Baran
  1981 *Mass Communication and Everyday Life: A Perspective on Theory and Effects.* Belmont, California: Wadworth.
Delia, Jesse G., Barbara O'Keefe, and Daniel J. O'Keefe
  1982 "The Constructivist Approach to Communication." In F. E. X. Dance (ed.), *Human Communication Theory: Comparative Essays. New York: Harper and Row.*
Ellul, Jacques
  1973 *Propaganda: The Formation of Men's Attitudes.* Trans. by Konrad Kellen and Jean Lerner, New York: Vintage Books.
Emmison, Mike
  1983 " 'The Economy': Its Emergence in Media Discourse." In H. Davis and P. Walton (eds.), *Language, Image, Media.*
Fisher, B. Aubrey
  1982 "The Pragmatic Perspective of Human Communication: A View from System Theory." In F. E. X. Dance (ed.), *Human Communication Theory: Comparative Essays.*
Habermas, Jurgen
  1979 *Communication and the Evolution of Society.* Trans. Thomas McCarthy, Boston: Beacon Press.
Hall, S., I. Connell, and L. Curti
  1976 "The 'Unity' of Current Affairs Television." *Working Papers in Cultural Studies* 9: 51-93.
Heiber, Helmut
  1972 *Goebbels.* Trans. John K. Dickinson, New York: Hawthorn Books.
Innis, Harold Adams
  1964 *The Bias of Communication.* 2nd ed., Toronto: University of Toronto Press.
  1972 *Empire and Communications.* Rev. ed., Toronto: University of Toronto Press.
Klapper, Joseph T.
  1960 *The Effects of Mass Communication.* New York: The Free Press.
Kornhauser, William
  1968 "Mass Society." In *Encyclopedia of the Social Sciences* 10: 58-64.
Lasswell, Harold
  1960 "The Structure and Function of Communication in Society." In Wilbur Schramm (ed.), *Mass Communications.* 2nd ed., Urbana: University of Illinois Press. Reprinted from Lyman Bryson (ed.), *The Communication of Ideas.* New York: Institute for Religious and Social Studies, 1948.

Lazarsfeld, Paul F.
 1941 "Remarks on Administrative and Critical Communications Research." *Studies in Philosophy and Social Science* 9: 2-16.
Lemert, James B.
 1981 *Does Mass Communication Change Public Opinion After All? A New Approach to Effects Analysis.* Chicago: Nelson Hall.
Littlejohn, Stephen W.
 1982 "An Overview of Contributions to Human Communication Theory from Other Disciplines." In F. E. X. Dance (ed.), *Human Communication Theory Comparative Essays.* New York: Harper and Row.
Luhman, Niklas
 1981 "The Improbability of Communication." *International Social Science Journal* 33 (no. 1): 122-32.
Melody, William H., Liora Salter, and Paul Heyer (eds.)
 1981 *Culture, Communication and Dependency: The Tradition of H. A. Innis.* Norwood, N.J.: Ablex.
Morley, David
 1983 "Cultural Transformations: The Politics of Resistance." In H. Davis and P. Walton (eds.), *Language, Image, Media.* Oxford: Basil Blackwell.
Pisarek, Walery
 1983 " 'Reality' East and West." In H. Davis and P. Walton (eds.), *Language, Image, Media.* Oxford: Basil Blackwell.
Pye, Lucien
 1963 "Introduction." In L. Pye (ed.), *Communication and Political Development.* Princeton, N.J.: Princeton University Press.
Sandman, Peter M., David M. Rubin, and David B. Sachsman
 1972 *Media: An Introductory Analysis of American Mass Communications.* Englewood Cliffs, N.J.: Prentice-Hall.
Schramm, Wilbur
 1954 "How Communication Works." In W. Schramm (ed.), *The Process and Effects of Mass Communication.* Urbana: University of Illinois Press.
 1955 "Information Theory and Mass Communication." *Journalism Quarterly* 32 (Spring): 131-46.
Shannon, Claude and Warren Weaver
 1949 *The Mathematical Theory of Communication.* Urbana: University of Illinois Press.
Smith, Henry Nash
 1950 *Virgin Land: The American West as Symbol and Myth.* New York: Random House.

Steinberg, Charles S.
  1970 *The Communicative Arts: An Introduction to Mass Media.* New York: Hastings House.
Tan, Alexis S.
  1985 *Mass Communication Theories and Research.* 2nd ed., New York: John Wiley.
Wiener, Norbert
  1967 *The Human Use of Human Beings: Cybernetics and Society.* New York: Avon Books.

Chapter 2

What is News?

On the surface, the question "What is news?" does not appear to be particularly difficult to answer. Nor, perhaps, does it seem to be a matter of overwhelming significance. Most people would probably assume that they know what news is, even though they might have difficulty putting it into words. But although we consume news on a daily basis, our familiarity with it does not necessarily mean that we understand its fundamental nature or appreciate its social role. News consists of factual accounts of what has happened recently that is of apparent interest or importance to people. But do these accounts amount to an integrated description of reality? Or are they merely raw data for the eventual formation of a meaningful picture of the world? Do they serve the interests and needs of the persons who consume them? Or are they really intended to enhance the power of those who disseminate them? Clearly, when we think about it further, there is much more involved in the question "What is news?" than first meets the eye.

We cannot, in fact, understand what news is simply by examining it in its present form. We need to know how news today differs from news a century or more ago. Otherwise, we run the risk of mistaking attributes of news that are merely temporary for those that are universal. We also eliminate the possibility of assessing current characteristics from a comparative historical perspective. For example, news is thought by many to serve primarily the vested socio-economic interests of power elites. The question, however, is whether it serves these interests to a greater or to a lesser extent than it once did. It would be quite surprising if evidence could not be found in every age and society to support the thesis that news has benefits for the ruling elite. But what we need to consider is whether these benefits have been increasing or decreasing as news has evolved.

Moreover, it is not enough to examine news as a finished product. We need to have some idea about the day-to-day operations of the news media, including the basis upon which a certain segment of reality comes to be regarded as news. The production of news has been seen by some scholars as having certain aspects in common with assembly-line work in factories. (Bantz *et al.*, 1980) It proceeds according to established routines in which each news worker performs a prescribed function. There is some autonomy within this process, but it is limited by the overriding concern to produce a certain kind of product with limited resources within a restricted period of time. We cannot, therefore, say what news is without reference to some of the constraints that govern its production.

Both of these considerations need to be kept in mind as we examine different conceptions of the nature of news in democratic societies. To this end, this chapter will begin with an account of the origins of news in the English-speaking world, keeping an eye to the particular segment of society that news served best in earlier times. The operation of a present-day Canadian television news-room will then be examined and some of the basic constraints on news production generally will be pointed out. Finally, when these two preliminary tasks have been completed, four conceptions of news will be analyzed and assessed with the aid of another "double polarity."

News existed long before there were newspapers or any other formal news vehicles. It travelled by word of mouth and later through personal correspondence, moving slowly and often arriving in a fragmented form. The development of a primitive news system began, not with newspapers, which were not introduced in Europe until the seventeenth century, but with the formalization of these interpersonal channels of information about current events. During the Middle Ages, European monarchs built up staffs of household messengers; they encouraged their diplomats and other foreign agents, both male and female, to operate as spies; and they instructed other officers of the Crown to gather information about local affairs. In England, some of the larger towns developed their own means for securing information; the mayor of London, for example, received news from his own accredited observers ahead of the royal messenger. News was also supplied by the country's merchants, while the greater financial houses of Europe developed their own intelligence systems. (Armstrong, 1948; Altschull, 1984)

Gathering information about current events was one thing; distributing it to the masses was quite another. In general, only a small fraction of what was learned by the government was ever passed on to the populace and then usually it was in a politically expedient form. Some events were made known by issuing proclamations, which were normally made public or "published" by word of mouth, but occasionally by posting copies of official letters. Government officials also prepared special narrative accounts of events for foreign consumption and distributed news domestically through bills and schedules. Their brief, factual news-bills provided the first official notification of most major events and were sometimes followed by lengthier news-letters. In most cases, however, the operation of these news vehicles lagged behind private correspondence. (Armstrong, 1948)

The only sources of counter-information for the medieval masses were rumours and hearsay. These were a more powerful force then than they are today, despite repeated attempts by governments to curtail them. For rumours, sometimes in the guise of ballads, rhymes, or prophecies, did not require literacy, credibility, or power to make their way in the world. They were regarded as dangerous by church and state because their own vehicles of information were so weak. Governments seldom tried to suppress rumours themselves; they concentrated instead on those who purveyed them. Over the centuries, increasingly severe penalties were introduced against rumour-mongers, as they were called, especially in times of civil tension. In England, for example, the *Statute of Westminster* provided for the imprisonment of anyone spreading falsehoods until he could produce his informant. English authorities also tried for a while to prevent rumours of internal disturbances from reaching the European continent, regardless of whether they were true or false. (Armstrong 1948).

It was only through a long slow process that the masses acquired better sources of information. That process began in the late fifteenth century with the invention and spread of the printing press, but the initial impact of printing was on knowledge rather than news. To understand why this was the case, it is necessary to recall that before printing, the only means by which medieval scholars could reproduce a text was to copy it by hand, which was a very time-consuming and labour-intensive process. Under these conditions, the preservation of knowledge, rather than its augmentation, was the overriding concern. With the introduction of printing, scholars were suddenly released from the problem of preservation. Books could be produced in much larger numbers and reprinted as required, without suffering from the corruption of their contents through repeated copying. As a result, however, print became closely associated with ideas of permanence and durability. It seemed unnatural to print something intended to be impermanent. The first tentative contact between news and print thus took the form of *books* of news, which, though it strikes the modern mind as a contradiction in terms, was a logical outcome of early notions of print.

The newsbooks of the sixteenth century evolved into the newspapers of the eighteenth century through a number of intermediate products. In seventeenth-century England, these went by a variety of names, including *corantos,* diurnals, and newsletters. Modelled on Dutch publications, the *corantos* first appeared in London in the 1620s and consisted of modest collections of such foreign news as the licensing authorities deemed acceptable for public consumption. The earliest English-language newspaper is generally considered to be *The Oxford Gazette,* which appeared for the first time in 1655 and became *The London Gazette* after 23 weekly issues. It was the result of the desire of members of the English court for tidbits of news following their removal to Oxford because of a plague in London.

Apart from its continuity (it appeared twice-weekly), *The London Gazette* differed little from the news publications preceding it. However, it soon spawned a number of imitators, including the *Publick Occurrences* of Benjamin Harris who had emigrated to Boston in 1690. This first attempt at a newspaper in America was suppressed by the Governor of Massachusetts after a single issue. But by the middle of the eighteenth century the newspaper was firmly established on both sides of the Atlantic. The first news sheet in Canada was the Halifax *Gazette,* established by John Bushell in 1752. Although a daily newspaper was begun in England in 1702, most colonial papers were issued on a weekly basis. Dailies were not common in the United States until the end of the eighteenth century and did not make their appearance in Canada until the 1840s. As in other areas of its history, British North America suffered from cultural lag in newspaper development.

Analyzed in terms of the primary constituency served, the development of English-language newspapers can be divided into three stages. During the first stage, which stretched from the late seventeenth to the early nineteenth century, newspapers were designed primarily to meet the needs of a relatively small political and commercial elite. In the course of the second stage, which spanned most of the nineteenth century, British and North American newspapers ceased to be merely the hand-maiden of the ruling classes and became an effective instrument of the rising middle classes. Finally, during the twentieth century, mainstream journalism began to reach down to the lower classes, which until then had been largely ignored except by the radical press. It is arguable, of course, that the middle classes have remained the segment of society best served by journalism. Nonetheless, a case can be made that the press is more genuinely democratic today than at any previous time in its history.

From the Glorious Revolution of 1688 to the accession of George III in 1760, English society was dominated by a small oligarchical elite of heterogeneous composition. It was from this elite that practically every member of Parliament was drawn. Moreover, representatives were chosen, not simply from this oligarchy to the exclusion of the rest of society, but by the three most powerful groups within it. Having acquired control over parliamentary revenue, the House of Commons was no longer controlled directly by the House of Lords. But elections for the House of Commons, which involved only 250,000 of Britain's six to seven million inhabitants, were still manipulated by the nobles and bishops who sat in the House of Lords and by the merchant princes who controlled town government.

It was for this oligarchy with its special information needs that the eighteenth-century newspaper was primarily designed. The first English newspaper was essentially a vehicle of government propaganda. But the curtailment of the *Licensing Act* in 1694 encouraged the development of newspapers that were not government-controlled. In 1712, the government passed the first of a series of Stamp Taxes with the apparent intention of taxing these papers into extinction. That did not happen, however, and the reason is not hard to find. The fact was that the English oligarchy needed newspapers in this period for both economic and political reasons. On the one hand, newspapers served as a bulletin board for the commercial community. On the other hand, they were required as an instrument of information and persuasion by the various political groupings and factions seeking either to preserve or acquire political power. It seems clear, therefore, that the Stamp Taxes were not designed to eliminate the news vehicles of the oligarchy, but rather to prevent the growth of a non-oligarchic press.

Other segments of society were not prohibited from reading newspapers, but they were deterred from doing so by both their cost and their content. In the early nineteenth century, the cost of American newspapers was still six cents an issue, or six to eight dollars for an annual subscription, and at this time the average urban worker earned less than 85 cents a day. It was possible to overcome this deterrent by sharing a newspaper or by frequenting one's favourite coffee-house where a selection of newspapers would be read aloud daily. But the content of these papers was intended for the select few, not for the untutored masses. Apart from a few cultural items, early English-language newspapers were devoted almost exclusively to domestic politics, foreign affairs, and commercial transactions. They contained very little local news and made no attempt to address the economic concerns of the urban or rural masses.

In its treatment of news, moreover, the eighteenth-century newspaper was more like an extended editorial. It set forth a certain amount of information considered useful for its particular clientele, but slanted its presentation along highly partisan lines. Indeed, its energies were spent less in gathering information than in reshaping it for the purposes of political persuasion. There were, in fact, very few reporters as such; most news came from travellers, merchants, friends of the editor, and other unpaid correspondents. It was not until the nineteenth century that foreign correspondents became paid employees. In terms of domestic politics, during the eighteenth century, English newspapers did use paid reporters to cover Parliament. But as late as the 1820s, some American newspapers relied upon letters from their members of Congress for coverage of Washington politics. The sources of news remained both informal and unreliable and no system was developed to check their accuracy. (Smith, 1978: 157-9; Schudson, 1978: 24)

The editorial confrontations among early eighteenth-century newspapers tended to arise from feuds within the oligarchy rather from than a struggle between classes. After 1760, however, this situation began to change. Upon ascending the throne, George III tried to reassert royal power by acting as if he were his own chief minister and exercising more control over the state bureaucracy. The clash that resulted not only weakened both the monarchy and the oligarchy but also released new pressures from the urban middle classes. Led by John Wesley, the Methodists began to attack both the moral laxity of the Anglican Church and the general depravity of the English oligarchy. At the same time, a group of radical reformers led by John Wilkes tried to force Parliament to allow reporting of its debates and provide legal recognition of the right of the individual not to be arrested on unspecified charges. Wilkes' reform movement was carried on during the 1780s by another radical group called the Dissenters, which agitated for universal male suffrage and parliamentary reform.

The reaction of the established order to these lower middle class rumblings was two-fold. First, the Anglican Church responded to Methodism with a reform movement of its own known as Evangelicalism. Through William Wilberforce, their spokesman in Parliament, the Evangelicals pressed for such reforms as the abolition of the slave trade. Secondly, the government responded to the Dissenters by eliminating the worst abuses of the patronage system and enacting a few other modest political reforms. The rest was taken care of by the French Revolution which, through its excessive violence, seriously undermined the political reform movement in Britain and gave the government a pretext for repressive measures. In 1789, for example, the government made it illegal for individuals to join together to purchase a newspaper. (Asquith, 1978: 100) Not until the end of the Napoleonic period did the English oligarchy again have to face the prospect of reform.

During the post-Napoleonic years, demands for political, economic, and social reform were renewed in Great Britain. Once again the pressure came from two main sources: a radical reform movement on behalf of the working classes; and a more moderate reform movement supported by the rapidly growing middle classes. Both movements sought to expand the suffrage, though by different degrees, and a limited victory was won by the middle classes in this regard with the passage of the Reform Bill of 1832. At the same time, the middle classes also waged a campaign to remove the remaining government controls on the press. Despite the relaxation of the law of libel by the *Libel Act* of 1792, the government had increased its newspaper subsidies in the 1790s and had steadily increased the Stamp Duty on newspapers until 1815. (Asquith, 1978: 98) But neither move had prevented the emergence of both an "unstamped" radical press and an increasingly influencial urban middle class press.

As it turned out, the real enemy of the radical press was not the government but the middle-class press. Through a series of complicated manoeuvres beginning in the 1830s, the middle-class press succeeded in having the obnoxious "taxes on knowledge" gradually reduced and eventually abolished. But it did so largely at the expense of the radical press. The reduction of the Stamp Duty made it possible for the middle-class press to lower the prices of their papers, increase their size, and publish more frequently. The fact that this served to squeeze out many of the radical papers came as no surprise to the government, for the middle-class press had pointed out this possibility in conducting its campaign against the Stamp Duty. (Curran, 1978: 53-6)

As the reform movement subsided in Britain during the second half of the nineteenth century, newspaper proprietors gradually began to run their newspapers less as political organs and more as omnibus publications ostensibly designed for the general reader. Through the use of what has come to be known as the "human interest" story, they tried to attract readers from all strata of society. The primary influence in this regard came from the United States, where freedom of the press had made more rapid progress than in either Britain or Canada. The stamp taxes were eliminated in America during the Revolution of 1776 and a guarantee of freedom of the press was included in the First Amendment to the Constitution of 1789. This did not immediately transform American newspapers, which remained an instrument of the propertied elite for some time thereafter. But during the era of Jacksonian Democracy, middle-class journalism made a triumphant appearance in America in the form of the so-called "penny papers." The first of these, the New York *Sun,* was set up by Benjamin Day in 1833; it was followed in short order by such papers as the New York *Herald* (1835) and the Boston daily *Times* (1836).

Most of the penny papers were independent of political parties and some even eschewed covering politics at all. All were less interested in political editorializing than in providing factual, timely, and entertaining accounts of events in ordinary life. They hired reporters and sent them into the courts and the streets to cover local events. They also invented, improved, and, in some cases, exploited the "human interest story" as a means of attracting large numbers of readers. Both strategies proved to be extremely successful and enabled the penny papers to make advertising their main source of revenue. Indeed, they worked so well that by the end of the nineteenth century, many of the established papers had become politically neutral and had begun to emphasize human interest content.

Despite their mass circulations, however, the penny papers still left major segments of society unserved. The farming community was poorly served and one could hardly tell that the urban working classes existed from reading most papers. This can be seen from the content analyses that historian Paul Rutherford undertook in connection with his detailed study of the daily press in late nineteenth-century Canada. For example, in 1896 *The Gazette* (Montreal) devoted 25.4 per cent of its news columns to information about economics. Of this, 24.8 per cent pertained to business news, while only 0.5 and 0.1 per cent dealt with labour and farm news respectively. While other Montreal papers generally devoted more space to labour and the farming community, their percentages in these categories were also very low. For labour coverage, the percentages were: *Herald,* 0.7;

La Presse, 3.1; *Le Monde,* 0.3; *La Minerve,* 1.0; and *La Patrie,* 4.3. For farm news, the percentages were: *Herald,* 0.1; *La Presse,* 2.2; *Le Monde,* 0.4; *La Minerve,* 2.3; and *La Patrie,* 0.1. (Rutherford, 1982: 70)

The extent to which this situation has changed is not clear. For reasons which are hard to discern, media researchers have carried out very few studies to determine whether non-elite groups are better served by newspapers today than a century ago. A small study of *The Toronto Star* conducted by Mark Stokes (under the author's supervision) found a modest but significant increase in the percentage of news devoted to non-elite groups during the period from 1904 to 1984. Particularly significant was the increased coverage of groups without formal organization. (Stokes, 1985) But this study was intended merely to test the waters and get a better idea of some of the problems to be encountered in this kind of research. A great deal more work will have to be done in this area before we can generalize about recent trends in proportions of news devoted to elite and non-elite groups in Canadian society.

There would, however, seem to be several forces that have been working on behalf of better news coverage for society as a whole. Foremost among these has been the increased professionalism of journalists. Since the turn of the century, journalists have become better educated and trained to practise their craft; they have developed professional associations, university programs, and elaborate data networks; and they have established standards of reporting and codes of ethical behaviour. They have also gradually refined their concept of objectivity. Initially, objectivity was taken simply to mean the suppression of bias and the maintenance of a strictly neutral stance. The growth of wire services reinforced this negative concept of objectivity as essentially the absence of subjectivity. But modern journalists have gradually come to realize its limitations. They have recognized that, above all else, objectivity demands a willingness to pursue the truth of a story wherever it may lead, regardless of the outcome.

Unfortunately, improvements in journalism have been compromised by other forces. Increased professionalism has been accompanied by the increasing involvement of commercial interests, for which news is merely a means of acquiring an audience. The requirements of advertisers are often opposed to the professional standards of journalists. For example, their desire to package television news as attractively as possible takes little account of what may be necessary from the standpoint of human understanding. Moreover, journalists have been plagued increasingly by what is known as government news management.

Since the end of the First World War, Western governments have sought to control the flow of information to the public less by censorship than by carefully prepared press releases and public relations campaigns.

The strategy is in part to so overwhelm the press with information that it becomes grateful for pre-packaged handouts. In Canada, T. Joseph Scanlon has shown how federal information services use the news media to manipulate public opinion. The problem is not only that "the news media stand ready to assist government in its attempts to manipulate public opinion," but also that there exist highly developed "publicity networks extending from government through advertising and public relations into the news media." (Scanlon, 1976: 83)

The operation of these contradictory forces should be kept in mind when we assess the performance of the news media in modern democratic societies. At the same time, however, we should also direct our attention to the basic question "What is news?" For in the final analysis, it may be that it is the underlying nature of news itself that causes some groups to be better served by the news system than others. We need to assess news, not by what we would like it to be, but by what its inherent nature will allow it to be. This does not mean that we should adopt an uncritical stance towards news as it is produced today. But neither should we measure it against a hypothetical product that never has existed and, in all likelihood, never will exist.

Although our concern is with the general nature of news, it is helpful to have a few concrete images in mind about what takes place in a news-room. In this section, therefore, a sketch is provided of a day in the life of a news-room. The news-room chosen is that of the CBC English network in Toronto. Broadcast news operations differ in a number of respects from print news operations. They produce fewer stories; they rely more on routine events; they make less use of regular "beats"; and they utilize the services of news agencies more extensively. (Golding and Elliott, 1980) Moreover, an operation such as the CBC national news-room obviously has much greater resources at its disposal than smaller radio and television news-rooms. But this does not mean that we need to define 'news' differently to accommodate its different species. Indeed, given the importance of broadcast news today, we should avoid forming generalizations about news that do not take into account the conditions under which broadcast news workers operate.

The production of "The National" by the CBC News Service takes place in somewhat shabby quarters on the fifth floor of the CBC Television building on Jarvis Street in Toronto. The workday begins about 6:30 a.m. when a person arrives to record items from the early American news shows. The first assignment editor arrives about 8:00 a.m. There used to be two senior assignment editors, one for foreign news, the other for domestic. Now there are three: one to assign reporters to cover foreign stories and two with domestic jurisdictions (Canada East and Canada West). The foreign assignment editor arrives first and begins his day by contacting the overseas bureaus and foreign correspondents. Later he has to make arrangements for material to be sent to Toronto by satellite. The domestic assignment editors work with CBC reporters in the regions and make use of land lines as well as satellites.

The day-long task of "deciding what's news" is carried out with the aid of various sources of information, including the wire services (Canadian Press, Associated Press, United Press International, Reuters); the most recent editions of major newspapers such as *The Times* of London, the New York *Times,* and *The Globe and Mail,* Toronto; and the CBC News Service's own diary or record of unfolding events. There are basically two kinds of decisions which have to be made as the day proceeds. The first type of decision is obviously about *what* stories to cover. More items are selected initially for potential coverage than ever make it into the final newscast. The assignment editors begin by drawing up a list called the "daily outlook." This consists of the broadest possible outline of potential news stories, including some items left over from previous newscasts. Throughout the day, this is whittled down from as many as 35 items to a final list of about 12.

The second kind of decision which has to be made concerns *how* particular stories are to be covered. This type of decision involves a variety of factors, including the availability of personnel, possible technical constraints, and the financial costs of different types of coverage. For example, it might be known that the American president will be giving a press conference later in the day. If the CBC simply relayed a feed of segments of the press conference, it might cost the News Service a few hundred dollars in transmission costs. Given the usual nature of such press conferences, however, it might be anticipated that the president will not really have very much to say. In this case, it might be better to have the CBC foreign correspondent in Washington do a live report summarizing the president's main points and adding some commentary of his own. This would normally run into extra costs, however, especially if studio time was rented from one of the American networks. So a decision would have to be made not simply in terms of what would work the best from the standpoint of content but also keeping in mind the relative costs involved. (Aitken, 1975)

Both kinds of decision making occur at the daily production meeting, called the "dayside/nightside" meeting because it is there that the people working during the day meet for the first time with those who will carry on during the evening. This kind of meeting remains a fixture in both print and broadcast news operations, though it is perhaps less important today than it once was. At the CBC, it used to be held at 4:00 p.m.; it is now held at 2:00 p.m. in part because of the movement of "The National" to an earlier time slot. The chief news editor together with the assignment editors and supervising producers draw up a "hit list" of stories and work out tentative story lengths. Only when their work is complete can the producer and lineup editor begin the demanding task of assembling the separate items into a balanced and coherent package for broadcast.

Although there are no rigid rules in this regard, those who prepare "The National" seem to strive for a reasonable balance between national and international news items. For example, on March 6, 1975, "The National" contained the following items (Aitken, 1975):

1. Guerrilla raid on Tel Aviv (2 mins., 25 secs.)
2. Ford's news conference on Cambodia (2 mins., 27 secs.)
3. Laid-off auto workers recalled (2 mins., 7 secs.)
4. Trudeau talks to Italian premier (1 min., 25 secs.)
5. Vancouver grain shipment strike (19 secs.)
6. CLC settles union dispute (25 secs.)
7. Capt. Brian Erb arraigned (1 min., 57 secs.)
8. Caouette on press "bribes" (17 secs.)
9. Montreal seeks lottery money (32 secs.)
10. Draft-dodgers in new bind (1 min., 51 secs.)
11. Rental housing shortage (3 mins., 37 secs.)
12. Washington's singing dogs (1 min., 19 secs.)

If the draft-dodger story is counted as international, there are seven domestic stories and five international ones. There is an even closer time split, with 10 minutes and 19 seconds worth of domestic news and 9 minutes and 27 seconds worth of international news. A few other general principles governing the organization of a television newscast can also be seen from this example. There is only one item longer than three minutes (the "ongoing" rental housing story) and it is placed next to last followed by the usual "brightener" at the end. There is an attempt to pair stories with a connection of some kind (*e.g.* the two union stories and the two Quebec stories).

As can be imagined, it is difficult to achieve a balance of national and international news on days when there happens to be a surfeit of one and very little of the other. However, there are various devices that can be used to get around this. For example, on March 5, 1984, "The National" contained the following items (author's analysis):

*1. Protest against cruise missile test (3 mins., 40 secs.)
   a) related court case
   b) NDP support
2. Trudeau honoured by Parliament (3 mins., 20 secs.)
3. Trudeau speech/birthday in Toronto (2 mins., 40 secs.)
4. Cabinet shuffle by Premier Levesque (2 mins., 10 secs.)
5. End of Lebanon-Israeli accord (1 min., 20 secs.)
6. Impending battle between Iraq and Iran (30 secs.)
7. Passport regulation (20 secs.)
8. Reagan and Cole (25 secs.)

9. Gulf purchase of Standard Oil (15 secs.)
10. Death of William Powell (45 secs.)
11. Special report on Aids (4 min., 50 secs.)

*The cruise missile material involved two closely related stories. If these are separated, the result would be a newscast of twelve items. For many years, "The National" always contained this number of stories, although a CBC spokesman has affirmed that this is no longer the case.

On this particular day, there were several domestic stories that seemed to warrant extensive coverage (relatively speaking). To provide this coverage, the time allotted to international news was reduced to a mere 3 minutes and 35 seconds (excluding the Aids report, which is hard to classify). But to retain some kind of overall balance, six international items were strung together in rapid succession after the opening four domestic stories.

The process of selecting, gathering, and structuring news items for a television or radio newscast obviously differs in a number of important respects from the assembly of a newspaper or news magazine. Broadcast news operations cannot afford to chase stories that might not work out as frequently as print news operations. They cannot provide as extensive coverage or coverage from as many angles. And they are under added pressure to increase or decrease coverage simply on the basis of likely audience interest (*e.g.* the 45 seconds devoted to the death of William Powell compared to the 15 seconds worth of coverage on the purchase of Standard Oil by Gulf). All news organizations, however, are structured to yield a uniform product in the face of variable events and resources. They all attempt to reduce the amount of uncertainty by advance planning and the creation of a normal working routine. Whatever news is, therefore, it is not simply a spontaneous, completely flexibile, and indeterminant response to current events.

Western conceptions of news have been formulated on the basis of a particular paradigm. The concept of a paradigm was first developed by Thomas Kuhn in a famous little book called *The Structure of Scientific Revolutions* (1962). As understood by Kuhn, a paradigm is any agreed-upon basis of scientific research; that is, any set of unquestioned theoretical or methodological principles within a field of enquiry. A scientific revolution, according to Kuhn, occurs whenever a research tradition within the natural sciences is overthrown and replaced by another one. However, the term quickly became a buzz-word within the academic community and was generalized to include less formalized bases of intellectual agreement than Kuhn originally had in mind. Scholars thus began to find — or, in some cases, bemoan the lack of — paradigms in economics, sociology, and so forth.

The key point about a paradigm is that it operates beneath the surface for the most part, at least until its use begins to create problems for its adherants. Only when it becomes incapable either of handling a significant number of new observations or of accommodating new ways of doing research does it come into full view. At that point, there are several things that can happen. Either the paradigm is bolstered by new arguments so that it survives more or less intact; or it is substantially modified, but not actually destroyed as such; or, finally, it is replaced by a new paradigm after, in many cases, a long and bitter struggle.

The nature of news has generally been examined on the basis of a "knowledge paradigm." That is, it has been taken for granted that news is – – or, at least, approximates or aspires to be — a form of knowledge. To be sure, this has not led to agreement about other aspects of its nature. On the contrary, there has been considerable debate about whether news is based on objective or subjective criteria of selection. According to some writers, certain events are selected as news because of inherent characteristics which they possess (*e.g.* immediacy, unusualness, social significance, human interest). According to others, however, the selection of news is governed by certain vested interests on the part of journalists and especially those who employ them. This debate has been interpreted as a confrontation between a commercial laissez-faire and a mass manipulative view of how news is manufactured. (Cohen and Young, 1973) The views in question differ not only in terms of their assessment of news criteria, but also with regard to their basic conception of knowledge. Nonetheless, both assume that news is best understood from the standpoint of knowledge.

The apparent weakness of the case for objective news criteria has made debate about the role of the press rather one-sided in recent years. Most of those who have studied the process of news production have become quite critical of current news practices. This is camouflaged to some extent by the fact that each new intellectual critique of the press is usually couched in the language of revelation. It is presented as if it were being discovered for the first time that the press does not provide an objective picture of the world. But there is certainly no shortage of media critics today; what is rare is to find someone prepared to defend the overall performance of the press against its many critics.

For those beginning the study of communication, the traditional emphasis on knowledge may seem strange. Why should news be approached almost exclusively from the angle of its relation to knowledge? Why, it might conceivably be asked, is it not considered from the standpoint of communication? The answer to this is rather paradoxical. On the one hand, the knowledge paradigm underlies the classical democratic view of the role of the press. According to this view, the press provides the information by means of which an enlightened public opinion is formed. News helps to create a knowledgeable citizenry capable of participating effectively in the democratic process. On the other hand, however, the knowledge paradigm also serves those who would criticize this view as having little or no foundation in fact. The main argument here is that the press currently provides an extremely biased and distorted picture of reality and is thus a very imperfect form of knowledge.

It becomes easier to defend the press if the traditional knowledge paradigm is replaced by a communications paradigm. News can then be seen as something that fosters a "meeting of minds" within society and helps to create a set of shared meanings. There is, of course, a more trivial sense in which the news media facilitate communication; namely, that they convey messages in the form of information to the general public. But that point does not provide a good basis for defending the press against its critics. More promising is the suggestion that news is actually an important vehicle through which people often convey their true thoughts and feelings to a larger audience; that it contains within it mechanisms for penalizing those who attempt to engage in propaganda; and that as a result it provides society with a safeguard against widespread public delusions.

The critical question is how this line of defence will stand up when we examine the issue of news criteria. For it was the question of news-worthiness that made adherants to the knowledge paradigm generally critical of the press. Considering news from the perspective of communication does not rule out the possibility that it still functions primarily to help the powerful to manipulate the weak. Given the two questions — "Is news a form of knowledge?" and "What is the basis of news selection? — four positions thus emerge. These are indicated in Figure 2 on p. 47.

To summarize in advance, Position A argues that through improved technology, increased professionalism, and substantial freedom of the press, journalists have been able to provide us with increasingly accurate and meaningful pictures of the world. (For the purpose of simplicity and editorial consistency, the pronouns 'he' and 'him' are used when referring to the journalist.) It is admitted that there are constraints upon the journalist, but it is held that journalists still do a reasonably good job of providing us with a preliminary picture of the world from which we can proceed to develop more refined versions. As such, journalism plays an important role in keeping the citizens of a democracy informed. Position B criticizes this viewpoint as naive. It argues that the "knowledge" contained within the news supports the ideology of the elite. In an attempt to counter this, Position C suggests that the knowledge paradigm be replaced by a communications paradigm. However, Position D replies by claiming that even when this is done, news still emerges as an elitist support mechanism.

Position A — News as a Preliminary Picture of the World

Position A sees news as an organized attempt to provide society with a picture of reality as it unfolds. It is not hard to find naive versions of this

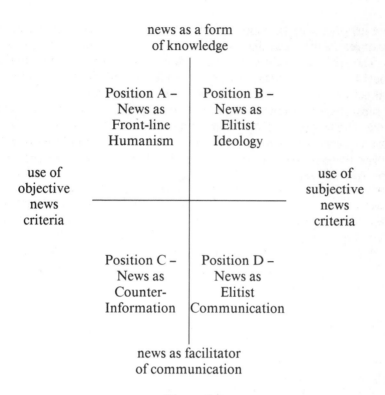

news as a form
of knowledge

Position A –
News as
Front-line
Humanism

Position B –
News as
Elitist
Ideology

use of
objective
news
criteria

use of
subjective
news
criteria

Position C –
News as
Counter-
Information

Position D –
News as
Elitist
Communication

news as facilitator
of communication

Figure 2

position, such as the idea that journalism holds up a mirror to reality. But
for the most part, adherants to this position would readily acknowledge
that the picture of reality provided by journalists is only a preliminary one
and is imperfect in many respects. What they would still maintain,
however, is that for all of its faults, news constitutes an essential starting
point for understanding the world in which we live. It extends our senses so
that, after a fashion, we are able to perceive events that would otherwise
remain outside our field of vision. As Walter Lippmann once said, it
furnishes us with the pictures that we carry around in our heads.

Viewed from this perspective, the journalist functions as a kind of
front-line humanist. This means two things principally. To begin with it
means that he is not a social scientist. The distinction between the humanities and the social sciences is, of course, a rather complex one. But to put
the matter as simply as possible, we might say that human perception poses
a radically different problem for each. For the humanist, the basic problem
is that we perceive too little. That is, we do not, without further reflection,
grasp the historical, the moral, or the religious dimensions of reality. We do
not sufficiently appreciate the subtleties of the human mind and the rich
texture of life. The task of the humanist, therefore, is to help us to see life

more fully not only through history and philosophy, but also by means of literature, poetry, and religion.

The problem for the social scientist, on the other hand, is precisely the opposite. It is rather that we perceive too much in the sense of indiscriminately absorbing information about all aspects of social reality. We do not separate perceptions about what is vital from perceptions about what is trivial. The task of the social scientist, therefore, is to discover, verify, and account for the more important relationships that occur within the parameters of human existence. In other words, the social scientist is concerned about constant relationships between types of events (*e.g.* television viewing and aggression) rather than relationships between specific events as such; or, insofar as the social scientist does concern himself with actual events, it is to derive data by which to test a hypothetical relationship and eventually establish a law governing certain event-types.

Seen in this light, the journalist obviously has a much closer affinity to the humanities than the social sciences. He is concerned with concrete events for their own sake and not simply to derive laws about event-types. His closest relative, indeed, is the historian, although the conditions under which the journalist operates make him, at most, a historian on the run. Indeed, the constraints upon the journalist are such that it is necessary, according to Position A, to describe him not merely as a humanist, but as a *front-line* humanist. He is the foot-soldier in the battle for human understanding, carrying out vital functions but seldom in a position to grasp what is happening in the overall campaign. He is under constant pressure to deal with immediate threats, lacking the time to measure all factors or weigh every contingency.

In the context of a news-room, this means that the journalist cannot reflect leisurely about the relative importance of different events. He needs certain rules of thumb or accepted guidelines for determining what is most newsworthy on a given day. Even so, journalists often make questionable decisions about what is important. On many days, they simply pursue the story that is easiest to obtain. In the final analysis, however, Position A assumes that the ultimate criterion of newsworthiness is social significance and that it is utilized to a reasonable degree. In a majority of cases, one event is selected for coverage over another because it is thought to be more important for society to know about it. It is then pursued by the journalist as far as his time, resources, and talent permit.

According to Position A, therefore, the journalist selects news on the basis of more or less objective criteria. That is, he does not simply select what interests him personally or what would serve the interests of a particular class. He does, of course, have to make a personal assessment of what is socially significant. And at times he has to include a certain amount of insignificant, but interesting material in order to capture and maintain his audience's attention. But that does not mean that the journalist's approach overall lacks objectivity.

The idea of the journalist as a front-line humanist underlay the classical democratic view of the role of the press. This view emerged during the nineteenth century as the English press tried to remove a number of remaining restrictions upon its freedom. In an effort to convince the government of the benefits of a free press, a number of Englishmen began to champion the press as a vital link between public opinion and government decision makers. In this regard, they ascribed to the press a two-fold role: to provide the information and ideas necessary for an enlightened public opinion; and to channel that opinion back to those in power. (Boyce, 1978) Better government, they argued, would result from a more informed and vigilant citizenry.

During the early years of the twentieth century, however, this optimistic assessment of the value of the press began to come under closer scrutiny. Both the assumption of rationality in political decision making and the belief in a rational public opinion were questioned. "Most of the political opinions of most men," wrote British political scientist Graham Wallas in *Human Nature in Politics* (1908), "are the result, not of reasoning tested by experience, but of unconscious or half-conscious inference fixed by habit." (Boyce, 1978: 38) Political action, Wallas argued, is based largely on accident, prejudice, and custom.

Even more damaging was the suggestion that the press could not, in fact, supply the information required for a rational public opinion. Foremost among those who began to have doubts about the ability of the press in this regard was a young American by the name of Walter Lippmann. Disenchanted by his own early experiences in politics, Lippmann began to reflect on the relationship between the intellectual and the politician in democratic societies. In a classic study entitled *Public Opinion* (1922), he reached the pessimistic conclusion that the press could never inform the electorate adequately for it to participate effectively in government policy making. The problem, as he saw it, was not with public opinion, but with the press itself. It is, he said, "too frail to carry the whole burden of popular sovereignty, to supply spontaneously the truth which democrats hoped was inborn." (Lippmann, 1965: 228) Lippmann wanted politicians to be guided in their decision making by organized intelligence produced by an intellectual elite, not by public opinion created by journalists.

Lippmann imagined this elite working in various public and private institutions and creating a body of knowledge and expertise on the basis of which public policy would be formed. Though he himself later became one of America's most distinguished journalists, he saw only a relatively minor role for journalism at this stage of his career. "The press," he wrote,

is no substitute for institutions. It is like the beam of a searchlight that moves restlessly about, bringing one episode and then another out of darkness into vision. Men cannot do the work of the world by this light alone. They cannot govern society by episodes, incidents, and eruptions. It is only when they work by a steady light of their own, that the press, when it is turned upon them, reveals a situation intelligible enough for a popular decision. (Lippmann, 1965: 229).

Lippmann's suggestion that "news and truth are not the same thing" (p. 226) could be interpreted to mean that news does not provide us with anything that could really be considered as knowledge. However, neither Lippmann nor most of his contemporaries were prepared to go quite this far. They admitted that news does not consist of formal, scientific knowledge. But they still considered it to be a form of knowledge with its own particular functions to fulfill. The clearest statement of this position was set forth by the American sociologist, Robert E. Park, in "News as a Form of Knowledge" (1940). Park imagined that different forms of knowledge might be placed along a continuum on the basis of their degree of precision. He then concluded that news is located at some point between a superficial and fragmentary personal "acquaintance with" certain events and a formal, exact, and verified "knowledge of" those events. News is more than one man's observation of reality, but less than history or sociology.

An interesting modification of Park's analysis has been worked out by G. Stuart Adam. Substituting journalism for news, Adam suggests that:

> . . . it is possible to imagine individual pieces of journalism at a number of stations along this imagined continuum, each station representing increasing descriptive richness, increasing complexity in the relations between phenomena described and increasing explanatory power. At one end of the continuum one would find journalism which would approximate mere gossip and rumor. Other pieces would be closer on the continuum, although never the equivalent, to exact pieces of scholarly knowledge derived from historical, philosophical or scientific investigation. (Adam, 1976: 9-10).

Like Park, Adam assumes that news is a form of knowledge, albeit a somewhat inferior one. He acknowledges that journalists are not in the business of producing rigorous scholarship, but concludes nonetheless that "the criteria by which journalism may be judged are similar in kind to the criteria we use to judge history, social science and literature." (Adam, 1976: 12) The position of Park and Adam provides a partial defence against Lippmann's pessimistic assessment of journalism's ability to provide us with a ready-made picture of the world. It suggests that journalism does, at least, assist us with the construction of a view of reality, even though it falls short of constructing that view itself. However, this position has been challenged on a number of grounds in recent years.

Position B — News as Elitist Ideology

Most media researchers today would reject the claim that the selection, gathering, and presentation of news are objective processes in the sense that they are determined primarily by the nature of reality itself. On the contrary, they would argue that it is not the attributes of events themselves, but the nature of news production, that determines whether something is newsworthy and how it is covered. As David Altheide has written, "events become news when transformed by the news perspective, and not because of their objective characteristics." (Altheide, 1976: 173) News is subjective in the sense that it is structured in accordance with the needs of the organization producing it. For example, audience interest in a television newscast can be maintained more easily if each item is cast in the form of a story with a beginning, a middle, and a conclusion. (Epstein, 1981: 129) This narrative structure is not necessarily inherant in reality; it is imposed upon it by news workers governed by the commercial necessity of attracting large audiences for their newscasts.

This does not mean that news can no longer be regarded as a form of knowledge. This would be true only if knowledge itself is assumed to be an objective reflection of reality. If, however, we regard knowledge as a social construction whose form and content is influenced by subjective as well as objective considerations, then news does not have to be excluded from the realm of knowledge. That knowledge should be seen in this manner is the basic assumption of the sociology of knowledge. All knowledge arises within, and is determined by, a particular social context. It is produced by individuals and groups with objectives, biases, and general ways of thinking which are socially derived.

Does this mean that all knowledge is ideology? Peter Berger and Thomas Luckmann point out that "the term 'ideology' has been used in so many different senses that one might despair of using it in any precise manner at all." (Berger and Luckmann, 1966: 204) However, they suggest a narrow definition that is particularly useful for the purposes at hand. "When a particular definition of reality comes to be attached to a particular power interest," they write, "it may be called an ideology." (p. 123) In other words, there are many subjective considerations that affect the production of knowledge. The desire to establish or maintain the power of a particular group in society is not the only such consideration, but it is a major one. Using the definition of Berger and Luckmann, an ideology exists when knowledge is created to bolster the power of an organization or class.

Can we say, then, that news is not merely knowledge but ideology? Does it construct a view of reality that benefits a particular power interest? Position B answers these questions in the affirmative, but does so in several different ways. According to some of its advocates, news is consciously created to serve the interests of the ruling class. Those who own the media are thought to exercise direct control over their employees in order to manipulate public opinion. According to others, media owners seldom interfere directly in the production of news. But news workers are aware of the interests of their employers and exercise a form of self-censorship. Still another group argues that the media serve as ideological agencies for the maintenance of class domination by indirect and unconscious means. There are thought to be inherent structural biases in news through which it unconsciously serves the interests of elites.

It is not difficult to find isolated cases of media owners directly controlling the production of news in order to manipulate public opinion. This kind of control was exercised by the American media baron, William Randolph Hearst, who used his newspaper chain to advance his own political interests. But it is more difficult to prove that this has been a widespread, sustained, and systematic practice among media owners. On the contrary, the evidence suggests that news operations are too large for owners to manipulate news coverage on a regular basis.

There are somewhat better grounds for concluding that control is exercised indirectly through a process of self-censorship by news workers. This argument was first set forth in a paper by Warren Breed entitled "Social Control in the Newsroom" (1955). According to Breed, newspaper publishers establish implicit news policies which help to maintain an existing system of power relationships. "Policy usually protects property and class interests," he wrote, "and thus the strata and groups holding these interests are better able to retain them." (Breed, 1960: 193) Breed argued that these policies are enforced indirectly by exploiting feelings of obligation or esteem as well as aspirations for promotion and achievement. The news worker "learns to anticipate what is expected of him so as to win rewards and avoid punishments." (Breed, 1960: 182) In particular, he learns what kinds of stories are acceptable and what topics are to be downplayed or ignored. Thus, he serves the interests of the elite by directing the public's attention towards some issues and away from others.

Since Breed's study appeared, the conception of news as elitist ideology has been refined even further. It is now maintained by some that journalists would serve the interests of the ruling class even in the absence of news-room controls. This is thought to be the case because of certain largely unconscious processes governing the selection of news that tend to favour the status quo and thus indirectly support existing elites. An interesting version of this argument can be found in Stuart Hall's article "A World at One With Itself" (1970).

According to Hall, news serves elites less through "the wilful, intentional bias of editors and newscasters" than through "the institutionalized ethos of the news media as a whole." (Hall, 1973: 89) Given the deluge of events confronting him, the journalist goes about his work on the basis of certain pre-conceived notions about reality. In particular, he assumes the existence of a consensus within democratic societies about the legitimacy of existing political and economic arrangements. When he is confronted with groups or movements that deny this legitimacy, he is at a loss over how to treat them. He "does not allow such phenomena an integrity of their own, but instead characterizes them as 'meaningless', 'immature' or 'senseless', as involving a *misunderstanding* of reality rather than an alternative interpretation of its nature." (Cohen and Young, 1973: 20) In so doing he diffuses the reality of alternative conceptions of the social order.

An interesting example in this regard is media coverage of nuclear disarmament groups. When these groups reappeared in the early 1980s, they had difficulty obtaining sustained and thoughtful coverage of their campaign. When they engaged in violence, that aspect of their campaign was reported, but their actual views were not examined very seriously. They were treated less as a minority group with a viewpoint worth hearing, than as a deviant minority whose ideas lie outside the democratic consensus. It is not simply that they imply that the leaders of the Soviet Union might actually be trustworthy; it is also that they assume that it would be possible to make changes in military policy that would depend upon a radical restructuring of society itself (*i.e.,* its demilitarization). Although journalists have had no difficulty relating to the sentiments of the peace movement, they have generally found themselves unable to see it as a practical proposition. They have thus tended to portray it as being out of touch with reality.

Position C — News as Counter-Information

Despite their very different assessments of its role, both Positions A and B take it for granted that news should be judged in relation to knowledge. There are, however, several reasons for questioning this assumption. First, knowledge is something that is built up by many persons over a substantial period of time. Its production is a cumulative and a collective process. While this is true to a degree in the case of news, each news story is not prepared in relation to what has been produced before or as a contribution to a larger whole. We speak of "advancing the frontiers of knowledge," but would not do so in the case of news. This is not to say that news does not deal with truth or that it consists simply of raw information without any analysis or interpretation. But each news story is a discrete entity; there is no attempt to integrate different news items into a systematic and comprehensive view of the world. There are no encyclopedias of news.

Position A suggested that the journalist is essentially a historian on the run. But when the historian constructs an account of a period of the past, he does so by integrating the observations of many different individuals who either participated in or witnessed the events being recounted. The result is to turn the reader of his account into a kind of supra-observer of the past, placing him in a position where he can see and understand far more than anyone who actually lived in the period in question. In the case of news, however, the consumer stays at more or less the same observational level as the journalist's sources. Only rarely does the journalist weave different observations together into a larger perspective.

This has led some people to make a very low estimate of what the journalist is able to accomplish with the time and resources at his disposal. Lippmann reduced the function of news to "signaliz[ing] an event." This, he took pains to point out, is not the same as the function of truth, which is "to bring to light the hidden facts, to set them into relation with each other, and make a picture of reality on which men can act." (Lippmann, 1965: 226) In a similar vein, Edward Jay Epstein has concluded that "journalists are rarely, if ever, in a position to establish the truth about an issue for themselves." (Epstein, 1975: 3) In his view, the problem is not simply that journalists have insufficient time and resources. It is also that they "lack the forensic means and authority to establish the truth about a matter in serious dispute." (p. 5) They are dependent for the most part on self-interested sources. They cannot compel witnesses to speak to them nor rigorously cross-examine them as if they were in a court of law, at least not without risking the loss of their future cooperation. And they can seldom challenge scientific data or even identify many of their sources in a scholarly manner.

An equally pessimistic estimate of journalism is to be found in Jacques Ellul's *L'Illusion politique* (1965). His complaint is not that journalism cannot arrive at the truth about events, but rather that it is packaged more to promote confusion and misunderstanding than a clear and logical view of the world. News overwhelms us with a profusion of events. It presents us, not with a coherent and meaningful view of the world, but with a "ceaseless kaleidoscope consisting of thousands of pictures, each following the other at an extraordinary pace." (Christians, 1976: 13) So besieged are we by the flood of news events that we are forced to erase most of it from our memory as a psychological defence. Aggravating this situation is the fact that journalism mixes significant events together with insignificant ones, severs the past from the present, and shuns the normal course of events in favour of the spectacular or catastrophic.

As long as news is regarded as a form of knowledge, it is difficult to defend it against these charges. But at this point, we should pause for reflection. We should ask ourselves whether these critiques actually hit the mark. They assume that journalism should provide us with a meaningful and comprehensive view of the world. But is this a useful or even appropriate way of looking at journalism? According to Position C, we need to shift our focus from the processes by which knowledge is created to the means whereby communication occurs. Indeed, we need to stop trying to see journalism in terms of knowledge at all. This would seem to be a natural step for communications researchers to take. However, they have been deterred from rejecting the knowledge paradigm for two reasons. First, since they themselves are in the business of producing knowledge, they tend to approach journalism from their own perspective. Secondly, the concept of communication most conducive to this kind of analysis is that which sees communication as a meeting of minds. But this concept has not been widely adopted within the academic community.

Even in the orthodox sense of the term, however, it is enlightening to see journalists essentially as facilitators of communication. For they spend much of their time telling us, not so much what has actually happened, but rather what different people think has happened. They are conveyor belts along which different views and opinions about events are carried to the public. This contributes to our understanding of events, but the process is less direct than we tend to imagine. Many stories that seem to be about an actual event are really little more than collections of opinion about that event.

A couple of examples should suffice to illustrate this point. A Canadian Press story with the headline "32,000 litres of waste containing toxic chemicals dumped into river" appeared in *The Ottawa Citizen* on December 21, 1985 (p. A12). It contained a few facts about an investigation of a spill at a petrochemical plant on the St. Clair River. But for the most part it consisted of statements about the spill by company spokesmen and officials from the Ontario Environment Ministry. Another Canadian Press story on the same page indicated in its actual headline that it was essentially a channel for opinion about a Supreme Court decision recognizing the rights of prisoners to *habeus corpus*. Entitled "Court decision hailed as major victory for justice behind bars," it conveyed the views of the chairman of the B.C. Law Society's civil liberties section, a University of B.C. law professor, and a spokesman for the federal penitentiary service.

It is clear from perusing any daily newspaper in Canada that these are not isolated examples. But it would be incorrect to suggest that every news story assumes this form. There are some stories that do not primarily channel the opinions of different sources to the reader, listener, or viewer. Such stories are concerned to establish facts about an event itself, rather than to simply relay observations about it. This kind of news story is not as pervasive as most people would probably imagine, but it certainly does exist. Does this mean that the journalists who prepare essentially factual stories are no longer engaged in facilitating communication? The answer to this question is no, but to understand why we need to broaden our conception of communication to embrace the notion of a "meeting of minds."

It would be unduly pessimistic to suggest that communication in the sense of an honest expression of thoughts or feelings never occurs of its own accord at either the personal or social levels of human interaction. At the same time, however, it would be naive to believe that deception and propaganda are rare and unnatural occurrences. On the contrary, deliberate distortion is a widespread and pervasive phenomenon. It ranges from the innocent colouring of facts in which we all engage to a degree to the perverse and sometimes dangerous hate literature which a number of groups continue to distribute. There are, however, two basic constraints upon deception at the social level. The first consists of various legal penalties that can be imposed under certain circumstances against those who consciously distort the truth. The second consists of what might be called the imperative of credibility. This is the principle that people will not generally distort the truth beyond the point at which they anticipate a loss in their credibility.

Several institutions contribute to the operation of the imperative of credibility as a check upon widespread public deception. One of the most important of these in modern democratic societies is the educational system. But even more important for society as a whole is the institution of journalism. For all of the abuse heaped upon it, the press still constitutes the most powerful countervailing force against deception and propaganda. By presenting the views of various sides on most issues, the press encourages people to be more open and honest in their public pronouncements than they would otherwise tend to be. Allowing most sides to be heard does not eliminate attempts to lead the public astray, but it does reduce their number and effectiveness. Moreover, the press also discourages deception by including information that makes it easier to assess the validity of any particular view.

This suggests that much of what we find in the news consists of what might be called counter-information. It provides us with a means of assessing the truthfulness of what various sources of information would have us believe. For example, if a government official tells us that Canada's oil reserves will last a hundred years, counter-information could consist of the findings of a recent study of the oil reserve situation or even of certain other contradictory statements made by the same official on a different occasion. In other words, what gives some information the status of counter-information is its relation to other information. It is determined to be news because of its bearing on other "news."

Can we extend this analysis to say that *all* news is counter-information? This suggestion is not quite so preposterous as it might sound at first. To see why this is the case, we need to return to the original question about news selection. On what basis are some events, or opinions about events, considered to be newsworthy while others are not? Or, given the present emphasis on communication, why is the press interested in some messages and not in others?

Stuart Hall has observed that the selection of news "rests on inferred knowledge about the audience" and that "news items which infringe social norms, break the pattern of expectations and contrast with our sense of the everyday . . . have greater news salience for journalists than others." (Hall, 1973: 86) He did not, however, take this idea to its logical conclusion and suggest that all news is counter-information. To do so, we need to assume, as Hall pointed out, that the journalist begins with some notion of how the public, or some segment of it, views the world. He might be wrong, of course; he might think that people believe that crime is on the increase, or that all politicians are corrupt, when this is not the case. But he starts with at least a rough idea of what people think about certain situations or aspects of reality.

What the journalist then proceeds to do, according to this line of argument, is to scan the flow of events for those occurrences that, if known, would require the public to modify its view of reality in some respect. (The occurrences in question would include the expression of viewpoints.) In other words, while he may talk in terms of news values such as relevance, human interest, and so forth, ultimately it is the anticipated effect on public perceptions that serves as the journalist's main criterion of news-worthiness. It is its status as counter-information (information that runs counter to public perceptions) that gives an event or opinion significance or social relevance.

While this fits nicely with a good deal of journalism, there are some cases that it does not seem to take into account. Why, for example, do the media cover murders and accidents in such detail? How do events such as these constitute counter-information? Are they not "news" simply because of our morbid fascination with other people's misfortunes? The response of Position C to this line of questioning will no doubt strike some readers as inadequate. But essentially the reply would be this. There is a tendency for the individual in Western societies to think that the world is a safer place than it really is — many of us go through life without coming face to face with very many tragic events. What news coverage of the deaths of others serves to do, therefore, is remind us on a continuing basis of an aspect of reality that we would prefer to forget. It is thus counter-information in that it prevents us from slipping into a view of reality that ignores the precarious nature of human existence.

Position D — News as Elitist Communication

Position D does not need to be examined at great length since it draws heavily from Position B and is essentially a counter-argument against Position C. Basically, while admitting that journalists facilitate mass communication, it insists that this is largely done in the interests of the elite. The voices that are heard with the aid of journalism are primarily elitist voices.

Adherance to this thesis is not restricted to Marxist literature. A Commission on Freedom of the Press held in the United States in the 1940s concluded that those at or near the bottom of the social pyramid are unable to express their views adequately through the mass media. "The development of the press as an instrument of mass communication," it asserted, "has greatly decreased the proportion of the people who can express their opinion and ideas through the press." (Fedler, 1973: 109) (It should be noted, perhaps, that the commissioners also argued that precious space in the mass media should not be used to give a voice to ill-informed points of view. Their essentially elitist position was that the public had a right to know, but only the informed viewpoint should be given expression.) In any event, A. J. Liebling put the essential point more bluntly. "Freedom of the press," he declared, "is guaranteed only to those who own one." (Tuchman, 1978: 169)

A number of studies could be cited in support of these claims. For example, a study of Boston newspapers conducted by E. N. Goldenberg in 1974 found evidence that "resource-poor" groups have difficulty gaining adequate press coverage. To attract attention, they sometimes resort to staged events. But this results in coverage that ignores the issues about which the groups are concerned. (Goldenberg, 1975)

However, there are other studies that contradict these findings. In a 1973 study of the coverage of two Minneapolis dailies, Frederick Fedler set forth two hypotheses: that "newspapers devote more space to established groups and their ideas, than to comparable minority groups and their ideas;" and that "minority group coverage is more violence-oriented than the publicity received by comparable established groups." (Fedler, 1974: 110) He found that over a ten-month period, the coverage of minority groups did indeed tend to focus on the more violent aspects of their activities. But he also found that, contrary to his first hypothesis, the minority groups consistently received more attention than established groups. He thus concluded that the "relationship between the media and groups seeking publicity seems far more complex than earlier articles suggested." (Fedler, 1974: 117)

More studies of this kind need to be conducted before any firm conclusions can be drawn about media coverage of elite and non-elite groups. However, it is also necessary to conduct longitudinal studies; that is, studies which seek to measure changes over a prolonged period of time. Only in this way shall we be able to tell whether minority groups are given better or worse coverage today than in earlier times. At the same time, it is necessary to devise more sophisticated techniques of content analysis in order to take account of journalistic devices such as the use of archetypes (see the discussion of Position B in Chapter 1). It is not simply the amount of coverage (*e.g.,* the number of column inches or stories), but the kind of coverage that determines whether minority groups are given a voice through the vehicle of news.

References

Adam, G. Stuart
  1976 "The Journalistic Imagination." In G. S. Adam (ed.), *Journalism, Communication and the Law.* Scarborough: Prentice-Hall.
Aitken, John
  1975 "Made to Measure." *Weekend Magazine* (May 10): 2*f.*
Altheide, David L.
  1976 *Creating Reality: How TV News Distorts Events.* Beverley Hills: Sage.
Altschull, Herbert J.
  1984 *Agents of Power: The Role of the News Media in Human Affairs.* New York: Longman.
Armstrong, G. A. J.
  1948 "Some Examples of the Distribution and Speed of News in England at the Time of the Wars of the Roses." In R. W. Hunt, W. A. Pantin, and R. W. Southern (eds.), *Studies in Medieval History: Presented to Frederick Maurice Powicke.* Oxford: Oxford University Press.
Asquith, Ivan
  1978 "The Structure, Ownership and Control of the Press, 1780-1855." In George Boyce, James Curran, and Pauline Wingate (eds.), *Newspaper History: From the Seventeenth Century to the Present Day.* London: Constable.
Berger, Peter and Thomas Luckmann
  1966 *The Social Construction of Reality.* New York: Doubleday.
Boyce, George
  1978 "The Fourth Estate: The Reappraisal of a Concept." In G. Boyce *et al.* (eds.), *Newspaper History.* London: Constable.
Breed, Warren
  1960 "Social Control in the News Room." In Wilbur Schramm (ed.), *Mass Communications.* 2nd ed., Urbana: University of Illinois Press. Reprinted from *Social Forces* (1955).
Canadian Broadcasting Corporation
  1977 "TV News: A Look Behind-the-Scenes." *Closed Circuit* (March 28): 4-5.
Christians, Clifford G.
  1976 "Jacques Ellul and Democracy's 'Vital Information' Premise." *Journalism Monographs.* No. 45.

Clarke, Debra
  1981 "Second-hand News: Production and Reproduction at a Major Ontario Television Station." In Liora Salter (ed.), *Communication Studies in Canada.* Toronto: Butterworths.
Cohen, Stanley and Jock Young
  1973 "The Process of Selection." In S. Cohen and J. Young (eds.), *The Manufacture of News: Social Problems, Deviance and the Mass Media.* London: Constable.
Curran, James
  1978 "The Press as an Agency of Social Control: An Historical Perspective." In G. Boyce *et al.* (eds.), *Newspaper History.* London: Constable.
Epstein, Edward Jay
  1975 *Between Fact and Fiction: The Problem of Journalism.* New York: Vintage Books.
  1981 "The Selection of Reality." In Elie Abel (ed.), *What's News.* San Francisco: Institute for Contemporary Studies.
Fedler, F.
  1973 "The Media and Minority Groups: A Study of Adequacy of Access." *Journalism Quarterly* 50 (Spring): 109-17.
Gans, Herbert J.
  1980 *Deciding What's News.* New York: Random House.
Goldenberg, E. N.
  1975 *Making the Papers.* Lexington: Lexington Books.
Golding, P. and P. Elliott
  1980 *Making the News.* London: Longman.
Hall, Stuart
  1973 "A World at One With Itself." In S. Cohen and J. Young (eds.), *The Manufacture of News.* London: Constable. Reprinted from *New Society* (1970).
Harris, Michael
  1978 "The Structure, Ownership and Control of the Press, 1620-1780." In G. Boyce *et al.* (eds.), *Newspaper History.* London: Constable.
Hofstetter, Richard
  1976 *Bias in the News.* Columbus, Ohio: Ohio State University Press.
Hughes, Helen MacGill
  1940 *News and the Human Interest Story.* New York: Greenwood Press.
Kesterton, W. H.
  1967 *A History of Journalism in Canada.* Toronto: McClelland and Stewart.
Lippmann, Walter
  1965 *Public Opinion.* New York: Free Press.

Park, Robert E.
1940 "News as a Form of Knowledge: A Chapter in the Sociology of Knowledge." *American Journal of Sociology* 45 (March): 669-86.

Ranney, Austin
1983 *Channels of Power: The Impact of Television on American Politics.* New York: Basic Books.

Rock, Paul
1973 "News as Eternal Recurrence." In S. Cohen and J. Young (eds.), *The Manufacture of News: Social Problems, Deviance and the Mass Media.* London: Constable.

Rutherford, Paul
1982 *A Victorian Authority: The Daily Press in Late Nineteenth-Century Canada.* Toronto: University of Toronto Press.

Scanlon, T. Joseph
1976 "How Government Uses the Media." In G. S. Adam (ed.), *Journalism, Communication and the Law.* Scarborough: Prentice-Hall.

Schudson, Michael
1978 *Discovering the News: A Social History of American Newspapers.* New York: Basic Books.

Smith, Anthony
1978 "The Long Road to Objectivity and Back Again." In G. Boyce *et al.* (eds.), *Newspaper History.* London: Constable.

Stokes, Mark
1985 "Access and Coverage: Non-Elite Social Groups and the Toronto *Star,* 1904-1984." Honours research paper: Carleton University.

Tuchman, G.
1978 *Making News.* New York: Free Press.

Chapter 3

What is the Ideal Press-State Relationship?

The *Charter of Rights and Freedoms* in the new Canadian Constitution states that the fundamental rights of all Canadians include: "Freedom of thought, belief, opinion and expression, including freedom of the press and other media of communications." (*Canada Act,* 1982, s. 2.) This ostensibly gives Canadians the same written guarantee that the Americans acquired in 1791 by the First Amendment to the United States Constitution, which declared that "Congress shall make no law . . . abridging the freedom of speech, or of the press." But it is not enough, of course, simply to have such words on paper. We need to look beyond the letter of the law to the legal and political reality. After all, Article 125 of the Constitution of the Soviet Union states that "the citizens of the U.S.S.R. are guaranteed by law (a) freedom of spech; (b) freedom of the press."

The reality in Canada is that freedom of speech and of the press are subject to a number of constraints. This does not entail that such freedoms do not exist, but it does mean that they are not regarded as absolute. In December of 1985, the Supreme Court of Canada made this clear in its decision in the case of Neil Fraser, who was dismissed from the public service for his scathing criticism of government policy. The court's unanimous judgment acknowledged that freedom of speech "is a deep-rooted value in our democratic system of government." But it also insisted that:

> [I]t is not an absolute value. Probably no values are absolute. All important values must be qualified, and balanced against, other important, and often competing values. The process of definition, qualification and balancing is as much required with respect to the value of "freedom of speech" as it is for other values. In the present case, the adjudicator determined that the value of freedom of speech must be qualified by the value of an impartial and effective public service. (Ottawa *Citizen,* December 12, 1985: A9)

Because the events in the Fraser case occurred before the *Charter of Rights* was proclaimed in 1982, the court's ruling took no account of its provisions. It is not, therefore, expected to be the last word on the issue of free speech and the public service. But future court decisions are unlikely to abandon the idea that freedom of speech is not absolute; the most that they might do would be to alter the legal qualifications imposed upon it.

Freedom of the press in Canada is also qualified by legal constraints. Journalists can be required by the judiciary to reveal their sources or face imprisonment, although only a few have been prosecuted to date for failing to disclose sources. (On the other hand, in the United States, the confidentiality of sources is protected by "shield laws.") The police can obtain a warrant from a Justice of the Peace to search a news-room for evidence that might assist them with a criminal prosecution. There are provisions to prevent the press from interfering with the right of accused persons to have a fair trial. Journalists can be charged with contempt of Parliament if their comments on its proceedings are considered libellous or scandalous. Private citizens as well as public officials can also sue the press for libel if they believe that their reputations or careers have been unfairly damaged. (Siegel, 1983: 57-61, 73-82)

The record of Canadian governments in safeguarding freedom of the press has been a mixed one at both the provincial and federal levels. In 1937, the Social Credit government of William Aberhart in Alberta passed *An Act to Ensure the Publication of Accurate News and Information.* Though an understandable reaction to sustained harrassment by the press, the Act was designed to give the government the power to censor newspapers and even to insert "rewrites" of stories considered to be misleading. (Adam, 1976: 155) It was never enforced, however, and was subsequently disallowed by the Supreme Court after being referred there by the federal government.

Unfortunately, the federal government failed to refer another Act attacking freedom of the press. The Quebec Padlock Law, enacted by the Union Nationale government of Maurice Duplessis in the same year as the Alberta Press Act, was supposedly intended to outlaw the use of any property in Quebec for distributing Communist literature. But it was actually used as a general instrument for censorship and repression until 1957 when it was finally declared unconstitutional. Professor Arthur Siegel relates that "political party interests were behind Ottawa's decision not to intervene in the Padlock Law, although Justice Minister Ernest Lapointe thought it was unconstitutional." (Siegel, 1983: 237)

Attacks on freedom of expression sometimes come from the most unexpected quarters. In December of 1985, for example, the Canadian Senate sought to prevent the release of a 79-minute National Film Board docu-drama called "The Kid Who Couldn't Miss." Produced by Paul Cowan of Montreal, the film questioned the exploits of Billy Bishop, a Canadian pilot who won a Victoria Cross during the First World War. It cast doubt as to whether a daring raid on a German aerodrome in 1971 had ever occurred. Upset by Cowan's apparent attempt to debunk Canada's most famous war ace, the Senate undertook hearings to defend not only Bishop's record but "the reputation of the country" and its heritage. As a result of Senate pressure, the NFB prepared a disclaimer to be included in the opening credits, indicating that the film had taken liberties with some of its details. (Riley, 1985: B4)

The senators who were upset by the Cowan film were not merely seeking to provide Canadians with another viewpoint on Bishop's career. Rather they were proceeding on the assumption that they had a duty and a right to protect the Canadian public against certain falsehoods not merely by exposing them as such but by actually preventing their circulation. They would no doubt have been extremely happy if the NFB had collapsed under their pressure and withdrawn the Cowan film from distribution. Moreover, if the NFB had done so, this would probably have pleased not only veterans' associations in Canada but many other Canadians as well.

There is a tendency to think that citizens in democratic societies are more or less agreed about freedom of speech and the press. But significant disagreements arise whenever specific cases are considered. A number of years ago, two researchers conducted an interesting study of American attitudes towards freedom of speech. Using a sample drawn from two university communities, where a libertarian viewpoint would tend to be the strongest, they found, as might be expected, that 90 per cent of those surveyed supported freedom of speech *in the abstract.* However, when the participants in the study were questioned further, two significant qualifications emerged. It was discovered that only 63 per cent would have permitted a speech against churches and religion, and that only 44 per cent would have allowed an avowed communist to speak on behalf of communism. (Prothro and Grigg, 1960)

The fact that Canadians are not of one mind about the nature and extent of press controls was illustrated early in 1985 when Ernst Zundel, a Toronto publisher who emigrated from Germany, was brought to trial for distributing a pamphlet entitled *Did Six Million Really Die?* Claiming that the Holocaust was a hoax perpetrated by the Jews to win German reparations for Israel, Zundel was found guilty of wilfully spreading false news. Many Canadians agreed with the court's assumption that it had a duty to suppress Zundel's views. But others believed that it was not only dangerous but misguided for the judicial system to try to act as an arbiter of history. They pointed out that one effect of the court's involvement was to give Zundel a far wider hearing for his unsubstantiated view than he would ever have received through his own efforts. As Zundel himself said at the trial's end: "It cost me $40,000 in lost work — but I got $1 million worth of publicity for my cause. It was well worth it." (Quinn, 1985: 42)

A final example may help to make the point that Canadians are not of one mind about the legitimate scope of free expression. In the spring of 1986, the student Press Club at Carleton University invited Glenn Babb, the South African ambassador to Canada, to take part in a public debate. The student council was so upset by this invitation that it withdrew recognition of the Press Club as an official club on campus. It rejected the argument of the Press Club that it was acting in accordance with normal journalistic practices. Instead, it said that allowing Babb to speak was equivalent to supporting the propaganda of apartheid. There was considerable support for the student council's position among both students and professors. However, when I asked my first year mass communication students on their final examination whether a newspaper should publish a letter to the editor by Glenn Babb, practically everyone who chose to answer this question made the case that it should.

It is clear from events such as these that the legitimate bounds of freedom of speech and of the press are still a matter of debate in Canada. In the case of freedom of the press, there are two basic reasons for this. First, different social groups as well as societies have varying social objectives, so that an appropriate press-state relationship for one is not always suitable for another. There is a natural tendency for groups in power to favour less freedom than groups seeking power. Secondly, even within a given social context, the changing nature of both the press and the state may necessitate a re-evaluation of their relationship. This, according to some observers, is precisely what has happened in Western societies where the growth of media conglomerates has called into question the relative absence of controls over ownership of the press.

During the five hundred years or so since the invention and spread of the printing press, several generally recognized "theories" of the press have emerged within the West. Though labelled as such, they are not really theories in the scientific sense of the term. Rather they are prescriptive formulations of the ideal relationship between the press and the state. They attempt to specify the extent to which the state should control the press and the form that state controls should generally take. Their validity does not lie, therefore, in the degree to which they conform to empirical reality, but rather in their ability to promote a certain kind of society. Nonetheless, their careful assessment in the light of what we now know about the media society remains one of the most important tasks for communications students.

Discussion of these different theories or conceptions of the ideal press-state relationship is facilitated by the use of another "double polarity" arising from two basic questions. The first question is essentially this. Under what conditions should the state be allowed to interfere with the freedom of the individual? This is obviously an extremely complex question. But basically it involves making a choice — or finding some middle ground — between the following two lines of response. On the one hand, there is the classical liberal response to the effect that the state is only justified in interfering with individual liberties in order to prevent one individual from doing harm to another. This is an essentially negative conception of the role of state, since it rules out state action to promote the actual good of the individual. On the other hand, there is the view that the state can interfere with human behaviour whenever it is necessary for the good of the state. This assumes that the state has a purpose of its own which transcends that of the individual.

These are, of course, extreme positions that would find few defenders in modern democracies. There is a consensus that the state exists for the purposes of the individual and as such is expected to take a number of positive measures to aid individual self-fulfillment. At the same time, however, there is still considerable debate as to how far the state should go in this regard. This becomes quite clear whenever new forms of state activity are contemplated. Certainly, in the case of the press, there is a significant polarization of opinion in this regard. Both sides subscribe to the unstated premise that the press generally operates so as to enhance freedom in society. But they disagree as to whether it is a mechanism which needs periodic adjustments and repairs or a natural system which works best when it is left alone. On the one hand, there are those who believe that the state must take certain steps to ensure that the press fulfills its proper role. On the other hand, there are those who insist that, except for providing a reasonable degree of protection for the individual, virtually any state interference with the press will ultimately compromise its role.

The second question involved in this chapter's double polarity concerns what has come to be known as the "self-righting principle." This is essentially the idea that public opinion is capable, in the long run, of sorting out truth from falsehood, provided that it is given an adequate opportunity to hear all sides of an issue. This principle was first developed by John Milton in a pamphlet entitled *Areopagitica* (1644). A recent version can be found in a dissenting opinion by Oliver Wendell Holmes, Jr. in *Abrams v. United States* (250 U.S. 616, 1919):

> When men have realized that time has upset many fighting faiths, they may come to believe even more than they believe the very foundations of their own conduct that the ultimate good desired is better reached by free trade in ideas — that the best test of truth is the power of thought to get itself accepted in the competition of the market, and that truth is the only ground on which their wishes can safely be carried out.

While many people pay lip service to this principle, their faith in it often wavers when specific cases arise. We can thus divide conceptions of the ideal press-state relationship on the basis of their response to the question: To what extent should truth be allowed to emerge through the operation of the self-righting principle? On the one hand, there are those who are prepared to let the self-righting principle do its work without interference. On the other hand, there are those who want to rush to its aid the moment that the particular "truths" in which they have a stake are put to the test.

Superimposing the basic lines of response to the above two questions yields four positions as in Figure 3:

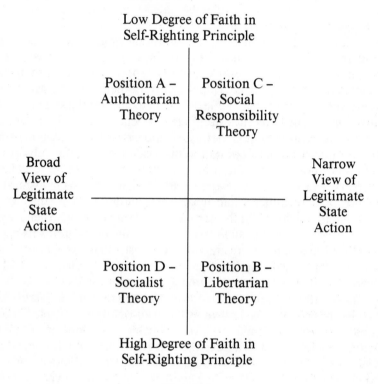

Figure 3

Positions A, B, and C have been labelled in accordance with Siebert, Peterson, and Schramm's book *Four Theories of the Press* (1956). However, a socialist position has been substituted for their Soviet-communist theory on the grounds that it is more relevant to the debate about freedom of the press in democratic societies. For the sake of convenience, the sequence of discussion will be: authoritarian, libertarian, social responsibility, and socialist positions.

Position A — The Authoritarian Theory of the Press

To understand the authoritarian theory of the press, it is necessary to recall the historical circumstances surrounding its genesis in the West. For it emerged during the same period as the modern state itself was first taking shape. We often forget that the state, as we know it, is a relatively recent product of history and one that emerged only after a long and at times violent struggle to secure its existence. In the process, it had to subdue a number of other interests, which included not only certain "ancient liberties" of the clergy and nobility but also, for a period of time, freedom of the press.

During the Middle Ages, political power was diffused among the church, the so-called territorial monarchies, the feudal landlords, the "free" cities, and the guilds of the towns. None of these entities possessed sovereignty; however, the idea of ultimate, indivisible, unquestioned power backed by the sanction of force was foreign to medieval society. There was no arbiter whose will was recognized as final in the event of a conflict of interests. Under these circumstances, the security of the individual was precarious at best, especially during the late medieval period when economic decline led to widespread conflict both within and between the competing political entities (*e.g.* the War of the Roses in England and the Hundred Years War between England and France). Only gradually was this situation altered through the slow transformation of the feudal monarchies into monarchical states possessed of sovereign power.

In England the process of state-building began during the reign of Henry VII (1485-1509), the first Tudor king, who rescued the country from civil war and restored social order. However, it was not completed in England until the late seventeenth century and took even longer in many other European countries. For it was not enough simply to develop the idea or even the substance of a political entity possessed of sovereign power; it was also necessary to agree upon the locus of sovereignty. For several centuries, the crown maintained that it was the repository of sovereignty. As Louis XIV put it succinctly, "L'Etat, c'est moi." But against this interpretation other claims were raised. In most cases, it required a lengthy and at times bloody struggle to resolve the issue of state sovereignty.

The value of the state itself was never questioned. It was assumed that it is only through the state that each person can realize their full potential and that the interests of the individual thus depend upon the security of the state. This led some philosophers to conclude that the state has a higher purpose than that of the individual; indeed, that it has a will and destiny of its own. But it was not necessary to take the argument this far to reach the conclusion that the dissemination of information and ideas by the press serves the interests of the state. It was enough to argue that the good of the individual depended upon "stability of government, the safety of the state, and the peace of the realm" and that these depended in turn on controls over the press.

The fact that this line of argument is not given much credence in Western democracies today should not blind us to its possible applicability in earlier times or other societies. It does not necessarily entail support for a tyrannical regime in which the press is merely an instrument of the government. On the contrary, it makes a good deal of sense in situations where the state is in an embryonic form and requires many forms of support for its further development. This was the case during the period when the press first emerged in the West and it has its counterpart in many developing countries today. This is not to say that freedom of the press cannot contribute to the security of the state. But it does so only when the state is already reasonably secure and democratic; where the state is fragile or undemocratic, a free press can threaten its very foundation. Only as the state becomes more mature does it become feasible to widen the range of tolerable dissent, though in retrospect it is clear that many states have continued to exercise strict controls for much longer than necessary.

The question of the press-state relationship was handled initially on an *ad hoc* basis. It arose in England following the introduction of the printing press by William Caxton in 1476. To their credit, Henry VII and his successors recognized the potential of printing to further the state-building process. But they also saw that it could undermine their own authority and sow the seeds of revolution and civil war. With the aid of their Privy Council, therefore, they used the extensive authority of the royal pre-rogative to build up an elaborate network of press controls. The first step taken was the appointment of an official or royal printer with a patent for the sole printing of parliamentary Acts and statutes. Shortly thereafter, additional printing "privileges" and patents of monopoly were granted to other selected printers as a further means of control.

Neither of these practices gave the state direct control over content. They did not enable the Crown to prevent the spread of obnoxious political or religious ideas. In 1529, therefore, Henry VIII promulgated a list of prohibited books and instituted a system of fines against transgressors. (This was 15 years before the first continental index.) Moreover, the following year he took steps to establish the first licensing system under secular control. Each book had to be scrutinized by an appointed licenser and given a stamp of approval before it could be printed or circulated. The Catholic Church had already experimented with licensing, but it had lacked effective means of subduing recalcitrant printers; its ultimate threat of excommunication meant nothing to persons committed to Protestantism. Under Henry VIII, however, "executions were substituted for excommunication, and fine and imprisonment for warning and censure." (Siebert, 1965: 46) While still making use of ecclesiastic licensers, Henry VIII turned most of their functions over to the state.

The next major step in the development of the licensing system occurred in 1557 when a printing craft organization known as the Stationers Company was granted a royal charter by Mary (1553-58). This amounted to a patent of monopoly over most forms of printing, though it was sub-divided among its master printers. In return for this monopoly, the Company assumed responsibility for administering and enforcing a large part of the licensing system. According to Siebert, the licensing system reached its peak under Elizabeth (1558-1603), who used it in her campaign to suppress Catholicism. She strengthened its apparatus by a set of royal injunctions in 1559 and a comprehensive Star Chamber Decree in 1586. By the end of her reign, however, the system was already beginning to break down as new strains were placed upon it. Apart from surviving Catholic non-conformists, Protestant sects such as the Puritans were spreading ideas that challenged the orthodoxy of the Anglican Church. A number of members of Parliament were also beginning to question the assumption that state sovereignty resided in the Crown. Together these groups provided a sizeable clientele for printers who were excluded from the privileged membership of the Stationers Company.

The licensing system itself was not openly attacked until the English civil war in the 1640s. Even then it managed to survive, albeit in a somewhat altered form. By the *Regulation of Printing Act* passed under Charles II in 1662, the licensing of printed materials was relinquished by the Stationers Company and taken over by two secretaries of state. This Act lasted until 1694 when it was finally allowed to expire for pragmatic reasons. Apart from the fact that it was difficult to secure men of ability to act as censors, the quantity of books and pamphlets had become too great for the system to handle. This not only made it impossible to check everything carefully, but it was also damaging the printing trade. At the same time, two new kinds of publications — newsletters and newspapers — had emerged which were excluded from the Act. In addition, the overthrow of James II during the Glorious Revolution of 1688 shifted power from the Crown to Parliament, opening the door for the development of a two-party system. To function effectively, however, this system required information, discussion, and criticism to a degree that was incompatible with licensing.

The abandonment of licensing was also influenced by the fact that the common law was thought to provide adequate protection against the expression of ideas dangerous to the state. By the late seventeenth century, the law of seditious libel had been given a broad interpretation to include any attack upon the representatives or policies of the state. During the late Middle Ages, a series of statutes known as the *Scandulum Magnatum* had been enacted to suppress disruptive rumours about the king and nobility. These had gradually fallen into disuse, but at the beginning of the seventeenth century they were rediscovered by James I, who was looking for additional means to control the press. The medieval statutes had provided that the objectionable matter was to be proven false in order to find the person who invented or disseminated it guilty. Moreover, to disseminate a false rumour was not considered as grave an offence as to invent it. Under these conditions, the *Scandulum Magnatum* were not a particularly effective means of discouraging criticism of the government.

James I quickly changed this situation by a drastic reinterpretation of the medieval statutes. Under common law, it was already the case that ordinary persons could win damages for defamatory statements made against them without having to prove the statements false. In 1606, the King's Court of Star Chamber extended this principle to the "Great Men of the Realm" in the case *de Libellis Famosis.* It became a criminal offence to accuse the state or its representatives (living or dead) of misdeeds, regardless of whether one could prove one's statements to be true. Truth was declared to be immaterial in cases of seditious libel; the only question was whether the state's reputation had been damaged. Indeed, it became the case that true accusations were considered to be even more libellous than false ones, since they presumably did more damage.

By the late seventeenth century, the law of seditious libel had become an extremely effective control over the press. Moreover, it was reaffirmed in the Tuchin case of 1704 when Chief Justice Holt laid down the following three rules: (1) seditious libel consists of whatever lessens the affection of the people for the government; (2) the only province of the jury is to determine whether the defendant published the offending material and whether the words published convey the meaning contended for by the prosecution; and (3) the province of the judge is to determine criminal intent (on the basis of the words alone) and the legality of the published language. These rules were intended to make criticism of the government tantamount to a crime against the state by eliminating the possibility of truth being used for a defence. The only acceptable defence was that one had not made the statements in question.

The law of seditious libel was not the only form of control over the press during the eighteenth century. Other means of controlling the press were used by the government, including the bribery of journalists, the purchase or subsidization of newspapers, and the imposition of stamp taxes on both the advertising and copy of newspapers. Walpole first introduced a subsidization program during the second quarter of the eighteenth century; it was revived during the later years of George III. The first *Stamp Act* was passed in 1712 after Anne had tried unsuccessfully to get Parliament to legislate against a veritable flood of allegedly seditious pamphlets and newspapers. Though abolished in America during the Revolution, these so-called "taxes on knowledge" were not eliminated in Britain until 1855.

It is difficult to find much of a defence for these kinds of press controls. They were never intended to protect the state, but only the vested interests of certain political factions. In the case of the law of seditious libel, however, there were reasonable men in this period who sincerely believed that it was necessary to protect the state by such legal means. One such individual was Dr. Samuel Johnson. Although Johnson fought for the right of the press to report the proceedings of Parliament, he also supported the right of the state to suppress dangerous ideas. "Every society," Johnson wrote, has a right to preserve public peace and order, and therefore has a good right to prohibit the propagation of opinions which have a dangerous tendency. To say the magistrate has this right is using an inadequate word: it is the society for which the magistrate is the agent. He may be morally or theologically wrong in restraining the propagation of opinions which he thinks dangerous but he is politically right. (Hachten, 1981: 63)

There is a tendency to think that the authoritarian conception of the ideal press-state relationship is restricted today to non-democratic states. But elements of the authoritarian outlook survive even within democratic societies. This is apparent not simply in the way that many people would deal with offensive published materials such as pornographic books and magazines and hate literature. It can also be seen in the criticism that is frequently levelled against the press as a whole whenever one segment of it acts irresponsibly.

Position B — The Libertarian Theory of the Press

Advocates of freedom of the press have had to contend with two general types of controls: pre-publication and post-publication. (Publication is used here in the broad sense to include both print and non-print forms of journalistic expression.) Both kinds of control continue to exist in Canada today. While there is no equivalent to the licensing system established in England by Henry VIII, there are censorship boards and other agencies that prevent certain kinds of material from being circulated. There are also legal penalties that can be imposed upon persons for making libellous statements in print or over the airwaves. In terms of public discussion, the main issue for democratic societies is how severe post-publication controls should be to maintain fair play without stifling healthy debate. However, the existence of pornography and hate literature has meant that the need for pre-publication controls is not yet a dead issue.

The argument for pre-publication controls (*e.g.,* licensing) over public discussion is based in part upon a low estimate of the ability of the average person to recognize and contribute to the formulation of truth. It assumes not only that the interests of the individual are subordinate to those of the state but also that the representatives of the state have superior access to truth. Truth is not to be found within the public as a whole, but is to be disseminated to it by a carefully controlled process. As previously explained, the elimination of the licensing system was not the result of any reversal in this belief. It came about for purely practical reasons. In the long run, however, the decision of a society to allow relative freedom from pre-publication controls depends upon a commitment to a fundamentally different conception of how truth emerges.

The single most important contribution to this conception is generally thought to have been made over three centuries ago by John Milton

(1608-1674). The pretext for Milton's attack upon the authoritarian defence of pre-publication controls was a new licensing law passed by the Long Parliament in 1643. Irritated by this law, which set up a Committee of Examinations comprised of 20 licensers, Milton issued a number of pamphlets without a licence, including one on divorce which was attacked as a "wicked book" by a Presbyterian member of Parliament. When the Presbyterians subsequently asked Parliament to enforce the licensing law against Congregationalist writings defending religious toleration, they also asked that it be used against Milton. Milton responded with his *Areopagitica,* which first appeared on November 24, 1644, unlicensed and without the imprint of a publisher or printer.

Milton began his case against the licensing system by arguing at some length that it had been invented by the Catholic Church to impede the Protestant Reformation and had been perfected thereafter by the Council of Trent and Spanish Inquisition. He conveniently ignored the contribution to effective and systematic licensing made by Henry VIII and his Tudor successors. He admitted, however, that evil persons might unwittingly devise something good. "Some will say, What though the Inventors were bad, the thing for all that may be good?" (Milton, 1644: II, 507) He proceeded, therefore, to develop a pragmatic argument against licensing; namely, that it would not — and could not — achieve the results intended. Given the tedious, unpleasant, and unrewarding nature of licensing, only the "ignorant, imperious, and remisse or basely pecuniary" would want the job. (Miltion, 1644: II, 530) Moreover, it would not deter persons intent on spreading evil ideas, but would only serve to prevent judicious readers from gaining a forewarning of dangerous ideas. It would also undermine the exercise of virtue by cloistering the individual against temptation and vice.

Even if licensing could be made to work, however, it should be rejected. For not only does it fail to produce the results desired; it also causes actual harm. "I lastly proceed from the no good it can do, to the manifest harm it causes." (Milton, 1644: II, 530) Milton observed that licensing acts as a "nursing mother" to sects and schisms. "It raises them and invests them with a reputation." (Milton, 1644: II, 542) He recognized that prohibiting a book or censuring a viewpoint often serves only to increase its circulation. He also believed that licensing seriously undermines the emergence of truth. It discourages originality in favour of mere conformity to the teachings of others. It also hinders truth from defeating falsehood within the intellectual arena.

It was this reference to the superior strength of truth over falsehood that secured Milton a hallowed place in the pantheon of libertarian thinkers. For it was the first expression of what later came to be known as the self-righting principle. "And though all the windes of doctrin were let loose to play upon the earth," Milton wrote, "so Truth be in the field, we do injuriously by licensing and prohibiting to misdoubt her strength. Let her and Falsehood grapple; who ever knew Truth put to the wors, in a free and open encounter. Her confuting is the best and surest suppressing." (Milton, 1644: II, 561) This faith in the ability of truth to defeat falsehood in a "free and open encounter" constituted a radical departure from the authoritarian theory of the press. For it meant that the state could no longer be thought to have a monopoly of truth; indeed, it implied that the state would hinder the emergence of truth if it placed controls upon discussion.

Having said this, however, an important qualification needs to be made. Milton's faith in the self-righting principle was not as complete as we might first imagine. While it is not inappropriate to label him a libertarian, he was a moderate libertarian at best. This becomes clear when we ask just how free and open Milton intended the encounter between truth and falsehood to be. That he did not go quite as far as the above statements might imply is suggested by the fact that he was later willing to serve as an official censor of newsbooks for Cromwell. The fact is that Milton still wanted to place rather severe post-publication constraints upon the press. His devotion to the self-righting principle was sufficient to favour the removal of pre-publication controls, but not the moderation of post-publication controls.

Milton believed that English society was founded upon revealed religion and thus especially favoured by God. As such it had an obligation to protect and propagate a body of religious doctrine and also to work out its full implications for the rest of the world. England was supposedly blessed with a greater degree of religious truth than any other nation, but it did not yet possess the whole truth. "For such is the order of Gods enlightening his Church, to dispense and deal out by degrees his beam, so as our earthly eyes may best sustain it." (Milton, 1644: II, 566) In effect, there remained a kind of grey zone between the black and white areas of revealed truth and demonstrated falsehood. What Milton wanted, therefore, was essentially the freedom for men like himself to roll back this grey area through the exchange of ideas. What he did not want was the freedom for men to disseminate known falsehoods as if they were true. He was prepared to tolerate "neighbouring differences" among Protestant sects, but not "open superstition" or "popery."

The problem for Milton, therefore, was how to control the deliberate dissemination of evil ideas without compromising the legitimate pursuit of goodness and truth. This problem was scarcely unique to the seventeenth century, even though the hostility between Catholics and Protestants has moderated considerably since then. We have our own varieties of seemingly dangerous writing, including communist attacks upon the foundations of democracy, hate propaganda against racial minorities, and pornography which assaults the dignity of women. Milton's answer was to abolish pre-publication censorship, but maintain post-publication controls; he wanted to do away with licensing, but retain the "book-burning principle." He thus proposed "that no book be Printed, unless the Printers and the Authors name, or at least the Printers be registered. Those which otherwise come forth, if they be found mischievous and libellous, the fire and the executioner will be the timeliest and the most effectuall remedy, that mans prevention can use." (Milton, 1644: II, 569)

There are several obvious difficulties with Milton's position. He neglected to explain how the state was to decide which books should be burnt by the executioner. He seems to have assumed that the state would act upon the advices of Protestant scholars like himself rather than those of "the mercenary crew of false pretenders to learning." But he did not indicate how the state was to know who belonged to which group. While implicitly rejecting the more recent idea of "community standards," he provided no clear guidelines for post-publication censors to follow. Milton was one of the first Western thinkers to grapple with the perplexing problem of how a community can remain free while pursuing goodness according to its own chosen standards. But he certainly did not solve the problem.

Two things were required before advocates of freedom of the press would be prepared to argue that *every* citizen should have the freedom to challenge *virtually any* of society's beliefs or values. The first requirement was the development of a greater faith in the self-righting principle. In Milton's day, the prevailing view of human nature was the *libertin* concept of man as a victim of his irrational passions. This view seemed to be confirmed by the political, economic, and religious turmoil of the period and it made it difficult to think in terms of an informed public opinion. During the Enlightenment of the eighteenth century, however, the pessimistic *libertin* assessment was replaced by a more optimistic belief in man's capacity for rational thought and action. Among the major contributors to this reassessment of human rationality were the English philosopher John Locke and the French *philosophe* Voltaire. Even man's passions underwent rehabilitation in the hands of romantic thinkers such as Rousseau.

The second requirement was to adopt a broader view of the benefits of the self-righting principle. Milton linked the self-righting principle with what might be called the "argument from civilization." He embraced the idea that truth will ultimately prevail over falsehood because it meant that human understanding could progress, especially in terms of religious truth ("to know God aright"). This linkage can be found in many later thinkers. In his 1779 draft of an Act to establish religious freedom in Virginia, for example, Thomas Jefferson declared that "truth is great and will prevail if left to herself, . . . she is the proper and sufficient antagonist to error, and has nothing to fear from conflict." During the eighteenth and nineteenth centuries, however, the self-righting principle was gradually linked as well to an "argument for democracy."

As long as the emergence of truth is seen as the only purpose served by the market-place of ideas, it might seem reasonable to conclude that freedom of the press should be restricted by effective state safeguards for both the beliefs and values of the community and the rights and reputations of its individual members. However, if the objective of a society becomes not simply the advance of "civilization" but the development of a *democratic* civilization, then it becomes necessary to adopt an even more libertarian attitude towards freedom of the press. That is, it becomes essential not only to eliminate most pre-publication controls but also to retain only a few moderate post-publication deterrents.

For the origins of this belief, we need to look not to Milton, who would have abhorred the suggestion that freedom of the press is desirable on democratic grounds, but to a short-lived opposition group in Parliament known as the Levellers. Led by John Lilburne, the Levellers did not explicitly justify freedom of the press in terms of the needs of democracy, but they did relate it to good government. As they pointed out in a petition to Parliament on January 18, 1649:

> ... if Government be just in its Constitution, and equal in its distribution, it will be good, if not absolutely necessary for them, to hear all voices and judgments, which they can never do, but by giving freedom to the Press, and in case any abuse their authority by scandalous pamphlets, they will never want advocates to vindicate their innocency. (Siebert, 1952: 201)

Despite combining the moderate statement that government would benefit from listening to "all voices and judgments" with the self-righting principle, the Levellers did not receive a sympathetic response to their petition. Parliament immediately enlarged the crime of treason to include seditious publications and attempted, albeit unsuccessfully, to obtain the conviction of Lilburne for such supposedly treasonous ideas.

The Levellers planted a valuable seed, but it was not harvested until the next century. Even then its first cultivators were careful to conceal their identity lest they suffer at the hands of the law for their unorthodox views. In a series of letters published in *The London Journal* between 1720 and 1723, two radical Whig thinkers, John Trenchard and Thomas Gordon, sought to work out some of the implications of the Levellers' suggestion that freedom of the press is essential for good government. In particular, they tackled the tricky question of how severe to make the law of libel. But they were not sufficiently confident in the current workings of that law to reveal their identities publicly. To avoid possible prosecution they took the pseudonym "Cato" and called their writings "Cato's Letters." Despite their anonymity, however, their writings were extremely influential, first in the American colonies and later in England.

Milton had wanted a free press in order that an intellectual elite might discover new truths; Trenchard and Gordon wanted a free press in order that there might be a free government. By a free government, they understood one in which the deeds of the governing parties are openly examined and publicly scrutinized. They spoke more of freedom of speech than of freedom of the press, but we can safely assume that they considered the former to embrace the latter. Although they did not believe that such freedoms should be absolute, they argued that the only theoretical constraint or limitation upon them should be that their exercise does not negate or infringe upon the rights of others. They concluded that in practice this means that the only restriction on freedom of speech should be the law of libel and that even it should be moderately interpreted.

Of what should this moderate interpretation consist? A careful reading of "Cato's Letters" reveals that Trenchard and Gordon did not reduce the question of libel simply to the matter of truth and falsity. Rather the key consideration was thought to be that of the public good. In "Reflections upon Libelling" (1721), they made a distinction between private and personal failings on the one hand and actions that affect the public on the other. With regard to the former, they insisted that:

> A Libel is not the less a Libel for being true. This may seem a Contradiction; but it is neither one in Law, or in common Sense: There are some Truths not fit to be told; where, for Example, the discovery of a small Fault may do great Mischief; or where the discovery of a great Fault can do no Good, there ought to be no Discovery at all: And to make Faults where there are none, is still worse. (Jacobson, 1965: 73)

In the case of the latter, however, they maintained that "the exposing . . . of publick Wickedness, as it is a Duty which every Man owes to Truth and his Country, can never be a Libel in the Nature of Things." (Jacobson, 1965: 74)

In other words, it would be libellous to expose the personal vices of a government official if these do not affect his public performance, but not libellous to criticize that performance if it harms the general interest. "It is certain, that we ought not to enter into the private Vices or Weaknesses of Governors, *any further than their private Vices enter into their publick Administration.*" (Jacobson, 1965: 77; emphasis added.)

Having interpreted libel in this manner, Trenchard and Gordon then proceeded to argue that the laws governing it should be applied leniently. They offered two basic reasons for this. The first was essentially a version of Milton's self-righting principle. They said that lies cannot hurt good men with clear reputations because upright men will always defend them and truth has many advantages over falsehood. The second was an expansion of the Leveller case for good government. They acknowledged that the wrongful accusation of innocent men in scurrilous writing is undoubtedly annoying to those involved. But they said that a far greater evil consists of not being able to accuse those who are truly guilty. To place rigid controls on the press might check a few errors and curtail a few minor mischiefs. But seditious libel seldom foments popular discontent or insurrection, while press controls open the door to superstition and ignorance, injustice and tyranny. "I must own, that I would rather many Libels should escape than the Liberty of the Press should be infringed." (Jacobson, 1965: 79)

The first use of "Cato's" argument that freedom of speech is an essential check upon oppression was made, not in England, but in the colony of New York when John Peter Zenger was prosecuted for seditious libel in 1735. Zenger's defence counsel proposed two radical departures from the precedents of common law. First, it contended that a plea of truth should be permitted as a defence against a charge of seditious libel. Secondly, it argued that the jury should have the right to decide both the legal and factual questions involved. Although there was no justification in law for either claim, the jury brought in a verdict of "not guilty" for Zenger. Moreover, while the case did not immediately change English law, juries were subsequently much less willing to convict publishers for seditious libel. (Levy, 1960, 1972)

It can be seen in the thought of a number of other eighteenth-century thinkers that it is possible to extend one's faith in the self-righting principle beyond that of "Cato." For example, "Father of Candor" was worried that the concept of truth as a defence might not provide adequate protection for a writer who unknowingly conveys a falsehood. He suggested that the court be required to prove that the author deliberately propagated the error. Only if proof was forthcoming should the accused be punished for libel. The historian and mathematician Francis Maseres likewise wanted to increase the court's burden of proof. Like "Father of Candor," he contended that maliciousness on a writer's part should be proven to establish his guilt. But he went even further by suggesting that a jury be shown, as a prerequisite of guilt, that the disturbing literature under consideration "actually occasioned that disturbance which it seemed to be intended to create." (Rivera, 1978: 48)

In 1770 the Reverend Phillip Furneaux set forth what is probably the most radical libertarian position of all. Furneaux advocated that governments ignore printed materials entirely and only concern themselves with the overt acts arising from them. According to Furneaux, opinions and beliefs do not as such endanger lives or property; they should not, therefore, be subject to scrutiny by the civil authority. "Punishing a man for the tendency of his principles," he wrote, "is punishing him before he is guilty, for fear he should be guilty." (Rivera, 1978: 49)

A less radical approach to the law of libel was espoused by the Canadian champion of freedom of the press, Joseph Howe. In 1835 Howe was accused of "seditiously contriving, devising and intending to stir up and incite discontent and sedition among His Majesty's subjects" because of a letter which he had published in the *Novascotian*. Signed "The People," the letter in question accused the magistrates and police of having fleeced the poor of at least a thousand pounds a year for the previous 30 years. During the century which had passed since the Zenger case, there had been a number of changes in the law of libel. In 1792, for example, the British Parliament had passed Fox's *Libel Act,* giving juries the right to decide not only whether the accused had published the objectionable statements but also whether they were, in fact, libellous. However, the effect of this was reduced by subsequent changes in procedural rules, so that in the period leading up to Howe's trial, prosecutions for seditious libel had met with considerable success. In a general sense, therefore, the Howe trial was the Canadian equivalent of the Zenger case.

In conducting his own defence, Howe adopted the general strategy of focusing on the notion that malice is one of the ingredients of a libel. Prior to the Howe case, maliciousness had usually been determined by examining the offending statements themselves to see if they were such as to disturb the public peace. But Howe argued that intention should be taken into account in determining malice:

> If, in resisting a burglar, I knock my friend upon the head, I cannot be convicted of crime; and if, in opposing a public robber, I utterly destroy his reputation by the exposure of his malpractices, the jury try me by my motives, not by the severity of the infliction, unless the punishment be utterly disproportionate to the crime. (Chisholm, 1909: I, 32)

Howe also contended that malice should not be decided simply on the basis of the offending statements. On the contrary, he should be given an opportunity to show "the state of my own mind at the time I published the letter." (Chisholm, 1909: I, 36) What he meant by this was that he should be able to set forth those facts which had led him to publish the letter. This was an ingenious ploy, for it enabled him to demonstrate not only that he had not acted maliciously but also that his claims about corruption were true. It allowed him to sneak the question of truth in through the back door.

Although there is no evidence to my knowledge of his having read Trenchard and Gordon, Howe's defence contains echoes of "Cato's Letters." He argued, for example, that his actions were not only lacking in malice but were, in fact, virtuous, because there was "a great and overwhelming public necessity" to know about the magistrates' conduct. His criticism was not a libel against the state, but an attempt to protect its reputation; instead of trying to breach the peace, he was actually trying to restore and preserve it. It was the magistrates who were guilty of sedition since "he who robs the subject makes war upon the king." (Chisholm, 1909: I, 40)

As in the Zenger case, Howe's acquittal did not immediately bring changes in the law of libel. But it was clear by Howe's day that authoritarianism was on the run. As the century progressed, libertarians in

Britain, the United States, and Canada won a series of important victories for freedom of the press. Libertarianism became not only a theory but a reality, embracing both the content of the press and its organization. It also had a new theorist to add to the pantheon of Milton, "Cato," Jefferson, and Howe. In 1859 John Stuart Mill published his essay *On Liberty.* In it Mill sought to establish "one very simple principle;" namely,

> . . . that the sole end for which mankind are warranted, individually or collectively, in interfering with the liberty of action of any of their number, is self-protection. That the only purpose for which power can be rightfully exercised over any member of a civilized community, against his will, is to prevent harm to others. His own good, either physical or moral, is not a sufficient warrant. (Mill, 1859: 592)

This principle might conceivably have been the basis for an argument for limited controls over the press. However, Mill seems to have advocated virtually absolute freedom of thought and discussion.

Mill justified complete freedom of expression on four grounds, which deserve to be quoted in full:

> First, if any opinion is compelled to silence, that opinion may, for aught we can certainly know, be true. To deny this is to assume our own infallibility.
>
> Secondly, though the silenced opinion be an error, it may, and very commonly does, contain a portion of truth; and since the general or prevailing opinion on any subject is rarely or never the whole truth, it is only by the collision of adverse opinions that the remainder of the truth has any chance of being supplied.
>
> Thirdly, even if the received opinion be not only true, but the whole truth; unless it is suffered to be, and actually is, vigorously and earnestly contested, it will by most of those who receive it, be held in the manner of a prejudice, with little comprehension or feeling of its rational grounds. And not only this, but fourthly, the meaning of the doctrine itself will be in danger of being lost, or enfeebled, and deprived of its vital effect on the character and conduct: the dogma becoming a mere formal profession, inefficacious for good, but cumbering the ground, and preventing the growth of any real and heartfelt conviction, from reason or personal experience. (Mill, 1859: 596-97)

It is doubtful whether anyone has made the case for freedom of expression more clearly, forthrightly, or persuasively than this.

Position C — The Social Responsibility Theory of the Press

By the late nineteenth century, the libertarian theory of the press had come to stand for three things. First, it insisted upon the absence of prior restraint over publication, including the gathering and presentation of news. Secondly, it called for a broad scope to legitimate criticism of government, with only moderate post-publication penalties for libellous materials. Thirdly, it opposed government interference with the business side of the press. It was argued that government measures affecting the operation of the press would undermine its freedom of expression. This was a reasonable enough conclusion to reach, given the way in which the stamp taxes had earlier been used to control the press. But it eventually led to suspicions that the real concern of media owners was not with freedom of expression, but with the freedom to continue certain exploitive business practices.

By the late nineteenth century, the general trend within the economy towards consolidation and concentration was starting to be reflected in newspaper ownership as well. Groups of newspapers under a single owner began to emerge, while the number of urban areas with two or more daily newspapers began to decline. At the same time as this form of "modernization" was occurring, however, newspapers were refusing to change in other ways. They remained hostile towards the unionization of their employees; they opposed wages and hours legislation; and they even reacted against the application of child labour laws to their carriers and news hawkers. They did so, moreover, on the grounds that theirs was a privileged industry that should be exempt from regulations affecting other industries.

Beginning about 1900, a number of American thinkers began to criticize these exploitive practices. Foremost among these critics were Will Irwin, Walter Lippmann, and Upton Sinclair. But it was not until the Depression of the 1930s that the American press was effectively challenged to change its ways. At that point, the press came into conflict with the New Deal legislation of President Roosevelt. The initial confrontation occurred in 1933-34 over the *National Industrial Recovery Act,* which required businesses to draft cooperative agreements increasing employment, shortening working hours, raising wages, and stabilizing profits. It also required collective bargaining and gave the President the authority to license businesses. The American Newspaper Publishers Association, which was given responsibility for the newspaper code negotiations, eventually conceded to wage and hour provisions, an open shop, and child labour regulations. It demanded that the President accept a clause declaring his commitment to the First Amendment, however, and shortly thereafter joined the National Association of Manufacturers and the U.S. Chamber of Commerce in lobbying against other New Deal legislation.

The American public did not buy the argument that social welfare measures such as the *Social Security Act* and the *Fair Labor Standards Act* constituted a threat to freedom of the press. It felt that newspaper owners were simply trying to avoid making reasonable adjustments to new socioeconomic conditions. In the presidential election of 1936, it gave is overwhelming support to Roosevelt, despite the fact that most newspaper editorials had come out in favour of the Republican candidate, Alf Landon. The following year, the Supreme Court dealt a further blow to the newspaper publishers. In *Associated Press v. National Labor Relations*

Board, the court declared in a 5 to 4 decision that "the publisher of a newspaper has no special immunity from the application of general laws." Publishers were required to recognize the American Newspaper Guild and were prohibited from firing an employee because of union activities. (Blanchard, 1977: 3-11)

This confrontation lent support to the view of some of the critics of the press that it was a representative of the socio-economic elite and did not reflect the views of the nation as a whole. It also contributed to the declining public image of the press resulting from such criticism. By the early 1940s, therefore, there was a growing feeling within newspaper circles that something needed to be done to ensure that Americans remained committed to the principle of freedom of the press. One attempt to resuscitate the image of the press was made by the American Society of Newspaper Editors, which felt that editors had been unfairly lumped together with owners. But their efforts were soon overshadowed by an initiative taken by Henry Luce, the publisher of *Time, Life,* and *Fortune* magazines. In 1942, Luce invited his personal friend and fellow Yale alumnus, Robert M. Hutchins, to head a commission to formulate a statement on freedom of the press. Hutchins, who was serving as President of the University of Chicago at the time, agreed to do so and set about organizing a group of scholars to that end. On February 28, 1944, he announced the creation of a 13-member Commission on Freedom of the Press.

The principal motive of Luce in providing $200,000 for this commission has often been overlooked in accounts of the Hutchins Commission. As Schudson has pointed out, it was not the practices of newspaper owners that caused Luce to be concerned about freedom of the press. What worried him was the increasingly organized and self-conscious control of news by government. Luce wanted the commissioners to make a statement about the dangers of governmental news management to freedom of the press. He did not, however, exercise any control over their deliberations, with the result that his own concerns were soon forgotten. Instead of addressing the question of news management, the commissioners focused on the impact of concentrated ownership on the performance of the press. Perhaps one reason for this was the fact that no one currently working for a newspaper was included on the commission.

The Hutchins Commission set forth the results of its deliberations on March 26, 1947, in a slim volume entitled *A Free and Responsible Press.* This report is generally credited with raising to the level of consciousness the idea that freedom of the press carries with it the obligation to act responsibly to society. The commission redefined a free press to mean one which reflects the views of all citizens and conveys the full spectrum of ideas in society. It concluded that in this sense, freedom of the press was in danger in America because of the growth of communications empires. It suggested that if the press did not clean its own house, government action might be necessary. But it clearly preferred the use of non-government mechanisms such as press councils to stimulate more responsible journalism from the press. It also proposed mandatory retraction and right of reply provisions.

The libertarian acceptance of the self-righting principle assumed the operation of a kind of "invisible hand" by which truth emerges from the competition of ideas. Each media outlet was thought to make a contribution to this process through its own unfettered activity. There was no need for it to do anything other than follow its own will. The social responsibility theory, however, reveals a distinct lack of faith in the natural workings of the press. It does not trust the media to achieve a reasonable balance of views of its own accord. It proposes, therefore, that the performance of the media be monitored so that its shortcomings can be corrected. It is still leery of government interference, but sees no reason why other instruments could not be used to ensure that the media fulfill their obligation to society.

Despite its ambiguity, the social responsibility theory of the press has been embraced by numerous American writers as transcending the limitations of libertarianism. It was clearly the preferred position of Siebert and his colleagues in *Four Theories of the Press*. In Canada, it was espoused by a Special Senate Committee on Mass Media created in 1969. One of the few persons to criticize the social responsibility theory has been John Merrill in *The Imperative of Freedom* (1974). "American journalists," he declared, "like most journalists in the Western world, while still chanting the tenets of libertarianism, are marching into an authoritarian sunset under the banners of 'social responsibility'." (p. 4)

Merrill accepted the premise that the press should act responsibly. But he asked whether the press's sense of responsibility should be self-determined or socially-determined. His answer was clear: if the journalist is to be personally accountable for the consequences of his actions, he must have the freedom and autonomy to direct his own behaviour. He must be able to determine for himself where his responsibility lies. His journalistic decisions cannot be determined collectively by society. Ironically, therefore, by advocating the imposition of journalistic standards from the outside, the social responsibility theory actually removes responsibility from the individual journalist.

Position D — The Socialist Theory of the Press

A Hegelian scholar looking at the history of theories of the press in the Western world would no doubt be tempted to see a dialectical progression. From the invention of the printing press until the eighteenth century, the authoritarian theory of the press was dominant. Then, during the eighteenth and nineteenth centuries, a libertarian theory emerged in opposition to authoritarianism and finally became ascendant. Finally, in the twentieth

century, the partial truths contained within authoritarianism and libertarianism were synthesized into the social responsibility theory of the
press, while what was false or excessive about each was left behind.

The only problem with this interpretation is that it ignores the fact that
there is more than one way of mediating between the authoritarian and
libertarian approaches. The social responsibility theory has a low degree of
faith in the self-righting principle in common with the authoritarian theory; it also adopts a restrictive approach to government activity in common with libertarianism. However, it is also possible in theory to combine
the high degree of faith in the self-righting principle of libertarianism with
the authoritarian acceptance of a broad scope to government activity. In
effect, this is what a socialist theory of the press would do.

The socialist approach should be clearly distinguished from the Soviet-communist theory of the press, which maintains that the press should
be a propaganda instrument of the communist party. "Soviet newspapers,"
writes Philip Short, "are, in Lenin's phrase, 'a collective organiser, agitator,
and propagandist'. Their role is not to inform, but to advocate, to crusade
and convince." To this end they present a monolithic view of the world
with no deviations from the accepted party line. Short relates that "in three
years of daily scrutiny of the main Soviet papers, in Moscow from 1974-76,
I found only one case where significant differences of view, indicating a
high-level debate on a question of political theory, were given clear public
expression, and that was over the attitude the Soviet Union should take to
Eurocommunism." (Short, 1982: 117)

The same thing is true of Soviet broadcasting. As Gorbachev's lieuten-
ant for ideology, Yegor Ligachev, stated a couple of years ago, "our television and radio broadcasts must be fully and totally political. Of course, this
does not mean that political slogans should resound in every program. But
all TV and radio programs should serve one aim — propaganda, the
clarification and implementation of the policy of the party." (McGillivray,
1985: A8)

It would be a distortion of the socialist view of the role of the press to
lump it together with this position. The socialist would argue, of course,
that before the press can function properly, capitalist institutions must be
drastically reformed. In this regard, the socialist position would be rejected
by both the libertarian and social responsibility theorists. But like the
libertarian and social responsibility theorists, the socialist would maintain
that freedom of the press is vital for a healthy democracy. He would not
subscribe to either the authoritarian or Soviet-communist view that the
press exists to serve the interests of the state as interpreted by its ruling
party.

In one respect, indeed, the socialist is closer to the libertarian than to
the social responsibility theorist. For once capitalist society has been
reformed, the socialist would be prepared to place substantial faith in the

self-righting principle. As we have seen, social responsibility advocates do maintain that under the conditions of unfettered private enterprise, the press is "freer" for some groups than for others. But their main remedy for this situation is an impassioned appeal for the press to accept a vaguely delineated and potentially stultifying concept of responsibility. The socialist, however, would be prepared to take much more decisive and extensive action (giving him one form of affinity with the authoritarian). To the horror of the libertarian and social responsibility theorist, he would argue that the government must take steps to restructure the media so that the self-righting principle can become operative. In particular, the socialist would hold that access must be created for groups and individuals poorly served by the private enterprise media.

Such steps could include the creation of publicly owned broadcasting facilities, financial support for community media projects, technical assistance for remote areas, and tax concessions for new media outlets. None of these measures would interfere directly with the existing content of the media. They would not deprive the journalist of any autonomy. Nor would they necessarily affect the degree of private ownership of the media, although the socialist would certainly not be opposed to regulating private ownership under certain conditions. What they would do is create new opportunities for ideas and viewpoints to emerge. For while the socialist theory rejects authoritarian controls over public opinion, it asserts the right of the citizens of a democracy to use their government to provide alternatives to the privately owned media. It embraces the self-righting principle, but insists that it can only work when there are assurances that all segments of society can participate in the search for truth.

References

Adam, G. Stuart
  1976 "The Sovereignty of the Publicity System: A Case Study of the Alberta Press Act." In G. S. Adam (ed.), *Journalism, Communication and the Law.* Scarborough: Prentice-Hall.
Beck, J. M.
  1974 " 'A Fool for a Client': The Trial of Joseph Howe," *Acadiensis* 3 (No. 2): 27-44.
Blanchard, Margaret A.
  1977 "The Hutchins Commission, The Press and the Responsibility Concept." *Journalism Monographs,* No. 49.
Chisholm, Joseph Andrew
  1909 *The Speeches and Public Letters of Joseph Howe.* 2 vols., Halifax: Chronicle Publishing Company.
Gross, Gerald (ed.)
  1966 *The Responsibility of the Press.* New York: Simon and Schuster.
Hachten, W. A.
  1981 *The World News Prism: Changing Media, Clashing Ideologies.* Ames, Iowa: University Press.
Hutchins Commission (on Freedom of the Press)
  1947 *A Free and Responsible Press.* Chicago: University of Chicago Press.
Jacobson, David L. (ed.)
  1965 *The English Libertarian Heritage: From the Writings of John Trenchard and Thomas Gordon in "The Independent Whig" and "Cato's Letters".* (Copyright © 1965 by Macmillan Publishing Company).
Kendall, Willmoore
  1960 "How to Read Milton's Areopagitica." *Journal of Politics* 22 (August): 439-73.
Kesterton, Wilfred H.
  1967 *A History of Journalism in Canada.* Toronto: McClelland and Stewart.
Levy, Leonard W.
  1960 "Did the Zenger Case Really Matter?" *William and Mary Quarterly* (Third Series)17: 35-50.

1972 *Judgments: Essays on American Constitutional History.* Chicago: Quadrangle Books.

McGillivray, Don

1985 "Free comment essential in our society." *The Ottawa Citizen* (December 20): A8.

Merrill, John Calhoun

1974 *The Imperative of Freedom: A Philosophy of Journalistic Autonomy.* New York: Hastings House.

Merrill, John C. and S. Jack Odell

1983 *Philosophy and Journalism.* New York: Longman.

Mill, John Stuart

1859 "On Liberty." In Vol. II of *Introduction to Contemporary Civilization in the West: A Source Book.* 3rd ed., New York: Columbia University Press, 1961.

Milton, John

1644 *Areopagitica; A Speech of Mr. John Milton For the Liberty of Unlicenc'd Printing, to the Parliament of England* (London); pp. 485-570 of *Complete Prose Works of John Milton; Volume II: 1643-1648.* New Haven: Yale University Press, 1959.

Ottawa Citizen (The)

1985 "Freedom of speech qualified by value of impartial public service" [excerpt from Supreme Court judgment signed by Chief Justice Brian Dickson]. *The Ottawa Citizen* (December 12): A9.

Prothro, James W. and Charles M. Grigg

1960 "Fundamental Principles of Democracy: Bases of Agreement and Disagreement." *Journal of Politics* 20 (May): 276-94.

Quinn, Hal

1985 "The Holocaust Trial." *Maclean's* 98 (March 11): 42-6.

Riley, Susan

1985 "Billy Bishop: Real Hero or Celluloid Fraud?" *The Ottawa Citizen* (December 7): B4.

Rivera, Clark

1978 "Ideals, Interests and Civil Liberty: The Colonial Press and Freedom, 1735-76." *Journalism Quarterly* 55 (Spring): 47-53*f.*

Rivers, W. L., W. Schramm, and C. G. Christians

1980 *Responsibility in Mass Communication.* 3rd ed., New York: Harper and Row.

Short, Philip

1982 *The Dragon and the Bear: Inside China and Russia Today.* London: Hodder and Stoughton.

Siebert, Frederick S.

1952 *Freedom of the Press in England 1476-1776: The Rise and Decline of Government Control.* Urbana: University of Illinois Press.

Siebert, F. S., Theodore Peterson, and Wilbur Schramm
    1956 *Four Theories of the Press.* Urbana: University of Illinois Press.
Siegel, Arthur
    1983 *Politics and the Media in Canada.* Toronto: McGraw-Hill
       Ryerson.

Chapter 4

Is Newspaper Concentration a Serious Problem?

From the invention of the printing press until the early years of the twentieth century, the form of media ownership was not a major issue in the English-speaking world. By the second quarter of the present century, however, two developments had begun to alter this situation. The first development, which provides the focus of this chapter, was a change in the nature of newspaper ownership. The second development, which will be examined in the next chapter, was the emergence of broadcasting. Together these developments have given rise to a sustained and often bitter debate about the nature of media ownership.

Throughout most of the nineteenth century, there were almost as many newspaper owners as there were newspapers. But in 1883, Joseph Pulitzer started the first modern newspaper group or "chain" when he purchased the New York *World* to go along with the St. Louis *Post-Dispatch*. Before long other American newspaper barons such as Edward W. Scripps, William Randolph Hearst, and Adolph Ochs decided to build their own chains. By 1900 Scripps owned nine daily newspapers in the American mid-west. The Hearst chain was smaller but more influential, embracing the San Francisco *Examiner,* the New York *Journal,* and papers in Chicago and Boston. In Canada the first group came into existence in 1897 when William Southam acquired *The Ottawa Citizen* to go along with the Hamilton *Spectator.* To these two papers the Southam Company Limited added the Calgary *Herald* in 1908 and the Edmonton *Journal* in 1912.

The first systematic investigation of newspaper ownership was conducted in the early 1940s by the Hutchins Commission in the United States. It was followed by the Royal Commission on the Press in Britain in 1947. (Subsequent British commissions on the press were held in 1961-62 and 1974-77.) Canada was even slower to become concerned about newspaper ownership. The Massey Royal Commission of 1949-51 made a passing reference to the importance of the print media, but it did not undertake to examine the problem of newspaper ownership. Moreover, while the Royal Commission on Publications chaired by Senator Grattan

O'Leary in 1961 established the federal government's right to regulate the fiscal affairs of the print media, it was more concerned with magazines than with daily newspapers.

It was not until the mid-1960s that there were calls for a full-scale enquiry into newspaper ownership in Canada. In 1963, Tommy Douglas, the leader of the New Democratic Party, urged the creation of a commission to investigate the increasing concentration of newspaper ownership. Two years later, the Saskatchewan Farmers Union made a similar call for a federal royal commission to investigate the growth of press monopolies. The Liberal government of Pierre Trudeau responded late in 1969, not with a royal commission, but by having Liberal Senator Keith Davey chair a Special Senate Committee on the Mass Media. The Davey Committee was the first serious investigation of newspapers in Canada. It conducted 43 days of hearings in Ottawa, received some 200 written briefs and research reports, and drew up a set of recommendations in a comprehensive report published in 1970.

The Davey Committee was unable to reverse or even slow down the process of newspaper concentration in Canada. During the 1970s, eight newspapers disappeared, including the Toronto *Telegram* and the Montreal *Star.* Thomson Newspapers did relinquish one of its newspapers, the Quebec *Chronicle-Telegraph,* to an independent owner, who turned it into a weekly. But in the fall of 1979, after a bidding war with industrialist Conrad Black, Thomson acquired eight newspapers at once through the purchase of FP Publications for $165 million. Included among the eight papers were *The Globe and Mail,* Toronto, and the *Winnipeg Free Press.* Less than a year later, on Wednesday, August 27, 1980, the Ottawa *Journal* and the Winnipeg *Tribune* were closed by their respective owners, Thomson Newspapers and Southam Inc. These closures left the *Free Press* owned by Thomson as the only daily in Winnipeg and the *Citizen* owned by Southam as the only daily in Ottawa. On the same day, moreover, Thomson sold Southam its one-third minority interest in the Montreal *Gazette* and 50 per cent interest in Pacific Press Ltd., which publishes Vancouver's two dailies, the *Sun* and the *Province.*

"Black Wednesday" sent shock waves not only through the journalistic community but into political circles as well. There were two reactions from the government: one legal, the other bureaucratic. The legal response came when the federal Department of Corporate and Consumer Affairs laid seven charges against Southam, Thomson, and a number of their subsidiary firms based on provisions in the *Combines Investigation Act.* (Southam and Thomson were acquitted in December, 1983.) The bureaucratic response came within a week of closure of the *Tribune* and *Journal* when Prime Minister Trudeau appointed a Royal Commission on Newspapers. Thomas Kent, a former editor of the *Winnipeg Free Press* and an advisor to the Liberal government in the 1960s, was named chairman of the commission. At the time of his appointment, he was dean of administrative studies at Dalhousie University. Assisting him were two co-chairmen: Borden Spears, a retired ombudsman for *The Toronto Star;* and Laurent Picard, a former president of the CBC.

The Kent Commission exercised a broad mandate. "Our task is to look at the industry as a whole," their final *Report* stated; "to suggest, if we can, a better course for newspapers in Canada; to recommend whether law or policy should be different for the future." (Kent Commission, 1981: xi) To accomplish this task, the commission spent approximately a year conducting public hearings, commissioning various research projects, interviewing newsmen, assembling their findings, and preparing a set of recommendations. The fruit of their labours, which cost $3.1 million, was published in August of 1981. Central to its recommendations was a proposed tax change that would reduce the net cost to a newspaper of spending more on editorial content. It also called for a ceiling on ownership and the use of capital cost allowances to encourage individuals to buy shares in newspaper companies. Virtually all of its proposals were attacked by the newspaper industry.

At the time of his appointment, Kent believed that the Liberal government fully intended to take action on the newspaper concentration situation. "I had the assurance, so to speak . . . that there was a real sense that there was a problem represented by the events of August, 1980," he later recalled. (Campbell, 1984: M5) But as he also soon realized, "by 1981 the Trudeau government was in disarray, confused by the economic problems with which it could not cope and by its ineptness in federal-provincial relations. With its popularity slumping, it was much less inclined to take on the newspaper publishers on an issue that offered little, if any, electoral benefit." (Kent, 1984: 2)

The Honourable James Fleming, who was multi-culturalism minister at the time and who had a background as a radio journalist, assumed responsibility for the Kent Commission report. In May of 1982, he announced in London, Ontario, that press legislation would soon by introduced — less severe than that called for by the Kent Commission but the first such legislation in Canada nonetheless. The proposed legislation was delayed, however, and in the fall of 1984 the Liberals were decisively defeated. With their overwhelming majority, the Progressive Conservatives were in a better position to take action on the ownership question without having to worry about short-term political repercussions. But the new government showed no interest in acting upon the recommendations of a Liberal-appointed commission. In fact, the only action it took was to reverse the Liberal government's position on cross-media ownership.

The problem of cross-media ownership is of more recent origins than that of newspaper concentration. It is the result of two processes of corporate diversification. First, media-based corporations have been expanding into non-media areas. Thomson, for example, has used profits from its extensive newspaper holdings in Canada, Britain, and the United States to expand into the Canadian department store business and acquire large holdings in travel and natural resources. *The Toronto Star* now accounts for less than 40 per cent of the revenue of the Torstar conglomerate.

Secondly, corporations with no media holdings initially have been acquiring various communications properties. In most cases, these acquisitions have remained secondary to the corporation's other activities. For example, S. Pearson and Sons in Britain has used profits gained from interests in oil, ceramics, banking and local newspapers to purchase such media properties as *The Financial Times,* Longman, and Penguin Books. In Canada, the Irving newspapers and radio stations in New Brunswick are a relatively small part of the Canadian and international operations of the Irvings.

The extension of the process of corporate diversification to the media has greatly complicated the problem of ownership. On the one hand, it has provided media properties with more security against economic downswings. But on the other hand, it has made those properties vulnerable to non-media considerations. This is particularly true of general conglomerates in which the media holdings are of recent origin. But it also applies to media conglomerates in which different kinds of media properties are subject to common control. Even in countries that have placed restrictions on the growth of media conglomerates, a number of cross-media situations have emerged.

In July of 1982, the Liberal government sent a directive to the Canadian Radio-Television and Telecommunications Commission indicating that broadcast licences should be denied if the licensee owned a newspaper in the same community. The directive said, however, that cases should be exempted where the denial would cause "exceptional and unreasonable hardship" on the licensee or harm to the public interest. As a result, the CRTC did not actually find itself compelled to deny anyone a licence renewal. For example, CFPL Broadcasting of London, Ontario, and the *London Free Press* were allowed to remain under common ownership on the grounds that they were providing good service and there was already sufficient competition in the London area.

The worst case of cross-media ownership exists in the Maritimes where K. C. Irving owns the morning and afternoon newspapers in Saint John as well as the New Brunswick Broadcasting Company, which operates the CBC affiliate in Saint John (CHSJ-TV) and several rebroadcasting stations. Following the government's 1982 directive, the CRTC informed the Irving interests that they should reorganize their holdings so as to dissolve this cross-media ownership by January 1, 1986, without depriving the province of CBC service. The New Brunswick Broadcasting Company responded by appealing to the Federal Court of Appeal, challenging both the constitutionality of the government's directive and the CRTC's application of it.

Although its appeal was dismissed in July of 1984, the company proceeded to apply for an extension of its licence beyond 1986. In January, 1985, it received permission to appeal from the federal court's decision. In March of the same year, the Attorney General of Canada countered by indicating that the government would intervene on the side of the CRTC and in support of the previous government's directive. However, by the following June, it had reversed its position and decided to revoke the directive rather than defend it in court. This left the CRTC without an effective weapon with which to deal with cross-media ownership (Bain, 1985: 54)

In the United States, on the other hand, cross-media ownership has declined sharply since the Second World War. In 1940, 23 per cent of radio stations were owned by newspapers in the same market; by 1950 this had declined to only three per cent, partly as a result of FCC regulation. As late as 1973, 16 per cent of the television stations in the top 100 markets were affiliated with newspapers. But the FCC subsequently prohibited newspapers from constructing or purchasing television stations that overlapped the same market. Moreover, in 1977 a U.S. Court of Appeals ordered that existing newspaper-broadcast combinations be broken up. (Compaine, 1978: 41)

Therefore, there are precedents within the English-speaking world for taking action to control the concentration of media ownership. (In 1984, after a heated debate, the French National Assembly approved a bill restricting the ownership of newspapers and magazines.) The question, however, is whether the current concentration of newspaper ownership in Canada is such as to warrant measures by the federal government. Is the lack of government action to date the result of political indecision? Or is the problem of newspaper concentration really not a very serious one?

There is no disagreement that since the turn of the century, newspapers have experienced the same concentration of ownership that has taken place in industrial organizations generally. There are, however, some significant differences between countries. To put the Canadian situation in perspective, it is helpful to begin by considering the state of concentration in the United States and Britain.

In the United States, the concentration of ownership has been largely a post-World War II phenomenon. At the turn of the century, there were only eight newspaper groups and still almost as many owners (2,023) as there were daily papers (2,042). By the late 1920s, the number of groups had increased to about 60, but only accounted for about 300 dailies. Over the next decade and a half, both the number of groups and the number of papers belonging to groups continued to increase moderately. As late as

1945 there were only 76 groups embracing 368 dailies. As a percentage of the total number of daily newspapers (1744 as of 1944), this was quite small (approximately 21 per cent). Although the circulations of the group-owned papers tended to be larger than those of the independents, accounting for more than a third of the total daily circulation, group ownership did not yet dominate the scene.

Beginning in the 1950s, however, the percentage of American daily newspapers belonging to groups increased rapidly. It reached 31 per cent by 1960, 47 per cent by 1970, and 62 per cent by 1980. At the same time, the circulation of group-owned papers also rose dramatically from 45 per cent in the 1950s to 61 per cent by the end of the 1960s to 75 per cent by 1980. (Compaine, 1979: 11, 17, 20; Bagdikian, 1980: 57-64; Bagdikian, 1983: 9) To keep this in perspective, however, two other trends are usually noted.

First, the number of different groups also increased steadily: from 31 in 1923, to 95 in 1954, to 167 in 1978. About one-third of these have owned only two newspapers. Secondly, while some of these groups are obviously much larger than others, the largest 25 per cent of newspaper firms account for a lower percentage of daily circulation today than a half century ago; the same is true for the largest 10 per cent. The 20 largest groups still only control about half of the daily circulation and the 50 largest only control two-thirds. There are, of course, some very large groups. The Gannet group has over 80 papers, the Thomson group over 50, and the Knight-Ridder and Samuel Newhouse groups over 30 papers each. Nonetheless, in 1978 the largest group in terms of total daily circulation, Knight-Ridder with 6.1 per cent, was still far short of the 10.4 per cent achieved by the Hearst group in 1946. Moreover, the percentage of daily circulation controlled by Gannett, Knight-Ridder, Hearst, Scripps-Howard, and Newhouse only rose from 20.4 per cent in 1946 to 23.2 per cent in 1978. (Compaine, 1979: 11, 17, 20, 22)

On the other hand, of the 677 independently-owned dailies still in existence at the outset of 1977, about 250 had circulations of less than 5,000, making them unattractive to group owners. Moreover, the others were being sought after at a furious rate. One hundred of these were purchased by chains in 1977-78 alone. Perhaps the most troublesome aspect of this consolidation and concentration has been the reduction in the number of cities with competing papers. In the United States, there were 502 cities in 1923 with two or more daily papers. But this number fell rapidly to 243 in 1933, 137 in 1943, 91 in 1953, 51 in 1963, and 37 in 1973. Of 1,536 cities with daily papers in 1978, only 35 or 2.3 per cent had two or more dailies, although another 20 cities had two papers operating under the agency shop provision of the Newspaper Preservation Act. The United States does have almost 10,000 other newspapers. But it is revealing that of the 1,100 or so dailies owned by groups in the late 1970s, only about 50 had local printed competition and only about half a dozen at the same time of the day. (Compaine, 1979: 11, 18; Bagdikian, 1980: 62-3)

Similar developments have been occurring in Britain. Between 1921 and 1937, the five largest corporations increased their percentage of newspaper titles from 15 to 43 per cent. After the Second World War, this process of concentration continued, with various companies jockeying for position. In the late 1940s, the top three companies were Beaverbrook Newspapers, Associated Newspapers, and Kemsley. By 1974 Kemsley had fallen by the wayside and the International Publishing Corporation was leading the pack with 29.6 per cent of the total circulation of daily and Sunday papers. Behind it were News International (18.7%), Beaverbrook Newspapers (15.8%), Thomson (7.3%), and Associated Newspapers (7.2%). The top five corporations thus controlled 78.6 per cent of daily and Sunday newspaper circulation.

There is evidence to suggest that this high degree of concentration may have reached its peak. In 1948 the three leading corporations controlled 46 per cent of the total daily and Sunday newspaper circulation. By 1961 this figure had increased to 65 per cent. As of 1976, however, it had declined slightly to 64 per cent. Moreover, between 1961 and 1976 the percentage of total daily newspaper circulation controlled by the three largest groups had declined from 67 to 49 per cent, while that of national daily circulation had dropped from 89 to 72 per cent. Although there was an increase in their share of national Sunday circulation from 84 to 86 per cent, their share of the total Sunday circulation dropped from 84 to 80 per cent. (*Royal Commission on the Press 1947-9 Report* (1949), Appendices 3 and 5; *Royal Commission on the Press 1961-2 Report* (1962), Appendices 2, 3, and 4; *Royal Commission on the Press, 1974-7 Final Report,* Annex 3.)

In Canada, the growth of newspaper groups began somewhat later than in the United States and Britain. But once under way, the concentration of ownership proceeded more quickly. This was partly because of the relatively small number of newspapers involved and the nature of Canada's corporate sector. The Southam Company Limited (which did not change its name to Southam Press Limited until 1964) remained the only newspaper group in Canada until the mid-1920s. At that point, the Sifton family, which owned the *Manitoba Free Press* (later the *Winnipeg Free Press*), gained control of the Saskatoon *Star-Phoenix* and the *Regina Leader-Post.* Clifford and Victor Sifton eventually divided their holdings and in 1959 the latter combined forces with a newspaper group built up by Max Bell to form the Sifton-Bell group — or Free Press Publications as it became known. In the meantime, the Southam group had continued to add to its holdings and a new competitor had entered the field in the person of Roy Thomson. After purchasing the Timmins *Press* in 1934, Thomson began buying up numerous small dailies and weeklies during the mid-1940s when many papers were suffering hard times. A quarter of a century later, the Thomson group controlled 30 Canadian dailies and over two dozen weeklies.

Together the Southam, Free Press, and Thomson groups controlled 49 of Canada's 116 daily newspapers by 1970. Twenty-eight other dailies were controlled by such groups as Irving, Péladeau, and Demarais-Parisien-Francoeur, leaving only 39 dailies in the hands of independents. In other words, by 1970 two-thirds of Canada's daily newspapers were group-owned (compared with 47 per cent in the United States). According to the Kent Commission, these groups accounted for 58 per cent of the total daily newspaper circulation: 60.4 per cent of English-language daily circulation and 49.2 per cent of French-language daily circulation. Among the English-language groups, FP Publications controlled 21.8 per cent of the English-language circulation; Southam Inc. controlled 21.5 per cent; Thomson Newspapers controlled 10.4 per cent; and a number of other smaller groups controlled the remaining 6.7 per cent. Together the three largest English-language groups also accounted for 44.7 per cent of the total daily newspaper circulation in Canada. In the case of the French-language groups, Gesca controlled 38.2 per cent of French-language daily circulation and Québecor controlled 11.0 per cent. (Kent Commission, 1981: 2-3, 9, 12)

A decade later, these figures had changed significantly. By 1980, 88 of Canada's 117 daily newspapers (119 before the closures on August 27) belonged to groups. In other words, almost three out of four dailies were now group-owned. According to the Kent Commission's statistics, these groups accounted for 77 per cent of the total daily newspaper circulation: 74.3 per cent of English-language daily circulation and 90.0 per cent of French-language daily circulation. Among the English-language groups, Southam with 14 dailies controlled 32.8 per cent of the total English-language circulation; Thomson with 40 papers controlled 25.9 per cent; the Sun Group with three dailies controlled 8.3 per cent; and a number of other smaller groups controlled the remaining 7.3 per cent. The group-controlled French-language daily circulation was split among Québecor with 46.5 per cent, Gesca with 28.8 per cent, and UniMédia with 14.7 per cent. (Kent Commission, 1981: 1, 2-3, 9, 12)

By 1985 only 26 of Canada's 112 newspapers were still independent, 27 if one counts *The Toronto Star*. The rest belonged to groups. In terms of the number of daily newspapers owned, the groups ranked as follows: Thomson (37); Southam (15); Sterling, mostly in British Columbia (10); Trans-Canada Group in Quebec (4), Irving in New Brunswick (5); Bowes in Alberta and Ontario (3), Toronto Sun in Ontario and Alberta (3), Uni-Média (Francoeur) in Quebec (3); Québecor (Péladeau) in Quebec (3); and Armadale (Sifton) in Saskatchewan (2). (Publicorp Development Communications, 1985: 297)

In terms of concentration, this places Canada well ahead of the United States. Moreover, as the Kent Commission *Report* showed, this concentration reaches even more alarming proportions when various regional and local markets are examined. For example, in seven of Canada's ten provinces (British Columbia, Alberta, Saskatchewan, Manitoba, New Brunswick, Prince Edward Island, and Newfoundland), a single group controls two-thirds or more of the total daily circulation. In New Brunswick, all of the English-language papers are owned by members of the Irving family, although control is split between James and Arthur Irving in the case of the papers in Saint John, and John Irving in the case of those in Moncton and Fredericton. In Manitoba, the Thomson chain accounts for almost 90 per cent of circulation. (Kent Commission, 1981: 1, 9)

The number of urban communities with two or more newspapers has been declining in Canada. At the turn of the century, there were 18 communities in Canada with two or more daily newspapers published in the same language and under separate ownership. This made for a total of 66 dailies in a competitive situation. By 1966 there were only nine communities with two or more dailies. This made for 75 dailies in a non-competitive situation. In 1970, there were 10 major Canadian cities with two or more resident papers; by 1981, there were only eight. In some cases (*e.g.* Vancouver), the two papers belong to one group (Southam). (Kent Commission, 1981: 8)

While there is no dispute about the increasing concentration of newspaper ownership in Canada, there is a debate as to how to interpret its significance and what should be done about it. There is no consensus as to whether there is sufficient scientific evidence to conclude that the current degree of concentration has serious negative effects. And there is certainly no agreement as to what steps, if any, should be taken by the government to deal with the situation. While many persons believe that strong government action is necessary, many others fear that this would do more harm than good. Once again, four positions can be distinguished on the basis of these two issues. These are indicated in Figure 4 on p. 100.

Position A — Laissez-Faire Approach

Position A advocates taking no measures with regard to the current pattern of newspaper ownership on two grounds. First, it claims that there is insufficient evidence to conclude that it has negative effects overall. On the contrary, it is argued that there is evidence to suggest that it has several important benefits. Thus, there is no demonstrated threat to the public interest. Secondly, government action would be undesirable, in any event, because it would necessarily threaten freedom of the press. This kind of argument has already been considered at length in connection with the press-state relationship. It will not be pursued in this chapter. But the

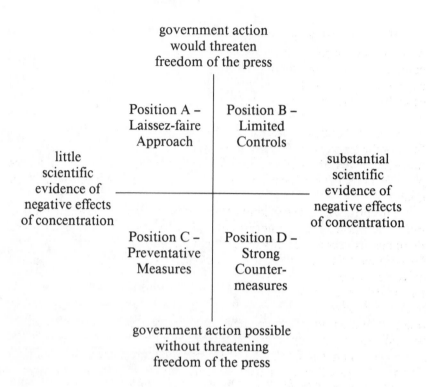

Figure 4

argument that there is no proof of serious negative consequences from the current concentration of ownership needs to be considered carefully. For the sake of convenience, it will be broken down into four sub-arguments. (Four counter-arguments will be presented in connection with Position B.)

The first argument usually made in support of Position A is that the consolidation of production in the hands of large corporations is one of the basic facts of modern economic life. It can be controlled to a degree, but it cannot be reversed without disrupting the entire economic system. Nor would it be advantageous to do so, for it takes advantage of the existence of *economies of scale* and this reduces the costs of goods and services to consumers.

In the case of the newspaper business, the average production cost per copy of a newspaper declines as the number of sold copies increases. There is a sizeable fixed cost in the preparation, printing, and distribution of the final product. It does not cost twice as much to produce a 100-page newspaper as a 50-page paper. Once a paper has paid for a wire service, for example, it does not increase its cost proportionately by making greater use of that service. Nor does it cost as much to print and distribute 100,000 copies of a single newspaper as it does to print and distribute 50,000 copies of two different newspapers.

During the nineteenth century, it was relatively easy for small independent newspapers to make a profit. Newsprint and labour were both comparatively cheap. But both of these resources have become much more expensive in the twentieth century, making it essential to take advantage of economies of scale either by merging two competing papers or by eliminating one of them outright. In the process, however, the newspaper business has generally become more economically stable. This has had many benefits, not the least of which is that it has made the employment of journalists more secure and reduced the need for sensationalism. It has also kept the price of newspapers down and provided resources for improving their quality.

This brings us to the second argument made in support of Position A. For in addition to the economies of scale within a one-newspaper town, there are also economic advantages that result from group membership. Group membership can cut the costs of preparing copy if news-sharing agreements are worked out or a central news bureau is created. Moreover, papers that might be forced to fold because of a temporary economic setback can be kept alive if they belong to a group. In addition, papers that operate from within the haven of a group can take bolder editorial stands without fearing the consequences from local authorities. "Editorial independence depends to a substantial extent on financial strength," Kenneth Thomson, head of an international media empire, told the Kent Commission. (Thomson, 1981: 5)

The third argument in support of Position A is that there is no scientific evidence that editorial quality has declined under monopoly conditions. In this regard, several studies could be cited. Nixon and Jones (1956), for example, found that the only significant differences between the content of competitive and non-competitive newspapers is that the former carry more news of accidents and disasters. Several subsequent studies (*e.g.* Rarick and Hartman, 1966; Grotta, 1970; Weaver and Mullins, 1975; Schweitzer and Goldman, 1975) have likewise failed to find significant differences between competing and non-competing newspapers. One study (Thrift, 1977) did find that independents provided fewer editorials on local topics after joining groups. But this is not necessarily a sign of poorer editorial quality. In addition, some journalists have suggested that the absence of direct competition enables them to select their assignments more carefully and research them in greater depth, since they do not have to worry about beating the opposition into print. (Stewart, 1981: 12, 86)

Finally, Position A argues that the pursuit of economies of scale is not inconsistent with the democratic requirement for diversity of ideas and information. Notwithstanding that no one has ever shown that a very high proportion of the population of cities with two newspapers actually reads both of them, there is, in fact, greater journalistic diversity today than there has ever been. The reason for this is that competition between papers published in one city has been replaced by competition between papers published in different cities but distributed over the same area. The number of cities with two or more of its own daily newspapers has obviously declined drastically. Nonetheless, the number of "media voices" in many communities is much greater today than at any previous time.

James N. Rosse has explained this in terms of an "umbrella hypothesis" concerning newspaper competition. According to Rosse, there are several levels of media activity. At the first and highest level, there are the large circulation newspapers in major metropolitan centres (*e.g. The Globe and Mail,* Toronto, *The Toronto Star,* the Montreal *Gazette*). At the second level, there are the newspapers produced in satellite cities (*e.g. The Ottawa Citizen*). The satellite cities receive the newspapers from the large metropolitan centres, but do not in turn distribute their own papers to those centres. At the third level, there are the local dailies produced in smaller communities. And at the fourth level, there are the weeklies and other specialized media. The "umbrella effect" refers to the fact that the higher levels encompass the lower ones in the sense that their media products are distributed to them. This can also be extended to include broadcast as well as other print media.

This point was made by several newspaper owners in their submissions to the Kent Commission. "We must recognize that most communities of any size have access to other communication voices in the form of radio, television, magazines and weekly newspapers," said Beland Honderich, president of Torstar. "Indeed, research for the Bryce Commission [on Corporate Concentration] suggested that the average Canadian is exposed to 100 or more media voices a week." (Honderich, 1981: 2) Kenneth Thomson was even more specific:

> Over the period 1970 to 1980 public access to information has been enhanced through the spectacular growth in major media. The number of daily newspapers has grown from 112 to 120, an increase of 7%. Community newspapers have grown from 890 to 1,090, an increase of 22%. Radio stations have grown from 388 to 543, an increase of 40%. Television stations have grown from 73 to 111, an increase of 52%. Consumer magazines have grown from 213 to 365, an increase of 71%. (Thomson, 1981: 9)

In addition to this point, it is also suggested that considerable competition between ideas occurs *within* the omnibus daily newspaper. This, to be sure, is a much more controversial claim. It assumes that newspaper owners do not control newspaper content. The time has passed when a William Randolph Hearst would seek to promote his presidential ambitions by personally directing a nation-wide chain of newspapers. But as we have seen in connection with Position C in Chapter 2, there are still grounds for suspecting that group owners affect editorial policy in a more general way.

There are, however, several studies that support the claim that concentration of ownership has not reduced the diversity of ideas. One study (Hicks and Featherstone, 1978) found little duplication of either news or editorial content in morning and evening newspapers in the same city under common ownership, even though these would normally be considered as a single "media voice." Moreover, while some American owners still insist upon a common editorial policy when it comes to endorsing political candidates, this is not the case in Canada. The evidence (*e.g.* Wagenberg and Soderlund, 1976) is rather that editorial endorsements of political candidates differ as much within newspaper groups as between them.

A general explanation of this is that day-to-day decision making within the modern corporation is no longer controlled by owners. During the nineteenth century, most owners actively intervened in the everyday operations of their firms. In the case of newspapers, proprietors doubled as editors. But as the corporation grew in size and complexity, the supervision of production was turned over to professional managers with the technical knowledge necessary to make production, finance, and marketing decisions. This transition was first heralded by Adolf Berle and Gardiner Means in *The Modern Corporation and Private Property* (1932) and came to be known as the "managerial revolution" after James Burnham's 1960 work by the same name. According to John Kenneth Galbraith, one of its effects is that corporations are less concerned to maximize profits in the short term than to ensure stable growth over the long term. (Galbraith, 1967: 60-71) As with the above points made in support of Position A, however, this one has also been subjected to criticism.

Position B — Limited Controls Approach

Position B refutes each of the four main arguments developed by Position A. These are: that economies of scale and other benefits result from having one-newspaper towns; that there are related advantages from group ownership; that the number of media voices has not declined; and that there is sufficient diversity of opinion within existing newspapers.

According to Position B, none of these arguments withstands closer scrutiny. First, consolidation of production is not absolutely necessary for the economic survival of newspapers. The main reason why groups are anxious to take over the remaining independents is that they are already profitable enterprises, especially where intra-urban consolidation has taken place. The real benefits of one-paper cities accrue to advertisers, who are able to reach the same audience at a reduced cost overall. Studies (*e.g.* Grotta, 1970) have shown that monopolistic conditions have not produced any monetary benefits for consumers; on the contrary, consumers have tended to pay higher prices for newspapers under monopoly conditions.

Moreover, wage rates for newspaper employees tend to be lower in monopoly situations. (Langdon, 1969)

Secondly, it does not require group membership to make a newspaper profitable. Most of the economies of scale that apply to intra-urban production do not apply to nearly the same extent in regional or national production contexts. Moreover, there is no economic rationale for allowing groups to expand without limitation. From a purely economic standpoint, it might be desirable to have, perhaps, 100 or so newspapers in Canada. It might also be preferable to organize these into groups of at least four or five papers in order to develop certain news sharing arrangements. But there is no economic justification for permitting these groups to become three or four times as large or to dominate entire regions.

Thirdly, according to Position B, it has been demonstrated that competition between newspapers improves their overall quality. A study prepared for the Kent Commission concluded that competition has clearly discernible positive effects. The coverage of local and regional news in Quebec City and Edmonton, for example, improved after the infusion of competition. (Fletcher, 1981) This conclusion was further substantiated by a subsequent examination of the comprehensiveness of the coverage of local government by *The Ottawa Citizen* and the *Winnipeg Free Press* before and after the closing of the Ottawa *Journal* (by Thomson) and the *Winnipeg Tribune* (by Southam) in August, 1980. It found that both the quantity and quality of municipal government news declined significantly when competition was eliminated. It also discovered that greater use was made of high profile sources (persons in positions of greater authority) at the expense of those lower down the decision-making ladder. (Trim *et al.,* 1983) This supported the Kent Commission's belief that the one newspaper town leads to a reduction in editorial expenditures and a concomitant decline in newspaper quality. (However, for a dissenting view on the Ottawa situation, see George Bain, "Good news in a one-paper town," *Maclean's,* August 25, 1986, p. 38.)

The response might be that the evidence merely points out that there are good newspaper groups and bad ones, just as there are good and bad independent newspapers. But the counter-argument to this is that a bad newspaper group can have a much more devastating effect overall than several bad independents. It is unlikely that with independent ownership, an entire region of Canada could end up being poorly served by its newspapers. But this is precisely what has happened in some of the regions of Canada under restricted group ownership.

Klaus Pohle's study of *The Lethbridge Herald* provides a good example of how the quality of a good independent can be eroded after being taken over by a group. Before it was acquired by Thomson Newspapers in early 1980 as part of the takeover of FP Publications, the *Herald* "enjoyed a good reputation in the industry for its commitment to quality journalism, spent a great deal of money in pursuit of what it deemed excellence, and was held in high regard by most of its staff and readership." (Pohle, 1984: 4) Although its circulation, which had been rising at about four per cent a year, was a modest 25,000, the paper had an editorial staff of 40 and a budget of about $1 million. It had appointed the first full-time consumer affairs reporter in Alberta. It also had a full-time investigative reporter on staff. (Pohle, 1984: 166, 15, 13)

After being taken over by Thomson, all of this changed. In June of 1981, six of the 14 members of the pressroom were laid off without notice or union consultation. The following May, two apprentice compositors were similarly dismissed. Those who remained found themselves doing more work for less pay. Moreover, although the paper and its circulation stayed the same size, there were sharp increases in both its price and advertising rates. (Pohle, 1984: 30, 31, 34, 37) Initially, there were not any changes in the news operation as such, except for reductions in travel allowances and meagre pay increases. "Complaints that pay increases were not in keeping with inflation were countered by lectures on the economics of the consumer price index and with suggestions that people should start vegetable gardens and shop for specials." (Pohle, 1984: 44)

But following the appointment of a new managing editor in July, 1982, the news-room itself became an object of "Thomsonization." Editorial authority was concentrated in the managing editor's office; editorial staff was steadily reduced from 40 to 28; editorial expenses were scaled down and subjected to tight controls; and editorial content was altered in accordance with the new philosophy of the managing editor. By the end of 1983, the staff of 175 full-time and part-time employees (as of December 1979) had been reduced to 119. (Pohle, 1984: 66, 68, 73) At the same time, there was a significant change in news content. Whereas previously, there had been an attempt to go beyond the basic reporting of local events and provide in-depth coverage of local issues, there was now a much greater emphasis on things such as garden parties, church bazaars, recipes, and beauty tips. (Pohle, 1984: 151) Although surveys revealed much less reader satisfaction with the new product, this reversal in the public's assessment of the paper was not accompanied by any dramatic decrease in subscriptions. As the only local paper in Lethbridge, the *Herald* was the sole means of access to such consumer services as classified advertisements, shopping specials, movie ads, and so forth.

The fourth counter-argument of Position B is that economies of scale cannot be considered in isolation from the special requirements for competition in news production. If competition is generally considered desirable in the production of automobiles and refridgerators, it is absolutely essential in the production of intellectual and artistic goods. As Andrew Osler has noted: "It is peculiar to the nature of information that it requires many independent approaches to processing and production if the many and varied requirements of the democratic marketplace are to be met." (Osler, 1983: 105) As we have seen, Position A did not deny this. Rather it argued that concentration of ownership has not reduced the diversity of information and ideas available to Canadians. It also supported this argument by reference to several formal studies.

The case for a loss of diversity as a result of the concentration of ownership is somewhat easier to make if the focus is shifted from newspapers exclusively to cases of cross-media ownership. Although one early study (Litwin and Wroth, 1969) published by the National Association of Broadcasters in the United States actually found improved coverage in a cross-media ownership situation, more recent studies (*e.g.* Stempel III, 1973) have found a significant loss of both quality and diversity in the news product in cross-media monopolies.

Position A concluded its case by suggesting that the fear that a few owners might exercise unwarranted influence over public opinion through vast media empires is without foundation. It argued that it would be impossible for owners to exercise such influence given the way in which power has been drawn down the corporate pyramid. However, this point is disputable. Graham Murdoch for one contends that the managerial revolution thesis blurs the distinction between the allocative control of corporate owners and the operational control of professional managers. According to Murdoch, corporate owners still possess the power — either directly or through their boards of directors — to define general corporate objectives and the scope of corporate activities. The control exercised by managers is limited to determining the effective use of resources that owners have allocated and to implementing policies upon which owners have decided. (Murdoch, 1982: 122) Newspaper owners would thus not be precluded from exercising control over general content through news-room policy, the targetting of certain markets, and determination of the financial commitment to excellence.

Moreover, media ownership critics from Robert Cirino in *Don't Blame the People* (1971) to Ben Bagdikian in *The Media Monopoly* (1983) have contended that the problem is not that media owners exercise their power on behalf of one political group or another. It is rather that through their influence, the media systematically support the ideology of corporate capitalism; that is, they seldom if ever carry stories critical of big business. This is in part because of the linkages between large newspaper companies and other corporate interests. It also reflects the need to stay on good terms with advertisers, who provide nearly 80 per cent of newspaper revenues.

Position B thus disagrees completely with Position A's assessment of the seriousness of the current situation. Its analysis of the effects of newspaper ownership concentration leads to the conclusion that something must be done. At the same time, however, Position B agrees with A that government action to rectify the ownership problem would threaten freedom of the press. It is feared that the cure would be worse than the disease. As a result, therefore, Position B advocates seeking essentially non-governmental means of alleviating the worst effects of the concentration of newspaper ownership.

This was essentially the approach of the Hutchins Commission in the United States. Although it proposed such things as mandatory retraction and right of reply provisions, it hoped essentially that the newspaper industry would recognize its social responsibilities and govern itself accordingly. In Britain and Canada, the advocates of minimal government interference have favoured the creation of press councils as an antidote to the worst effects of concentrated newspaper ownership. This kind of self-monitoring device was recommended by the first royal commission on newspapers in Britain. The Davey Committee also urged the newspaper industry to create a voluntary national press council. (Voluntary press councils were subsequently established in Ontario, Quebec, and Alberta.)

The Hutchins Commission did suggest hesitantly that if the newspaper industry did not act more responsibly, it might be necessary to use the federal anti-trust laws to control the growth of newspaper groups. These laws have been used to a degree since then to prevent groups from buying additional papers in regional markets where they are already strong. But this has not prevented groups such as that owned by Thomson from expanding by leaps and bounds. Moreover, in 1970 the American government passed the *Newspaper Preservation Act,* which allowed failing newspapers to be operated jointly with another newspaper to cut costs. Similarly, while a cross-media ownership rule was established in 1975 preventing newspapers from acquiring radio or television stations in their own communities (and vice-versa), it contained a grandfather clause that allowed existing arrangements to be maintained.

The second royal commission on newspapers in Britain led to the establishment of guidelines for newspaper acquisitions under merger and monopoly legislation passed in 1965. However, "the net result has been one ruling against the purchase of a weekly by a group operation." (Kent Commission, 1981: 16) According to Lord McGregor, the third royal commission "was urged by several groups to recommend the creation, by or through government intervention, of new agencies to control the press. It rejected all such proposals on the ground that government intervention would undermine the independence of the press and soon involve persons who owed their position to government acting in practice as censors." (Osler, 1983: 112)

Position C — Preventative Measures Approach

Position C seems on the surface to be contradictory. On the one hand, it disagrees with Position B that the current newspaper ownership situation is grave. But on the other hand, it also disagrees with Position A that the government should not intervene to control newspaper ownership. It favours government action, despite the fact that it does not consider the current newspaper ownership pattern to constitute a serious problem. How can this be?

The main argument presented by Position C in defence of group ownership is that the modern newspaper requires far greater resources than its predecessor to fulfill its democratic role. There are several reasons for this, including the increased complexity and more rapid pace of life in the late twentieth century. But first and foremost is the fact that newspapers today must confront and somehow overcome political and bureaucratic machinery adept at news management. If newspapers are to present not only the truths that government would like us to know but also those that it would prefer to keep hidden, then they need more resources at their disposal than would be possible under conditions of independent ownership. It is only the large newspaper backed by the strength of a group that can systematically engage in the kind of investigative journalism necessary for a healthy democracy.

At the same time, however, advocates of Position C are prepared to admit that there are limits as to what is required in this regard. The development of strong groups does not necessitate national, regional, or even intra-urban newspaper monopolies. Position C is prepared, therefore, to allow measures that would keep the growth of groups under control. It would not be adverse, for example, to temporarily "freezing" the current pattern while further studies are conducted and further proposals are considered. Beyond this it would also favour in principle permanent measures designed to prevent an increase in the current degree of newspaper concentration. It does not agree with Position B that such steps would necessarily infringe upon freedom of the press. However, it does agree that it would be dangerous to attempt to break up groups that now exist.

This was essentially the position of the Special Senate Committee on the Mass Media of 1969-70. Apart from recommending the creation of a voluntary national press council, it proposed the establishment of a federal Press Ownership Review Board with the power of disapproval over any purchases of, or mergers between, newspapers or magazines. The board was to operate on the assumption that "*all* transactions that increase concentration of ownership in the mass media are undesirable and contrary to the public interest — unless shown to be otherwise." Appeal against its rulings was to be to the Federal Court of Canada. However, this recommendation was not acted upon.

In his submission to the Kent Commission, Beland H. Honderich, president of Torstar Corporation, also adopted the preventative measures approach. He admitted that the concentration of newspaper ownership could have an effect on the diversity of opinion. "Group ownership," he said,

> does place in the hands of relatively few people the power to control what their newspapers publish. Even if this control is not exercised directly, it is exercised indirectly through budget controls and the selection of publishers and editors. For the same reason that independent newspaper publishers tend to hire people that reflect their opinions, the owners of group newspapers select people whose opinions do not vary too greatly from their own. My reading of Canadian newspapers suggests that group ownership has tended to restrict the variety of opinion available to the public. (Honderich, 1981: 3)

He thus concluded that newspaper mergers, like business mergers generally, should be subject to an objective review on the basis of their individual merits. He suggested that the federal *Combines Investigation Act* might be amended to require newspaper companies to show that mergers above a certain size would provide significant benefits for Canada. (Honderich, 1981: 4)

Position D — Counter-Measures Approach

Position D agrees with B that the current ownership situation is serious. It also maintains that government action is possible without threatening freedom of the press. Strong action is thus favoured to deal with the current situation, including measures to reverse the growth of groups. For example, in 1975 the United States government introduced a capital gains tax incentive to encourage the break-up of such combinations. The best example of this position, however, is the Kent Commission.

Like the Davey Committee before it, the Kent Commission bemoaned the state of the media in Canada and laid most of the blame on the fact that "concentration engulfs Canadian daily newspaper publishing." (Kent Commission, 1981: 1) "Too much power is put in too few hands," it declared; "and it is power without accountability." (Kent Commission, 1981: 220) It proposed that no newspaper group be allowed to control more than five per cent of the total national daily circulation. Existing groups with more than five per cent would be allowed certain concessions, but would be forced to divest themselves of some properties. For example, Thomson would be required to sell either *The Globe and Mail,* or all of its other newspapers. It also proposed the creation of a "Press Rights Panel" with the authority to review all proposals for newspaper ownership changes, including closures, and to monitor journalistic performance generally.

The legislation proposed by the Minister of State for the Liberal government did not go this far. It sought to eventually limit the newspaper holdings of any single owner to 20 per cent of the country's total average daily newspaper circulation. Southam and Thomson, both of which exceeded this proposed 20 per cent limitation, would be allowed to retain their dailies for the time being, but would not be permitted to expand further. The Minister also suggested that the Canadian Radio-Television and Telecommunications Commission should be encouraged to use its regulatory powers to break up local mixed-media monopolies and oligopolies.

In addition, he outlined plans for a Canadian Advisory Council on Newspapers with the aim of "receiving complaints about press reporting in daily newspapers that are not members of effective press councils, promoting public debate, complementing the press councils and ombudsmen that already exist locally, and reporting biennially on the state of the industry on the basis of its own research and analysis." (Fleming, 1982) Had it been enacted, the proposed legislation would not have gone nearly as far as the Kent Commission recommended. However, it would have meant an unprecedented degree of government regulation over the Canadian newspaper industry.

References

Audley, Paul
1983 *Canada's Cultural Industries: Broadcasting, Publishing, Records and Film.* Toronto: James Lorimer.
Bagdikian, Ben
1980 "Conglomeration, Concentration, and the Media," *Journal of Communication* 30 (Spring): 59-64.
1983 *The Media Monopoly.* Boston: Beacon Press.
Bain, George
1985 "A Tory turnabout on ownership." *Maclean's* (June 24): 54.
1986 "Good news in a one-paper town," *Maclean's* (August 25): 38
Borstell, Gerald H.
1956 "Ownership, Competition and Comment in 20 Small Dailies." *Journalism Quarterly* 33 (Spring): 220-22.
Campbell, Murray
1984 "Requiem for the Kent report on ownership." *The Globe and Mail,* Toronto (November 15): M5.
Central Office of Information
1984 *Britain 1984.* London: Her Majesty's Stationery Office.
Clement, Wallace
1975 *The Canadian Corporate Elite: An Analysis of Economic Power.* Toronto: McClelland and Stewart.
Compaine, Benjamin M.
1979 "Newspapers." In B. M. Compaine (ed.), *Who Owns the Media? Concentration of Ownership in the Mass Communications Industry.* New York: Harmony Books.
Davey Committee (Special Senate Committee on Mass Media)
1970 *Report.* Ottawa: Queen's Printer.
Fleming, James (Honourable)
1982 "Government proposals on Freedom of the Press in Relation to the Canadian Daily Newspaper Industry." An address on May 25 to the Graduate School of Journalism at the University of Western Ontario.
Fletcher, Frederick
1981 *The Newspaper and Public Affairs.* Ottawa: Queen's Printer.
Galbraith, John Kenneth
1967 *The New Industrial State.* Boston: Houghton Mifflin.
Goldenberg, Susan
1984 "The Thomson empire." *Content* (September/October): 8-11.

Gormley, William T., Jr.
    1976 "The Effect of Newspaper-Television Cross-Ownership on News Homogeneity." Ph.D. thesis: University of North Carolina.
Grotta, Gerald L.
    1970 "Changes in the Ownership of Daily Newspaper and Selected Performance Characteristics, 1950-68: An Investigation of Some Economic Implications of Concentration of Ownership." Ph.D. thesis: Southern Illinois University.
    1971 "Consolidation of Newspapers: What Happens to the Consumer?" *Journalism Quarterly* 48 (Summer): 245-50.
Hicks, Ronald G. and James S. Featherstone
    1978 "Duplication of Newspaper Content in Contrasting Ownership Situations." *Journalism Quarterly* 55 (Autumn): 549-53.
Honderich, Beland
    1981 "Remarks . . . to Royal Commission on Newspapers." (February 9): 4 pp.
Kent Commission (Royal Commission on Newspapers)
    1981. *Report.* Ottawa: Supply and Services Canada.
Kent, Tom
    1984 "The Commission revisited." *Content* (September/October): 2-3.
Kesterton, Wilfred H.
    1967 *A History of Journalism in Canada.* Toronto: McClelland and Stewart.
Langdon, John Henry
    1969 "An Intra Industry Approach to Measuring the Effects of Competition: The Newspaper Industry." Ph.D. thesis: Cornell University.
Litwin, George and W. H. Wroth
    1969 "The Effects of Common Ownership on Media Content and Influence." Washington, D.C.: National Association of Broadcasters.
McDayter, Walt and Russell Elman
    1971 "In the Shadow of Giants: Concentration and Monopolies in the Media." In W. McDayter (ed.), *A Media Mosaic: Canadian Communications Through a Critical Eye.* Toronto: Holt, Rinehart, and Winston.
Murdoch, Graham
    1982 "Large Corporations and the Control of the Communications Industries." In Michael Gurevitch, Tony Bennett, James Curran, and Janet Woollacott, (eds.), *Culture, Society and the Media.* London: Methuen.

Nixon, Raymond B. and Robert L. Jones
  1956 "The Content of Non Competitive vs. Competitive News-
      papers." *Journalism Quarterly* 33 (Summer): 299-314.
Osler, Andrew M.
  1983 "From Vincent Massey to Thomas Kent: The Evolution of a
      National Press Policy in Canada." In Benjamin D. Singer (ed.),
      Communications in Canadian Society. Rev. ed., Don Mills:
      Addison-Wesley.
Pohle, Klaus
  1984 "The Lethbridge Herald: A Casestudy in 'Thomsonization'."
      M.J. thesis: Carleton University.
Publicorp Development Communications
  1985 *Matthews List.* Pointe Claire, Quebec: Publicorp.
Rarick, Galen and Barrie Hartman
  1966 "The Effects of Competition on One Daily Newspaper's Con-
      tent." *Journalism Quarterly* 43 (Fall): 459-63.
Rosse, James N.
  1975 *Economic Limits of Press Responsibility.* Stanford, Calif.: De-
      partment of Economics, Stanford University.
  1978 "The Evolution of One Newspaper Cities." Paper presented at
      the Federal Trade Commission Symposium on Media Con-
      centration, Washington, D.C.
  1980 "The Decline of Direct Newspaper Competition." *Journal of
      Communication* 30 (Spring): 65-71.
Schweitzer, John C. and Elaine Goldman
  1975 "Does Newspaper Competition Make a Difference to Readers?"
      Journalism Quarterly 52 (Winter): 706-10.
Seacrest, T. C.
  1983 "The Davey Report: Main Findings and Recommendations."
      In Benjamin D. Singer (ed.), *Communications in Canadian
      Society.* Don Mills: Addison Wesley.
Siegel, Arthur
  1983 *Politics and the Media in Canada.* Toronto: McGraw-Hill
      Ryerson.
Southam Communications Ltd.
  1984 *1984 Corpus Almanac and Canadian Sourcebook.* Vol. I, Don
      Mills: Southam Communications Ltd.
Stempel III, G. H.
  1973 "Effects on Performance of a Cross-Media Monopoly." *Jour-
      nalism Monographs.* No. 29.
Stewart, Walter
  1981 *The Only Side of the Street, The Journalists.* Ottawa: Queen's
      Printer.

Thomson, K. R.
    1981 "Opening Remarks to the Kent Commission." (April 13): 16 pp.
Thrift, Ralph R., Jr.
    1977 "How Chain Ownership Affects Editorial Vigor of News-
        papers." *Journalism Quarterly* 54 (Summer): 327-31.
Trim, Katharine, Gary Pizante, and James Yaraskavitch
    1983 "The Effect of Monopoly on the News: A Before and After Study
        of Two Canadian One Newspaper Towns." *Canadian Journal
        of Communication* 9 (no. 3): 33-56.
Wagenberg, Ronald H. and Walter C. Soderlund
    1976 "The Effects of Chain Ownership on Editorial Coverage: The
        Case of the 1974 Canadian Federal Election." *Canadian Jour-
        nal of Political Science* 9 (December): 682-89.
Weaver, David H. and L. E. Mullins
    1975 "Content and Format Characteristics of Competing Daily
        Newspapers." *Journalism Quarterly* 52 (Summer): 257-64.

Chapter 5

What Form Should Broadcast Ownership Take?

At the same time as newspaper ownership was beginning to become a cause for concern, a second development presented governments with an additional and more urgent media ownership problem. This was the emergence of radio after the First World War as a medium of popular entertainment. Because of the nature of the radio spectrum, it was not possible, even in theory, for everyone with the means and desire to establish a broadcast station. There were only a limited number of radio frequencies available, making it necessary to work out an allocation system or face chaos on the airwaves.

Britain was the first English-speaking country to consciously adopt a particular broadcasting system, followed closely by the United States. Canada equivocated until December of 1928, when the Liberal government of Mackenzie King established a Royal Commission on Radio Broadcasting under Sir John Aird. Some of the recommendations made by the Aird Commission were modified by the House of Commons Special Committee on Radio Broadcasting, chaired by the Honourable Raymond Morand. But the committee did act upon the recommendation of public ownership in drafting the *Canadian Radio Broadcasting Act, 1932* (22 & 23 Geo. 5, c. 35). A publicly owned Canadian Radio Broadcasting Commission was created by Parliament to provide nation-wide radio programming for Canadians.

The CRBC proved to be a short-lived experiment in public broadcasting. But despite its several failings, its performance was sufficient to sustain the belief that national public broadcasting might be made to work if it were reorganized on a more solid basis. In 1935 another Special Committee on Radio Broadcasting was set up to examine the situation. It recommended replacing the CRBC with a Crown corporation with full control over its staff and budget. The result was the *Canadian Broadcasting Act, 1936* (1 Edw. 8, c. 24), which established the Canadian Broadcasting Corporation with stronger organization, more assured financing, and better guarantees that it could act independently of the government of the day.

The 1936 Act provided a sound basis for both public and private broadcasting during the late 1930s and 1940s. Except for licensing, it gave the CBC full regulatory powers over the private stations. By the early 1950s, however, a number of developments had created a need to reconsider the basis of Canadian broadcasting. These included the maturation of the private radio stations, the arrival and rapid growth of television, the steadily increasing strength of monopoly capitalism, and the emergence of a less elitist concept of the arts and culture. The first major review of the Canadian broadcasting system was conducted in connection with the Royal Commission on National Development in the Arts, Letters, and Sciences in 1949-51 under the chairmanship of Vincent Massey. The Massey Commission made a number of valuable suggestions for improving Canadian broadcasting, but it remained for the most part within the tradition of the Aird Commission.

In contrast to the Massey Commission, the Royal Commission on Broadcasting chaired by Robert Fowler in 1955-57 constituted a major turning point in the history of the Canadian broadcasting system. It paved the way for the passage of the *Broadcasting Act, 1958* (7 Eliz. 2, c. 22) by the Conservative government of John Diefenbaker. The 1958 Act radically altered the broadcasting system by transferring the regulatory functions of the CBC to a new agency called the Board of Broadcast Governors. It did not, however, achieve greater harmony; it left the relationship between the CBC and the new authority unclear and failed to specify the role that the Corporation was to play within the revised system.

It was to rectify this situation in part that the Liberal government of Lester Pearson asked Robert Fowler to chair the Committee on Broadcasting in 1965. Fowler II provided the stimulus for yet another broadcasting Act, though one which still reflected its chairman's views imperfectly. The *Broadcasting Act, 1967-68* (16 & 17 Eliz. 2, c. 25) was intended to establish the main contours of the Canadian broadcasting system for several decades to come. Beginning in the 1970s, however, the broadcasting environment was beset with a series of new technologies, including multi-channel cable television, satellite broadcasting, videodiscs, videocassettes, and videotex, which were only dimly perceived by the architects of the 1968 Act.

By the late 1970s, therefore, the feeling was growing in some circles that revisions to the Act would be necessary if Canadians were to meet the challenges of the new broadcasting environment. In 1982 the Federal Cultural Policy Review Committee chaired by Louis Applebaum and Jacques Hébert set forth a particularly controversial blueprint for revising the broadcasting system. Its recommendations were not acted upon, but the belief remained that a new broadcasting Act was necessary. In the spring of 1985, therefore, Communications minister Marcel Masse appointed a seven-member Task Force on Broadcasting Policy. It was chaired by Gerald Caplan, former federal secretary of the New Democratic party, and Florien Sauvageau, a Quebec broadcaster and Laval University communications professor. Its unanimous 731-page report, which was released in Ottawa on September 22, 1986, was the first major report on broadcasting in Canada since 1965. In the years to come, Canadian broadcasting history may well be divided into two periods: BC (before Caplan-Sauvageau) and AC (after Caplan-Sauvageau).

The debate about what form broadcast ownership should take has revolved around two main considerations. The first of these has to do with the relative complexity of the objectives set for the broadcasting system. On the one hand, countries in which broadcasting is tied closely to only one or two major goals have tended to opt for a unitary system; that is, one with either full public ownership or complete private enterprise. The straightforward nature of their aims has made the choice of a broadcasting system comparatively easy. On the other hand, countries with numerous, diverse, and perhaps even contradictory ends for the broadcasting system have been predisposed towards some form of mixed ownership. A unitary system of one form or another has seemed insufficiently flexible to facilitate a variety of goals. In cases where broadcasting objectives have grown more complex over the years, there has usually been pressure to shift from a unitary to a dualistic or mixed form of ownership.

The second important consideration has to do with the relative amount of faith in public enterprise. In countries with an uncompromising private enterprise ideology, the idea of public ownership has generally been equated with government control. But in other countries there has developed the idea of a public corporation operating at arm's-length from the government, though ultimately responsible to the public through its elected representatives. The basic argument for such corporations has been that they are able to pursue goals that would not be fulfilled by private enterprise, while at the same time not being subject to the constraints of a government department. However, even in countries such as Britain and Canada that have been prepared to establish public corporations in certain fields, the commitment to them has been qualified. There has been an ongoing debate as to their efficiency, effectiveness, and legitimate scope.

Superimposing the polarities that exist with regard to these two considerations provides a framework for examining four basic systems of broadcast ownership. These are indicated in Figure 5 on p. 118. Instead of discussing these broadcasting systems in the abstract, each will be examined with reference to a particular example. System A will be represented by the early British broadcasting system; B by the current British system; C by the American system; and finally, D by the Canadian system.

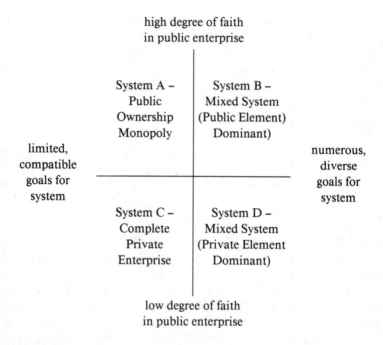

Figure 5

Position A — Public Monopoly of Broadcast Ownership

The public monopoly of broadcast ownership that existed in Britain from the late 1920s to the early 1950s was the result of a unified vision for broadcasting combined with a strong commitment to public enterprise. When both of those elements were subsequently eroded, the British opted for a mixed form of broadcast ownership, though one in which the public element was still dominant.

Radio broadcasting began in Britain shortly after the First World War when the Postmaster General granted licences to the Marconi Company and a few other radio manufacturers to broadcast news, weather, and music. But the Post Office soon became concerned that competition between these private companies might lead to chaos on the airwaves. Under western European arrangements, Britain had access to only two wavelengths capable of providing nationwide reception throughout the day and night. After lengthy negotiations, therefore, six of the companies involved were consolidated in 1922 into the British Broadcasting Company. Its revenues were derived from royalties on the sale of radios; 50 per cent of licence fees charged to owners of receiving sets; and payments from sponsors, who were restricted to having their names mentioned on the programs which they financed.

From a technical standpoint, it is conceivable that Britain might have continued indefinitely with this commercial monopoly of radio broadcasting. It was a reasonably satisfactory way of handling the wavelength problem. However, it did not ensure that broadcasting would serve the best interests of the community as a whole. Ironically, the person most concerned in this regard was J. C. W. Reith, the General Manager of the British Broadcasting Company. Reith believed that broadcasting should be used to uplift the cultural tastes and standards of the general public. But he thought that this vision could only be realized through the agency of a publicly owned corporation free from the constraints of a commercial operation. The result was the creation of the British Broadcasting Corporation under a Royal Charter on January 27, 1927. The shareholders in the Company were bought out and radio broadcasting became a public monopoly.

The creation of the BBC may have owed something to the growing strength of socialism in Britain. Certainly, arguments on behalf of public ownership met with a more favourable reception from the Labour party then in power than they would have received from the Conservatives. Public ownership of broadcasting was also aided by the fact that the telephone and telegraph systems had already been brought under government control. But the BBC has by no means been an agency of government propaganda. From the very outset, it has insisted upon and successfully maintained its independence from government. It has been able to do so for a number of reasons, including its independent source of funding (annual licence fees) and the fact that the members of its Board of Governors have not been political patronage appointments.

On the surface, to be sure, the BBC has been subject to two forms of government control. First, the Postmaster General can order the BBC not to broadcast matter that he deems to be improper. Secondly, he can compel it to broadcast announcements considered to be in the public interest. But these two provisions do not mean exactly what they say. The understanding is that they constitute a kind of reserve power for the government; that is, they are to be exercised only in the event that the BBC should severely abuse its monopoly. During the first quarter century of the BBC's existence, only once the government ordered the BBC not to make a particular broadcast (an interview with a German submarine commander and a British officer whom he had captured during the First World War). In 1985 the BBC did yield to government pressure not to air a program containing a sympathetic portrait of a member of the IRA. But the response from journalists, who staged a short strike, was indicative of the continuing commitment to a politically independent BBC.

The idea of a public corporation was a relatively new one at the time of the BBC's creation and was easily subject to distortion. Asa Briggs has shown that Lord Reith, who served as the BBC's first Director-General, had two main points in mind when he defended the Corporation against its critics. First, he regarded the management and staff of a public corporation as dedicated public servants, who did not need the stimulus of profits to motivate them. Secondly, he insisted that he and his colleagues were not government servants like those who worked in the Civil Service; rather they were managing their own business and should be allowed to do so free from political or bureaucratic interference. He believed that under these conditions, the public corporation was well adapted not only to broadcasting, but also to other kinds of enterprises. It was, he thought, "a precedent for similar advances towards a better world in other domains where great services are handicapped by too definite State control or where the public is handicapped by there being too little State control." (Briggs, 1961: 416)

Position B — Mixed System of Broadcast Ownership: (Public Element Dominant)

Beginning in the 1930s, the British public was exposed to European commercial broadcasting through the development of relay exchanges. The favourable reaction was indicated by the fact that 40 per cent of those polled in a 1946 survey wanted to abolish the BBC's radio monopoly and allow the introduction of commercial stations. This did not immediately redound to the benefit of the commercial radio lobby. The monopoly of the BBC over radio broadcasting was retained until 1972, when the *Sound Broadcasting Act* authorized the establishment of 60 commercial stations. But it did encourage advocates of commercial television.

After a short period of experimentation during the late 1930s, the BBC had been forced to abandon television broadcasting during the Second World War. But when it resumed television broadcasts after the war, those who favoured commercial television began to push their case. A small but dedicated lobby known as the Popular Television Association was formed by Norman Collins, a former BBC controller who had been passed over for promotion. It received support from various ideological quarters, including intellectuals such as Malcolm Muggeridge and A. J. P. Taylor. Apart from arguing that broadcasting should be allowed to perform its function as "a great marketing device," it suggested that the BBC was an anti-democratic instrument of the upper classes.

The cause of the BBC was taken up by Lord Reith, who charged that commercial television would undermine the nation's intellectual and moral standards. When it became clear that the Conservative government was less sure than Reith about this effect, the BBC's Board of Management proposed the creation of a second BBC television service to be financed by advertising. However, the government ignored this attempt by the BBC to preserve its monopoly by selling its soul. In 1954 an Act of Parliament was passed authorizing the creation of the Independent Television Authority, thereby ending the longstanding monopoly of the BBC. Under its initial mandate, the ITA was expected to build and operate new television stations and oversee the activities of 15 program-producing companies located in various areas of Britain. Each company was to derive revenue from the sale of time to advertisers; in return it was to pay a levy to the Exchequer along with fees to the ITA for broadcasting its programs.

Although its first chairman was the distinguished Sir Kenneth Clark, ITV was essentially a workingman's and middle-class network. It quickly won public acceptance, capturing 70 per cent of the British viewing audience within a few years. It also generated sizeable profits for its backers. Though criticized in the 1962 report of the Pilkington Committee on Broadcasting for failing to "satisfy the varied and many-sided tastes and interests of the public," it probably had a beneficial effect on the BBC. The BBC had become somewhat lethargic by the post-war period. Its television operation was dominated by people who had been trained in radio and lacked the incentive and vision to develop the full potential of the new medium. For example, from 1946 to 1953, the BBC television newscast treated viewers to a picture of a clock while a radio announcer read the news. Even when the BBC finally put a live news-reader on the screen, there were still no pictures of events or persons in the news to accompany the script. Competition from ITV did not immediately spur the BBC out of its complacency. But under the leadership of Hugh Greene, who was appointed Director General in 1960, the BBC began to change its ways.

The Pilkington Report led to the passage of a new Television Act in 1964, subjecting the ITV schedule to closer scrutiny and levying a stiff tax on advertising. It also prompted the government to award the BBC a second channel as a reward for its good performance. In 1964 British viewers acquired a choice between popular entertainment and journalism on BBC1 and more esoteric and experimental programming on BBC2. This ensured that the BBC would remain the paramount element within the broadcasting system. By carefully scheduling its programs so as to take advantage of the "inheritance factor" of audience viewing, the BBC began to reclaim the audience that it had lost in the 1950s. With the additional aid of its second channel, which enabled it to make use of the principle of complementary programming, the BBC was able to achieve a 50 per cent audience share by the mid-1960s.

Many of the fine programs that North Americans tend to associate with the BBC, however, are actually productions of the independent television companies (*e.g.* "Upstairs, Downstairs"). While dependent upon commercial sponsorship, ITV avoids its worst abuses by preventing advertisers from becoming associated with particular programs and by enforcing a code of standards and practices designed to prevent misleading advertising. Together with the Welsh Fourth Channel Authority, it serves the regions more effectively than would be possible through the nationally oriented BBC. The British have thus come by a formula in broadcast ownership that has much to recommend it. The British broadcasting system is relatively free from political pressures on the one hand and from advertising pressures on the other. It is not always in pursuit of the mass audience, but provides an impressive range of high standard programming.

The most significant change to this system in recent years has been the establishment of a fourth television network by an Act of Parliament in 1981. Intended to encourage innovation and experimentation and serve audiences ignored by mainstream television, Channel 4 went on the air in November of 1982. After a shaky start, it has won considerable praise for its documentaries, arts coverage, educational programs, and esoteric movies. It purchases most of its programming from independent producers, using funds derived from a fixed percentage of the revenues of the Independent Television network. In return, the ITV companies are permitted to sell advertising time on the new network. Even though it still attracts less than ten per cent of the British viewing audience, Channel 4 has apparently been responsible for a rapid increase in the number of independent television production companies in Britain. (*Maclean's,* September 22, 1986: 41.)

Position C — Private Enterprise Broadcasting System

The earliest and most sustained commitment to private enterprise in broadcasting is to be found in the United States. The Americans have not allowed private interests to operate without any restraints. But they have favoured the minimum of regulation consistent with a reasonable degree of order on the airwaves. Public ownership has never been seriously considered. The private broadcasting interests have been able to capitalize on the strong commitment to freedom of the press to equate public enterprise with government control. In 1932, for example, the National Association of Broadcasters prepared a handbook entitled *Broadcasting in the United States* in which it declared that: "Under a system such as that of Great Britain, radio becomes one of two things. An instrument of government propaganda or an utterly colorless and wasteful means of communication."

The Americans learned very early that complete freedom of the airwaves would lead to chaos. Lack of regulation in the early 1920s had enabled the privately owned stations to jump frequencies, increase wattage, and change hours of operation almost at random. This had been accompanied by a flood of hard-sell commercials and scurrilous religious broadcasts. The situation became so bad that the public turned to the government for relief. The result was the creation of the Federal Radio Commission in 1927 to regulate the private broadcasters. Its authority was divided with the Interstate Commerce Committee and the Department of

Commerce, however, and it was forced to operate under a series of yearly mandates. Although it managed to restore a degree of order, it was thus an extremely weak and timid agency. It was also blatantly biased towards commercial radio. When the FRC began its work, 90 of the 732 stations in existence were run by educational institutions. By 1932 only 33 of these were still operating. The rest had been eliminated through forced power reductions, compulsory time-sharing arrangements, and repeated changes of frequency.

On July 1, 1934, the United States government passed a new Communications Act, replacing the FRC with the Federal Communications Commission. A single regulatory body comprised of seven commissioners appointed for seven-year terms, the FCC was given authority to regulate all radio communication as well as all interstate and foreign telegraph and telephone service. However, the government passed up the opportunity to provide for non-commercial broadcasting. During the course of debate, Senators Wagner and Hatfield introduced an amendment which would have allotted 25 per cent of broadcasting facilities to religious, educational, cultural, agricultural, labour, and other non-profit organizations. Shocked by this possibility, the National Association of Broadcasters wrote to all senators urging them "not to destroy the whole structure of American broadcasting" and the Wagner-Hatfield amendment was defeated.

The FCC has two kinds of power. First, it has the statutory power to prevent certain kinds of broadcast material (*e.g.* lotteries, rigged quiz shows, false distress messages, deceptive advertisements, obscene language). In this regard, it can also require stations to provide equal opportunity for candidates for public office to make use of the airwaves. Secondly, it has the statutory power to require stations to operate in the public interest. It can refuse to grant or renew a licence — licences are granted for three years — to a station unless it can demonstrate that it will serve the interests of the community as a whole. These provisions have led some observers to suggest that there is too much regulation under the American system. But they have not always meant in practice what they imply on paper. In restricting licences to three-year periods, Congress assumed that the airwaves belonged to the public; that is, that the broadcaster acquired no ownership rights over the frequency assigned to him. For this reason, Congress also gave the FCC power to regulate chain ownership. However, this has not prevented the growth of powerful broadcasting networks.

The members of the FCC are appointed by the President and have on occasion been influenced by personal ties and friendships. When lobbying the FCC directly has not proven productive, broadcasters have been able to appeal to Congress, which has the power to investigate the FCC and pass legislation superseding its regulations. Should they fail to influence Congress, broadcasters can also take their case to the courts, which can pass rulings affecting both FCC decisions and Congressional legislation. Even

The Media Society: Basic Issues and Controversies

citizens' groups can challenge FCC policy by initiating litigation in the courts. (Krasnow and Longley, 1978: 27-68, 94-103)

One of the weapons used to curtail the power of the FCC has been section 326 of the *Communications Act,* which specifies that: "Nothing in this Act shall be understood or construed to give the Commission the power of censorship ... and no regulation or condition shall be promulgated or fixed by the Commission which shall interfere with the right of free speech by means of radio communication." This has made it difficult for the FCC not only to require certain kinds of programming (*e.g.* children's programs, educational programs) as necessary for the public interest but also to deal effectively with problems such as the excessive amount of violent programming.

The weakness of the FCC has also been clear in the case of the regulation of commercials. In 1946 the Commission issued a handbook entitled *Public Service Responsibilities of Broadcast Licensees* (popularly known as the "Blue Book") in which it stated that the elimination of excessive numbers of commercials would be considered as a program service factor relevant to the public interest. But it was not until 1963 that the FCC finally decided to take concrete action to control the number and frequency of radio and television commercials. By that time, the National Association of Broadcasters had worked out a set of guidelines for advertisers. However, the NAB codes were only voluntary; in 1963 more than half of all radio stations and over a quarter of the existing television stations still did not subscribe to them. Moreover, even those that did subscribe found ways of getting around them. Nonetheless, when the FCC attempted to make the NAB codes compulsory, it was met with strong resistance and backed down completely, thereby opening the door to even more commercials.

It was not simply the number of commercials that bothered critics. It was also the way in which sponsors controlled the nature of programming. In *The Sponsor* (1978), Eric Barnouw has shown how the means used to achieve such control have changed over the years. Initially, when advertisers took control of radio in the early 1930s, they were involved in the actual production of programs. They decided upon program material and even made last-minute changes from the "sponsor's booth." When television was introduced, this kind of direct participation was no longer practical on a wide scale. Instead, advertisers began to purchase entire programs offered by the networks. Many had their product name associated with the program (*e.g.* "U.S. Steel Hour", "Goodyear Television Playhouse", "Revlon Theater"). But they were no longer engaged in the production process. Rather their control was exercised simply by choosing to sponsor some types of programs and not to sponsor others.

The results of this soon became apparent. By the mid-1950s, advertisers had come to realize that there was a serious discrepancy between their commercial messages and the themes of many of the live dramatic productions which they were sponsoring. As Barnouw has related, the commercials offered clear-cut solutions for life's trials; their message was that by purchasing a certain toothpaste, hair shampoo, floor wax, or automobile, one's problems at home or at work would soon disappear. But the dramas of writers such as Paddy Chayevsky offered no such solutions; on the contrary, they suggested that personal problems are often rooted deep within the psyche or stem from fundamental social and economic problems. Before long, therefore, the advertisers abandoned the provocative anthology series, despite strong audience support for them, and began buying time on quiz shows such as "$64,000 Question" and pre-shot westerns, of which there were 30 in prime time alone by 1958.

As commercial time became increasingly expensive, the purchase of entire program series gave way to the buying of "spots" on different programs. This reduced the risk of being tied to a loser for an entire season and increased the exposure that a commercial might achieve. Moreover, it still enabled advertisers to determine collectively what kinds of programs would be produced as well as when they would be aired. For example, there used to be a number of children's programs on early evening television; these were moved to Saturday mornings at the behest of advertisers. Similarly, when advertisers decided that there was not enough football on television, Monday night football was introduced.

Through surveys conducted by ratings services such as A. C. Neilsen and the American Research Bureau, sponsors are able to ascertain not only the size of a program's audience but also its demographic makeup. This enables sponsors to target certain audiences through their choice of programs. As a result, audience size is no longer the only criterion for program survival. Some programs have been able to survive with small but affluent audiences (*e.g.* "Star Trek"), while others with older audiences have been cut despite good ratings (*e.g.* "Beverly Hillbillies"). The targeting of audiences gives credence to the argument of Dallas Smythe in *Dependency Road* (1981) that programs are merely a device to create an audience for a commercial message.

Defenders of the American broadcasting system counter that audiences control program content through the ratings system. But this claim is questionable. The ratings are designed to indicate whether one program is more popular than others in the same time slot; they do not measure absolute popularity. CBS's "M*A*S*H", which eventually became one of the most popular programs ever broadcast, did poorly in the ratings when it was first shown opposite NBC's "Chico and the Man." It went to the top of the ratings only after being moved against weaker competition. The public thus has no way of indicating that it would like more variety in its programming and better program balance. Moreover, the ratings tend to make programming very conservative; producers aim less at pleasing an audience than at avoiding its displeasure.

The introduction of the Public Broadcasting System has provided American viewers with a worthwhile alternative to CBS, NBC, and ABC. But because of its reliance on voluntary subscriptions, PBS has constituted only a minor threat to the domination of American television by the three commercial networks. A much greater threat to the old triumvirate has come from the growth of independent stations, pay television, and videocassette recorders. Between 1976 and 1986, the major networks' share of the viewing audience dropped from 93 to 73 per cent (*Maclean's,* September 22, 1986: 38) With the launching of a fourth commercial network, Fox Broadcasting Company, by the Australian-born media magnate Rupert Murdoch in October of 1986, this share declined even further. Ironically, while constituting the greatest threat to indigenous television programming in other countries, the American broadcasting system is perhaps the one most imperilled by recent developments in television technology.

Position D — Mixed System of Broadcast Ownership (with Private Element Dominant)

The members of the Royal Commission on Radio Broadcasting created by Mackenzie King on December 6, 1928, were initially divided as to whether Canada should follow the American or the British pattern of broadcast ownership. While Charles Bowman, editor of *The Ottawa Citizen,* favoured some form of public ownership, both Sir John Aird and Augustin Frigon leaned towards a private enterprise system. But several factors conspired to win Aird and Frigon over to Bowman's position.

Before undertaking a series of public hearings across Canada from mid-April to July of 1929, the Aird Commission visited the facilities of NBC in New York as well as several European broadcasting agencies. In Europe the commissioners were impressed not only by the BBC but also by the German broadcasting system which combined federal and state control. But while at NBC, they learned that the American network considered Canada to be within its broadcasting orbit. According to Bowman in *Ottawa Editor* (1966), the chairman of NBC said that his network intended to give Canada "complete coverage as in the United States."

It soon became clear to the commissioners that the privately owned stations in Canada could scarcely be counted on to counter American cultural imperialism. For as Frank Peers has shown in *The Politics of Canadian Broadcasting, 1920-1951* (1969), the private stations were incapable of providing for even Canada's most basic broadcasting needs. By 1929 there were 40 radio stations in the United States with a capacity of between 5,000 and 25,000 watts. By contrast, in Canada there were only two stations with a 5,000 watt capacity, one in Ontario, the other in Manitoba. Five others were between 1,000 and 1,800 watts; all the rest were 50, 100, or 500 watts. One-half of the total transmitting power was located in Montreal and Toronto, providing fair service for those areas but leaving many rural areas with no service at all. Coverage was especially poor in Quebec, the Maritimes, and British Columbia. Even in urban centres the situation was far from satisfactory owing to the American monopoly of good frequencies; in Toronto, for example, three stations were forced to share the same wavelength.

Of the 95 channels available to Canada and the United States under international regulations, Canada was able to obtain exclusive use of only six along with shared use of 11 others. Even the negotiated allocation was not secure; in the mid-1920s, a Chicago station run by the Zenith Radio Corporation began using a frequency assigned to Canada. The programming provided by the Canadian stations was irregular and generally uninspiring. It consisted mostly of music, especially after 1926 when Canadian newspapers took action to exclude news from radio. The poor quality of programming reflected the nature of station ownership. Except for a few stations run by religious organizations, most were operated either by newspapers trying to stave off competition for advertising revenues or by radio manufacturing firms seeking to create a market for their receiving sets. Neither expected to make any money from their radio operations as such. They were not motivated, therefore, to expend more on programming than was necessary to secure their limited objectives. Moreover, some were thinking of affiliating with American networks.

There was one exception to this situation which may have influenced the Aird Commission. Under the inspiration of its President, Sir Henry Thornton, the Canadian National Railways had begun installing radio sets on its trains in the early 1920s as a way of attracting more customers. Shortly thereafter radio stations were built in Ottawa, Montreal, Toronto, Moncton, and Vancouver, creating the first coast to coast network service in Canada. The schedule of programs, which included concerts, comic opera, school broadcasts, and historical drama, provided a hint of what an adequately funded national radio service might accomplish. But the CNR could expend only limited funds on radio. Even by the end of 1929, it was providing just three hours a week worth of national broadcasts.

The fact that Canadians were listening to American stations more than Canadian ones disturbed the members of the Aird Commission. For they envisaged that broadcasting might make a valuable contribution to Canadian nationhood. "At present the majority of programs heard are from sources outside of Canada," they stated. "In a country of the vast geographical dimensions of Canada, broadcasting will undoubtedly become a great force in fostering a national spirit and interpreting national citizenship."

They also believed that broadcasting could become "an instrument of education . . . in the broad sense, not only as it is conducted in the schools and colleges, but in providing entertainment and informing the public on questions of national interest."

The Aird Report, submitted by the Commission to the Minister of Marine on September 11, 1929, proposed that all broadcasting in Canada be undertaken by a publicly owned national agency to be called the Canadian Radio Broadcasting Company. This company was to be "vested with the full powers and authority of any private enterprise, its status and duties corresponding to those of a public utility." It would operate a national radio network in English and French by means of seven 50,000 watt stations located across the country (a Maritime station together with one in each of the other provinces). While these facilities were being built at an estimated cost of $3 million, a provisional service would be provided by taking over some of the existing private stations on a temporary basis and closing down the rest. The private stations would receive compensation, but would be excluded from further broadcasting. Eventually local stations might be added to the high-power ones, but these would be operated by the proposed company. In other words, private broadcasting was to be eliminated.

The Aird Report has been heralded as a landmark in the development of a national broadcasting system in Canada. However, if it had been implemented, it is doubtful that it would have provided the basis for a truly national system. The proposed Canadian Radio Broadcasting Company was to have been administered by a board of 12 directors, three representing the federal government and nine representing the provinces. Each provincial director was to head a provincial advisory council, which would have full control over the programs in its area. No provision was made for a company manager, and it was not clear who was to appoint the provincial directors. The result would probably have been a collection of more or less independent provincial broadcasting operations, rather than a system capable of stimulating greater national consciousness and unity.

Following the submission of the Aird Commission Report, the Department of Marine began work on draft legislation. However, on October 23, 1929, the stock market crashed and the climate of prosperity in which the Aird Commission had operated was soon shattered as Canada plunged into the Depression. On June 30, 1930, the House of Commons dissolved for an election and the Aird Report was temporarily shelved. For some observers, its fate seemed sealed when the Liberals were defeated by the Conservatives on July 28, 1930. For the new Prime Minister, R. B. Bennett, and his colleagues were strongly committed to private enterprise. Bennett had once been a solicitor for the CPR and continued to have close ties with its president, E. W. Beatty, who wanted to operate his own private radio network.

Moreover, the delay in considering the Aird Report gave its opponents an opportunity to organize a campaign against it. In addition to the CPR, these opponents included: prosperous private radio stations such as CKAC Montreal and CFRB Toronto; several leading newspapers, including *La Press,* The *Montreal Star, The Toronto Telegram,* and *The Financial Post;* the Canadian Manufacturers' Association; numerous corporations; and even the CNR, which stood to see its own broadcasting network taken over. Mobilizing these opponents was a new organization, the Canadian Association of Broadcasters (CAB), which had been established by the private radio broadcasters in 1926.

Supporting the Aird Report were a number of newspapers that did not own radio stations, most academics and educators, the churches, women's groups, labour and farm groups, and other assorted organizations such as the Canadian Legion. But they lacked any means of working together and thus initially did not exert much pressure upon the government. In October of 1930, therefore, Graham Spry and Alan Plaunt from Ottawa created an informal voluntary association called the Canadian Radio League (CRL) to campaign on behalf of a publicly owned national broadcasting system.

Working on a shoe-string budget, Spry and Plaunt prepared pamphlets setting forth their objectives, recruited other young, public-spirited Canadians, and obtained endorsements from prominent Canadians and various organizations across the country. In between his appearances before the Minister of Marine and the 1932 Parliamentary committee, Spry also found time to lobby the Prime Minister personally. "The question," he told the Morand Committee, "is whether Canada is to establish a chain that is owned and operated and controlled by Canadians, or whether it is to be owned and operated by American interests. The question is, the State or the United States."

Because of the Depression, the CRL proposed a modification to the Aird Commission's recommendation of complete public ownership. It suggested that there also be a number of small, short-range commercial radio stations which would serve local needs and feed free programs from the publicly owned high-power stations. Thus, the door was opened for private broadcasting once again. The report of the Morand Committee adhered closely to the CRL's blueprint for the broadcasting system. On May 26, 1932, Parliament created the Canadian Radio Broadcasting Commission (CRBC) with a mandate to develop a national broadcasting system. It said that it wanted to protect Canadian national sovereignty against American incursions; extend broadcasting to all settled parts of the country; and use the limited natural resources of the airwaves to foster national consciousness and unity. It gave the CRBC extensive regulatory power, including authority not only to issue or cancel licences but also to buy, lease, or expropriate any existing private station. But it did not give the

CRBC adequate financial and structural support for its successful operation.

It soon became necessary, therefore, to pass a new Broadcasting Act through which the Canadian Broadcasting Corporation came into being on November 2, 1936. The *Broadcasting Act* of 1936 gave the CBC authority to create, equip, maintain, and operate broadcasting stations; to originate, purchase, and exchange programs; and to work out arrangements with the private stations for the broadcasting of programs. The CBC could "prescribe the periods to be reserved periodically by any private station for the broadcasting of programmes of the Corporation" and "control the character of any and all programmes broadcast by Corporation or private stations." It could also "prohibit the organization or operation of chains of privately operated stations." To carry out these functions, it was given direct access to revenue from licence fees and other sources and was allowed to borrow money. A new administrative structure made a firm distinction between regulatory and general policy matters on the one hand and day-to-day operations on the other. The former were to be taken care of by a Board of Governors, the latter by a general manager, assistant general manager and their staff.

The *Broadcasting Act* of 1936 still envisaged the complete nationalization of radio and called for an increase in coverage by means of new CBC stations and the affiliation of private stations. However, the Minister of Marine, C. D. Howe, soon told the CBC that it should leave station construction to the private sector and become a program-production agency only. Public opinion, he said, did not support public ownership of broadcast facilities. Under the chairmanship of Leonard W. Brockington, a brilliant lawyer from Winnipeg, the CBC held firm in its resolution to improve its station facilities and gradually secured funds for capital expansion. But Howe countered by refusing to increase the listening fee, which forced the CBC to carry sponsored American programs in addition to its own unsponsored programs. (Smythe, 1981)

At the 1936 parliamentary committee on broadcasting, the private broadcasters and advertising interests had lobbied for regulation by a government agency. They were prepared to allow a public broadcasting organization to continue, but they wanted to restrict its activities to the production and distribution of programs. During the Second World War, the private broadcasters kept a low profile on this issue. But led by the CAB, they took it up again with a passion after the war. The CBC, they complained, "is at one and the same time competitor, regulator, prosecutor, jury and judge." This argument did not meet with much success initially, in part because of the CBC's lenient regulatory approach. The Massey Commission acknowledged that the private stations were useful to the business community and constituted "a possible outlet for local talent." But it saw no reason to alter the relationship between the public and private sectors, especially since the main contribution of many of the latter had been to carry some of the programs produced by the CBC. "We are resolutely opposed to any compromise of the principle on which the system rests and should rest." (Massey Commission, 1951: 26, 284)

The "principle" in question was that of a "single national system," but this has meant different things to different observers. For the Massey Commission, it ruled out the development of two independent groups of radio stations. The Massey Commission did conclude that the private stations should be licensed for five (instead of three) years and should be granted the right to appeal to a Federal Court. But it believed that the private stations should continue to be regulated by the CBC and should not be permitted to form their own separate networks. It also recommended that no private television stations should be licensed until the CBC television service was firmly in place. Moreover, it proposed that all private television stations be affiliated to the CBC and be regulated by it.

However, since then less restrictive conceptions of a single national system have emerged. The first of these was espoused by the Fowler Royal Commission, which thought that the main requirement of a "single national system" was that the public and private broadcasters work together towards a common purpose. In other words, it was not necessary for the public broadcaster to regulate the private broadcasters. Indeed, the Fowler Commission agreed with the CAB that it would be better to have this role performed by a separate public agency. It thought that the CBC had done little to force the private stations to improve the quality of their programming and increase the amount of Canadian content.

The process by which this new regulatory agency emerged and evolved has been charted in great detail by a number of Canadian scholars (*e.g.* Babe, 1979; Peers, 1979; Foster, 1982). The Fowler Commission proposed the creation of a Board of Broadcast Governors to direct and supervise the entire broadcasting system. It was to consist of 15 members appointed for five year terms and removable only by a joint address of the Senate and House of Commons. The CBC would retain its paramount network position, but would be responsible to the new board in policy matters. The BBG would in turn be responsible to Parliament.

The *Broadcasting Act* of 1958 accepted some parts of the Fowler Commission Report, while rejecting others. It created a Board of Broadcast Governors as recommended, but separated it completely from the CBC. It gave it general jurisdiction over both the CBC and the private stations, though less authority than Fowler had considered necessary. The BBG could not, for example, attach special conditions to licenses. As established by the 1958 Act, the BBG was to consist of three full-time salaried members (a chairman, a vice-chairman, and one other) appointed by the Governor in Council for seven years, along with 12 part-time members appointed for five years. The CBC Board of Governors was transformed into a Board of

Directors, rather than abolished as Fowler recommended, and left nominally responsible to Parliament for its overall performance.

The creation of the Board of Broadcast Governors to regulate the broadcasting system marked the beginning of a steady shift away from a mixed system in which the public element is dominant, to one in which the private element is dominant. The creation of the BBG was not in itself a serious blow to the CBC. With no regulatory problems to worry about, it could get on with the job of broadcasting. However, there were two features of the 1958 Act that lessened the CBC's control over its own destiny. First, unlike the BBC, which is responsible to Parliament rather than the IBA, the CBC was to be regulated by the BBG in much the same fashion as the private stations. Secondly, it lost a certain amount of control over its finances. Instead of receiving statutory grants derived from an excise tax on the sale of television sets, its operating and capital funds were to be provided by annual appropriations. This not only made long term planning difficult but also made the Corporation more susceptible to political pressure.

The 1965 Advisory Committee reaffirmed the idea of a single system in which the public and private sectors share the same national broadcasting objectives. It also asserted that in any basic conflict between the two sectors, the interests of the CBC must prevail. Upon reviewing the performance of the BBG, however, it concluded that a stronger regulatory authority — to be called the Canadian Broadcasting Authority — was necessary to make this system work. The BBG, it argued, had not taken a very active role in improving the level of programming, particularly in the case of the private stations. Although it had introduced Canadian content quotas, for example, it had frequently failed to enforce them and had, in any event, created so many loopholes as to render them largely ineffective. "We believe," Fowler stated, "that . . . enforcement of Canadian content by universally applicable regulations is impractical. The individual capacity of each broadcaster should be reviewed from every angle at the time the license is issued, and appropriate requirements for Canadian content should be made a contractual engagement as a condition of the license itself." (Fowler Committee, 1965: 49)

The *Broadcasting Act* of 1968 replaced the BBG with the Canadian Radio-Television Commission. It did not give the CRTC as much direct authority over programming as Fowler's proposed Canadian Broadcasting Authority would have had, but it did provide the CRTC with a stronger organization, full licensing powers, and a clearer mandate. (In 1976 the CRTC took over the regulation of cable from the Canadian Transportation Commission and was renamed the Canadian Radio-Television and Telecommunications Commission.) The 1968 Act made a significant modification to the concept of a single national system by differentiating between the goals for the system as a whole and those of the CBC. But it still assumed that the private sector should contribute to the development of Canadian culture.

In order to help realize the ideal of a single national broadcasting system, the CRTC developed the strategy of giving the private stations and networks considerable protection from normal market forces in return for certain promises of performance and acceptance of Canadian content quotas. (Babe, 1979) There is widespread agreement, however, that despite various refinements in this strategy over the last 15 years, its results have been decidedly poor, especially in terms of television broadcasting. (Babe, 1979; Hardin, 1985; Wolfe, 1985) The private sector has continued to use various loopholes in the content regulations to pack the prime time television schedule with popular American programs. It has also limited its own production largely to the most inexpensive kinds of programming, while purchasing American drama and comedy series at a fraction of their original cost. This should not be particularly surprising, however, given the economic realities that confront Canadian television broadcasters. It costs $900,000 to produce one episode of "Seeing Things", whereas an episode of an American program such as "Remington Steele" can be purchased for about $50,000. (The general rule of thumb is that it costs ten times as much to make a Canadian program as to buy an American one.)

What we need to ask ourselves is not why the private sector has failed to live up to its end of the bargain. It is rather why the CRTC ever struck such a bargain in the first place. A number of years ago, the American historian Gabriel Kolko set forth a revisionist interpretation of the so-called age of reform in late nineteenth and early twentieth-century America. What he suggested was that the numerous "reforms" won by the populist and progressive elements (*e.g.* wages and hours legislation, safety regulations) were not really major concessions by the corporate elite. Rather they were diversionary handouts that prevented any major structural changes from taking place. By the same token, it could be argued that Canadian content regulations have functioned in much the same way. They have brought about a few minor concessions in programming policy by the private stations and networks. But they have also served to divert attention from the need for a fundamental change of approach to broadcasting in Canada. Despite the periodic outcries of the private sector against their unfairness, the fact is that they have done a great service to the private sector by preserving the myth of the single system.

The single system is a myth for several reasons. First, after 35 years of television broadcasting in Canada, the public and private sectors have not yet managed, through their combined efforts, to provide viewers with a satisfactory "Canadian schedule" in prime time. The viewer who sits down in front of his or her set between 7:00 and 11:00 p.m. has no guarantee that he or she will actually be able to watch a Canadian production. Because the CRTC defines prime time as 6:00 p.m. to midnight, broadcasters can fulfill most of their 50 per cent Canadian content quota during the less popular first and final hours. Nor have the major Canadian networks ever attempted to co-operate to build an identifiably Canadian schedule through their combined resources. On the contrary, they have each gone their separate ways, often putting blockbuster American productions against some of the best indigenous Canadian programming. Moreover, the CRTC has never done anything to try to facilitate co-operation in this regard. Instead, it has set about devising increasingly complex content regulations which would do justice to medieval scholasticism.

Secondly, the most natural division of labour among public and private broadcasters in Canada has never been implemented. Broadcasting is expected to promote national consciousness and foster a greater sense of identity. What this means in a Canadian context, of course, is that it must meet the distinctive needs of the different regions, cultures, and linguistic groups. To do so, moreover, two things are required: (1) the means must be provided whereby these different elements can communicate with each other and with Canada as a whole; and (2) it is necessary that they be able to communicate among themselves. Without a national broadcasting system, it would be impossible to satisfy the first requirement. But national broadcasting does not, in and of itself, provide the different constituencies within Canada with adequate opportunies for their own self-expression. A logical division of labour would be for the public sector to serve the first of these needs while the private sector serves the second. However, that has never been the way in which the Canadian broadcasting system has actually worked.

Thirdly, the concept of the single system ignores the main value of a mixed system of ownership; namely, protection against excessive commercial propaganda as well as against the possibility of government propaganda. On the one hand, the existence of a commercial-free public broadcasting sector serves as a check against excessive commercialism by providing the viewers with an alternative. On the other hand, the private sector provides a measure of protection should the public sector fall prey to government propaganda. In other words, the value of a mixed system of ownership lies precisely in the way that it pits the public and private sectors against each other. There is no need for perfect harmony within the broadcasting system; on the contrary, there are substantial benefits from a degree of confrontation. As the Fowler Committee observed, "if the union of public and private elements produces clashes of opinion and controversy within the system, it is all to the good in an institution engaged in public information and the formation of public opinion." (Fowler Committee, 1965: 13)

The single system is thus more rhetoric than reality. It distorts what broadcasting can and cannot be expected to accomplish in Canada. It also undermines our willingness to provide adequate support for the public sector, since it assumes that private broadcasters can carry a substantial portion of the burden. As long as regulators continue to subscribe to it, they will keep trying to accomplish things through private enterprise that can only be carried out by public enterprise. While the record of public broadcasting in Canada is hardly an unblemished one, its overall performance has been fairly closely related to the level of support which it has received.

For several decades, the CBC never received adequate capital support to build a first-rate system of radio stations. It was thus not until the mid-1960s that the coverage of stations owned and operated by the CBC reached the level recommended by the Aird Commission 35 years earlier. However, when television was introduced, the CBC had by most accounts adequate funding for the task at hand. The result was that television was available to 60 per cent of the population by 1954 and to 85 per cent by 1957. This constituted the fastest growth of television coverage in the world. Moreover, in the mid-1950s, Canadian production of live television programs was second in number only to that of the United States.

In recent years, Canadians have become increasingly ambivalent about the merits of public enterprise. While there has always been a strong belief in the necessity of a predominately private enterprise economy, this has not precluded government participation in large national projects, such as the building of the CPR and the St. Lawrence Seaway. Where private enterprise has been considered incapable of carrying out projects that would serve the national interest, Canadians have supported government involvement on their behalf. Nonetheless, there has been a declining incentive to make broadcasting a project of national enterprise. Instead, there has been a growing desire to treat it as a "cultural industry," with the emphasis on industry rather than on culture.

This approach is reflected in a number of recent reports and studies on broadcasting. The Applebaum-Hébert Committee, which was established by the Honourable Francis Fox on August 28, 1980, did not originally intend to say much about broadcasting. However, its final report included a number of highly controversial recommendations for the broadcasting system. The committee believed that to remain competitive in the midst of rapidly increasing program choice, Canadian broadcasters would have to draw more effectively on the available creative resources. Thus, it focused its attention on the relationship between the established networks and the independent production industry. In particular, it recommended that "with the exception of its news operations, the CBC should relinquish all television production activities and facilities in favour of acquiring its television program material from independent producers." (Applebaum-Hébert Committee, 1982: 292) Although Applebaum-Hébert insisted that the CBC was still "the key element in the system, fundamental to its operation" (p. 288), this proposal would, if enacted, fundamentally alter the place of the CBC within the overall system. Clearly, it would be a severely weakened and demoralized CBC that would remain.

Part of the appeal of Applebaum-Hébert's approach stems from its attempt to instill private enterprise virtues into a broadcasting system which has successfully eluded them to this point. Under normal conditions, competitive market structures make industries more productive and efficient and lead to the production of higher quality goods. However, in the case of television broadcasting in Canada, private enterprise principles have been largely inoperative. Competition, such as it has existed, has provided no incentive to the efficient production of quality Canadian programs; it has simply led to a scramble to secure the best American programming. To get around this situation, the Applebaum-Hébert strategy was to try to secure the benefits of competition at the level of independent production houses, rather than at the level of broadcast ownership. To do so, however, they still considered it necessary to provide a reasonably assured market for the product of the independent production industry. (This, of course, corrupts the concept of a competitive independent production segment.) It is for this reason that the CBC would be forced to give up most of its own production and then rely on purchases from independent companies.

There is a certain plausibility to this argument, especially if one agrees with Applebaum-Hébert that the "privileged position" of the CBC has led to "a hardening of creative arteries and protection of the institutional status quo." However, apart from the fact that it provided no concrete evidence of a vigorous and healthy private production industry, there are several points which the Applebaum-Hébert Committee failed to consider. First, public enterprise has always been able to take on larger and riskier projects than private enterprise. Secondly, the CBC would lose a great deal of control over the quality and content of programming. Thirdly, many of the most talented producers and performers would probably head to the United States once they have achieved success in Canada. It is well documented that the CBC has served to restrict the outflow of Canadian talent by providing the compensation of greater security than is usually available within private enterprise.

In spite of this, the balance of ownership within the Canadian broadcasting system has shifted steadily in the direction of private enterprise. In television the process began in 1961 when stations in eight cities were allowed to link up to form the Canadian Television (CTV) network. It continued in the early 1970s with the creation of a private francophone network in Quebec and the licensing of the Global network in Ontario. And it has carried on in the 1980s with the rejection of the CBC's application for a second English and French network; the granting of pay television licences to exclusively private interests; and the failure of CBC funding to keep pace with inflation. When the pay television licences were granted, it was on the condition that the networks provide 50 per cent Canadian programming and invest 45 per cent of their gross revenues in Canadian production. But this was later reduced to 30 per cent Canadian content and 20 per cent of gross revenues. Only the emergence of provincial networks such as TV Ontario has stemmed the increasing domination of Canadian television by private interests.

For advocates of public broadcasting, one of the few encouraging developments in recent years has been the report which the Task Force on Broadcasting Policy submitted in September, 1986. In the most comprehensive study of broadcasting in Canada's history, the Caplan-Sauvageau task force concluded that Canada is in the midst of a serious cultural crisis owing to the lack of home-grown content on prime-time television. The reason for this, it argued, is not because Canadians do not like to watch Canadian programs. On the contrary, it found that Canadians watch their own programming in almost the same proportion as it is available. The problem is that Canadians are swamped by American programs. In the case of English-Canada, only 28 per cent of the programming available is Canadian. Indeed, for every hour of Canadian drama shown to cable television subscribers, there are 24 hours of American drama. In fact, Canadians with cable actually have better access to American programming than people living in Manhatten.

Not unexpectedly, the Task Force report was critical of the performance of the private television stations. As a result of various protective devices, the private broadcasters were found to be reaping enormous profits, while at the same time putting very little back into the system in terms of quality Canadian programming. For the CTV affiliates which systematically deprive the network of the funds necessary to produce better programming, television had become virtually a licence to print money.

However, the report was even more critical of the CRTC for having allowed this situation to develop. The CRTC, it said, had failed to carry out its mandate. By its refusal to hear competing bids when broadcast licences come up for renewal, it had practically turned the airwaves into private property. It had, in fact, never revoked a television licence. On the contrary, it had coddled the private television broadcasters financially through its acceptance of two policies which increased television revenues by millions of dollars every year. Since 1976 Canadians have not been permitted to deduct from their taxes the costs of advertising on U.S. border stations (as they can if they advertise in Canada). At the same time, broadcasters have been allowed to simulcast or substitute Canadian signals and commercials for U.S. ones on cable when the same show is broadcast on both channels. The Task Force acknowledged that most of the necessary regulations for more quality Canadian programming in prime time already exist. But it criticized the CRTC for not implementing its own policies.

In contrast, its report indicated strong support for the CBC. The CBC, it stated, should be the "centre-piece" of the Canadian broadcasting system. While critical of the size of the Corporation's bureaucracy, it supported the longstanding suggestion that the government commit itself to a level of financial support for the CBC over its entire licence period. This, it thought, would enable the CBC to draw up realistic five-year plans and use its resources more efficiently.

The Task Force made four basic proposals with regard to television. First, the CBC should increase its Canadian content from the current 80 per cent to about 95 per cent by dropping most of its American programs. Secondly, the private stations should increase their Canadian content to 45 per cent between 7:00 p.m. and 11:00 p.m. Thirdly, the CBC should be allowed to create a separate channel on the basic cable service dedicated exclusively to news and public affairs. And fourthly, a new commercial-free public superstation called TV Canada should be created. It would be carried on the basic cable service in both French and English and would show only Canadian programming. It would be independent from the CBC and be devoted to children's shows, National Film Board documentaries, arts programs, and more programs devoted to the regions. It would also serve as a repeat channel for the best programs from the public broadcasters.

The Task Force estimated that it would cost about $275 million to implement these proposals. Increasing Canadian content on CBC television would cost about $90 million, while its proposed all-news channel would cost between $25 and $30 million. (The Corporation's loss of commercial revenue from phasing out its foreign programming would amount to as much as $140 million.) TV Canada's budget was placed at $45 million in the first year, increasing to about $100 million after five years. The Task Force believed that these funds could be secured without unduly burdening taxpayers. "We are saying there is a lot of money [$3 billion] in the system," Caplan said at the time of the report's release, "and that the Government is in a position to redistribute it from its own revenues, from very small accretions of taxation, from very small add-ons to our cable revenues, from larger contributions from the private system." (Winsor, 1986: A3)

More specifically, it was proposed that about $110 million be raised by imposing a five per cent tax on sales and rentals of videocassettes, VCRs, and satellite dishes. In addition, cable television subscribers should be required to pay an extra 25¢ a month for the CBC all-news channel and an extra 75¢ a month for the English and French TV Canada channels. Beyond that, the Task Force thought that private broadcasters should pay more for their licences; that the federal government should give an extra $72 million a year to the CBC for purchasing independent productions; that the Broadcast Fund, which subsidizes television production, should be increased from $55 million currently to $75 million by 1988; and finally, that the federal government should create a 150 per cent business tax deduction for the purchase of commercials bought on certain kinds of Canadian programs.

The initial response to the Task Force report was generally favourable. Michael Hind-Smith, head of the Canadian Cable Television Association, expressed opposition to further levies on cable subscribers and said that there is no evidence of public support for the proposed new channels. But most other reactions were positive. The Minister of Communications, Flora MacDonald, praised it as a practical report and said that it was "full of good ideas for the next 10 to 15 years and on into the next century." (Winsor, 1986: A3) She even went on record that the government would respond with a new broadcasting Act "within this mandate." Pierre Juneau, President of the CBC, welcomed the report's support for public broadcasting and said that it killed the myth that there are easy solutions to the problems of Canadian broadcasting. A spokesman for the Canadian Association of Broadcasters indicated that his organization supported the report in principle, though considerable negotiation would be required. Columnist Jeffrey Simpson was particularly glowing in his praise. "With lucid prose, relentless logic and a sure eye for the possible," he wrote, "the Task Force has charted an exciting and distinctively Canadian future for television and radio." (Simpson, 1986: A6)

When the Caplan-Sauvageau report is examined carefully, however, it is less clear whether its proposals would provide the most effective means of strengthening the Canadian broadcasting system. Even if the government could reconcile pouring over $200 million more into television broadcasting at a time when the federal government has an annual deficit of over $30 billion, it is questionable whether the Task Force's blueprint would be the best way to spend it. It is difficult to criticize the general goal of raising the quantity and quality of Canadian television programs. But ironically, while the Task Force called the CBC's multichannel strategy "extravagant," the same can be said of its own proposal for three new channels.

For several years after the introduction of satellites, converters, and hand-held channel selectors, there was much talk of the benefits that would soon accrue from having a hundred or more channels. But it did not take very long for most people to realize that the steady increase in available channels was not being accompanied by a significant increase in the number of good programs. While there is an understandable fear that Canadian channels are being overwhelmed by an ever larger number of American ones, the solution to this is not to create as many new Canadian channels as possible. Rather it is to support the number of channels that is consistent with high quality programming. One good channel still remains better than two bad ones. This probably means that in addition to improving its current English and French network offerings, the CBC could operate second channels in English and French with a reasonable increase in funding. But it probably rules out the creation of two additional channels in English and French as the Caplan-Sauvageau task force recommended.

Second channels run by the CBC could carry the same kind of programming proposed for TV Canada as well as substantial news and public affairs programming. (They might even incorporate the parliamentary channel which Caplan-Sauvageau proposed taking away from the CBC.) Moreover, they could do so without creating a new bureaucracy and without reducing the incentive of the private broadcasters to maintain the quality of their news and public affairs. Apart from the fact that public demand for an all-news channel has not been demonstrated, it is important for the news system as a whole that there be a reasonable balance between the public and private broadcast news sectors. It is also vital that any new channels that are created not further erode the place of the CBC within the overall system, which is clearly what would happen if an independent TV Canada were to be created. For within a few years, no doubt it would be competing against the CBC for federal funds.

The only problem with the suggestion that the CBC acquire the equivalent of BBC1 and BBC2 is that it has already been made before and rejected. Having spent over $2.5 million, the Task Force on Broadcasting Policy obviously felt compelled to come up with an array of new proposals of its own. When the Canadian broadcasting system is examined in a comparative perspective, however, a simpler strategy for improving its performance would still appear to be worth considering. This would consist of abandoning the attempt to get the private television sector to produce more Canadian drama, but insisting that it provide a better balance of foreign drama and maintain the quality of its news and public affairs. At the same time, it would gain the benefits of the elimination of commercials on the CBC, but would be given much less protection from normal market forces. The CBC, for its part, would be relied on to provide a variety of Canadian programming for the nation as a whole. It would be expected to eliminate all foreign programming, but would be permitted to create second channels in English and French. It would also be given significantly increased funds over longer time periods with adequate allowance for inflation.

References

Aird Commission
>1929 *Report of the Royal Commission on Radio Broadcasting.* Ottawa: King's Printer.

Allard, T. J.
>1979 *Straight Up: Private Broadcasting in Canada, 1918-1958.* Ottawa: Canadian Communications Foundation.

Applebaum-Hébert Committee
>1982 *Report of the Federal Cultural Policy Review Committee.* Ottawa: Supply and Services.

Audley, Paul
>1983 *Canada's Cultural Industries: Broadcasting, Publishing, Records and Film.* Toronto: James Lorimer.

Babe, Robert
>1979 *Canadian Broadcasting Structure, Performance and Regulation.* Ottawa: Supply and Services Canada.

Barnouw, Eric
>1966 *A Tower in Babel.* Vol. I: To 1933 of *A History of Broadcasting in the United States.* New York: Oxford University Press.
>1968 *The Golden Web.* Vol. II: 1933-1953 of *A History of Broadcasting in the United States.* New York: Oxford University Press.
>1970 *The Image Empire.* Vol. III: From 1953 of *A History of Broadcasting in the United States.* New York: Oxford University Press.
>1975 *Tube of Plenty: The Evolution of American Television.* New York: Oxford University Press.
>1978 *The Sponsor: Notes on a Modern Potentate.* New York: Oxford University Press.

Bowman, Charles A.
>1966 *Ottawa Editor.* Sidney, B.C.: Gray's Publishing.

Briggs, Asa
>1961 *The Birth of Broadcasting.* Vol. I of *The History of Broadcasting in the United Kingdom.* London: Oxford University Press.

1965 *The Golden Age of Wireless.* Vol. II of *The History of Broadcasting in the United Kingdom.* London: Oxford University Press.
1970 *The War of Words.* Vol. III of *The History of Broadcasting in the United Kingdom.* London: Oxford University Press.
1979 *Sound and Vision.* Vol. IV of *The History of Broadcasting in the United Kingdom.* London: Oxford University Press.

Bunce, Richard
1976 *Television in the Corporate Interest.* New York: Praeger.

Burns, Tom
1977 *The BBC: Public Insitution and Private World.* London: Macmillan.

Caplan-Sauvageau (Task Force on Broadcasting Policy)
1986 *Report.* Hull, Que:" Supply and Services Canada.

Clyne Committee
1979 *Telecommunications and Canada.* Hull, Que.: Supply and Services Canada.

Curran, Charles
1979 *A Seamless Robe: Broadcasting Philosophy and Practice.* London: Collins.

Ellis, David
1979 *Evolution of the Canadian Broadcasting System, 1928-1968.* Ottawa: Department of Communications.

Emery, Walter B.
1969 *National and International Systems of Broadcasting.* East Lansing: Michigan State University Press.

Foster, Frank
1982 *Broadcasting Policy Development.* Ottawa: Franfost Communications.

Fowler Commission
1957 *Report [of the] Royal Commission on Broadcasting.* Ottawa: Queen's Printer.

Fowler Committee
1965 *Report of the Committee on Broadcasting.* Ottawa: Queen's Printer.

Globerman, Steven
1983 *Cultural Regulation in Canada.* Montreal: Institute for Research on Public Policy.

Hardin, Herschel
1985 *Closed Circuits: The Sellout of Canadian Television.* Vancouver: Douglas & McIntyre.

Johnson, Brian D. *et al.*
1986 "TV Boils Over." *Maclean's* (September 22): 38-40.

Krasnow, Erwin G. and Lawrence D. Longley
  1978 *The Politics of Broadcast Regulation.* 2nd ed., New York: St. Martin's Press.
Massey Commission
  1951 *Report [of the] Royal Commission on National Development in the Arts, Letters and Sciences, 1949-1951.* Ottawa: King's Printer.
McFadyen, Stuart, Colin Hoskins, and David Gillen
  1980 *Canadian Broadcasting: Market Structure and Economic Performance.* Montreal: Institute for Research on Public Policy.
Nolan, Michael
  1984 "Canada's Broadcasting Pioneers: 1918-1932." *Canadian Journal of Communication* 10 (no. 3): 1-26.
Peers, Frank
  1969 *The Politics of Canadian Broadcasting, 1920-1951.* Toronto: University of Toronto Press.
  1979 *The Public Eye: Television and the Politics of Canadian Broadcasting 1952-1968.* Toronto: University of Toronto Press.
Simpson, Jeffrey
  1986 "An exciting vision." *The Globe and Mail,* Toronto (September 23): A6.
Smythe, Dallas W.
  1981 *Dependency Road: Communications, Capitalism, Consciousness, and Canada.* Norwood, N.J.: Ablex.
Therrien Committee
  1980 *The Eighties: Decade of the Proliferation of Broadcasting, Satellites and Pay Television.* Hull, Que.: Supply and Services Canada.
Weir, E. Austin
  1965 *The Struggle for National Broadcasting in Canada.* Toronto: McClelland and Stewart.
Winsor, Hugh
  1986 "Boost Canadian content, task force recommends." *The Globe and Mail,* Toronto (September 23): A3.
Wolfe, Morris
  1985 *Jolts: The TV Wasteland and the Canadian Oasis.* Toronto: James Lorimer.

Chapter 6

Where is Communications Technology Leading Us?

The impact of new communications technologies is an important component of the larger debate over technology and society. Although concern about communications technology is of more recent origins than concern about technology in general, its roots can be traced back to the introduction of the printing press. While many rejoiced over the convenience of printing, others were disturbed about its implications for employment and the permanency of records. (Eisenstein, 1979) Similarly, there were mixed reactions to the invention of the telegraph and motion pictures four centuries later. (Czitrom, 1982: 6-21, 30-59) However, it is only with the emergence of more recent electronic media — radio, television, and computer networks — that a full-fledged controversy has developed over where new communications technologies are leading us.

An interesting prelude to this controversy occurred around the turn of the century. In 1888 Edward Bellamy, a New England journalist, published a utopian novel entitled *Looking Backward* which anticipated, among other things, the electronic distribution of information and entertainment to people in their homes. Julian, the central character in this novel, falls asleep in 1887 and wakes up in Boston in the year 2000. To his surprise he finds that the squalor and injustices of the late nineteenth century have been replaced by general well-being based on a system of public capitalism. He also discovers that new communications technologies have eliminated the necessity to leave one's home for entertainment or religion. "There are some who still prefer to hear sermons in church," Julian's host, Doctor Leete, explains at one point,

> but most of our preaching, like our musical performances, is not in public, but delivered in acoustically prepared chambers, connected by wire with subscribers' houses. If you prefer to go to a church I shall be glad to accompany you, but I really don't believe you are likely to hear anywhere a better discourse than you will at home. I see by the paper that Mr. Barton is to preach this morning, and he preaches only by telephone, and to audiences often reaching 150,000. (Bellamy, 1976: 273)

When *Looking Backward* appeared in England, the acclaim that greeted it in America was not as readily forthcoming. The poet and literary journalist Lionel Johnson said that it was "of an ugliness so gross and so pestilent, that it deserved the bonfire and the hangman, the fate of no worse books in a bygone age." (Faulkner, 1973: 339) An equally vehement critic was the socialist poet, William Morris, who could not abide the way in which Bellamy had restructured capitalist society. Taking as his own ideal the Marxian vision of a society in which the worker gains personal fulfillment from the fruits of his labour, Morris could not imagine how this would be possible if all industry was subject to the strict regulations of a single national authority. He countered Bellamy's work by writing a utopian romance of his own called *News from Nowhere* (1891) in which he depicted a peaceful, contented, aesthetically-pleasing existence in a highly decentralized rural society. The implication was that in their haste to reform the world, men like Bellamy were creating a form of life that is so mechanized, sanitized, and regimented that there is little joy or satisfaction left for the individual.

Morris's central concern was overlooked by H. G. Wells when he decided a decade or so later to construct yet another utopia. "Were we free to have our untrammelled desire," he wrote in *A Modern Utopia* (1905), "I suppose we should follow Morris to his Nowhere, we should change the nature of man and the nature of things together; we should make the whole race wise, tolerant, noble, perfect — wave our hands to a splendid anarchy, every man doing as it pleases him, and none pleased to do evil, in a world as good in its essential nature, as ripe and sunny, as the world before the Fall." (Wells, 1905: 7) Instead Wells decided to proceed on a more "practical plane." His utopia consisted of a scientifically planned welfare state run by experts and assisted by a state-funded research institute. Every citizen is adequately housed and nourished; the state assists people in finding employment and, if unsuccessful, provides them with publicly supported work; and the sick, the incapacited, and the aged are all taken care of at the state's expense.

Although Wells did not foresee the kind of communications network anticipated by Bellamy, he did envisage a system of "organized clairvoyance" based on a central index to all the world's inhabitants. Housed in Paris, this index would classify every citizen by means of unalterable physical traits such as fingerprints. It would maintain records of personal data such as marriages and criminal convictions and keep track of the location of every individual at all times.

A little army of attendants would be at work upon this index day and night. From sub-stations constantly engaged in checking back thumb-marks and numbers, an incessant stream of information would come, of births, of deaths, of arrivals at inns, of applications to post-offices for letters, for tickets taken for long journeys, of criminal convictions, marriages, applications for public doles and the like. A filter of offices would sort the stream, and all day and all night for ever a swarm of clerks would go to and fro correcting this central register, and photographing copies of its entries for transmission to the subordinate local stations, in response to their inquiries. So the inventory of the State would watch its every man and the wide world write its history as the fabric of its destiny flowed on. (Wells, 1905: 164-5)

It was not until the advent of computers that the index foreseen by Wells became a practical possibility. But even before then, a number of thinkers began to worry about how new communications technologies might be used as a instrument of social control. Foremost among these was George Orwell, whose *Nineteen Eight-Four* (1948) imprinted a nightmarish image of a totally monitored population on the minds of his readers. Orwell did not believe, however, that the future he depicted was pre-determined. He offered a warning of what might happen rather than a prophecy of what is inevitable. Thus, he left the door open for others to argue that new communications technologies, if used properly, could lead to a more peaceful, integrated, and prosperous world.

During the late 1970s and early 1980s, the computer industry underwent a phenomenal growth. Then, for a short spell in the mid-1980s, this upward movement tapered off. Sales of home computers fell and profits within the computer industry as a whole declined. This has been reversed, however, by the appearance of a new generation of faster, smarter, and friendlier computers utlizing amazing improvements in semi-conductor technology. The time and cost to process data have been greatly reduced and new kinds of functions for computers have become possible. Computers can now recognize speech and convert it into text; they can read documents and store their contents; they can even recognize human gestures and monitor behaviour. Through what are known as "expert systems," moreover, they are beginning to approach the frontiers of artificial intelligence by mimicking human problem solving in specialized contexts. In 1985 the most powerful computer was the Cray-2 built by Cray Research; it was 100,000 times faster than the best personal computer. However, even this computer was soon being challenged by a new breed of "minisupercomputers" that link together thousands of microprocessors.

Going hand in hand with these advances in computer technology is the development of fiber optics. Until 1980, practically all phone calls and computer data were transmitted by an electric current passing through copper wire. But this technology is now being replaced by hair-thin glass filaments that carry intense beams of light projected by tiny lasers. By having a pulse of light stand for "one" and no light represent "zero," computer-coded information can be generated by rapidly turning the beam of light off and on. The advantages of fiber optics over copper wire are three-fold. First, much greater amounts of information can be sent in a fraction of the time. According to one estimate, 25 million words (or the contents of almost 500 magazines) can be transmitted with fiber optics in one second; to do this over a copper wire would take 21 hours. (*Business Week,* 1984: 168) Secondly, fiber optics has much greater channel capacity than copper wire. And thirdly, the need for expensive equipment to amplify and retransmit a signal being sent over a long distance is greatly reduced.

Apart from providing better and cheaper telephone service, fiber optics could thus solve the major problem of handling the rapidly growing traffic between computers. It could make possible the development of vast computer-based information networks. Satellites will probably still be used for a long time to transmit data around the world. But fiber optics is likely to replace satellites fairly rapidly as the basis of contintental information networks. Moreover, it is also envisaged by some that fiber optics will be used to speed up the transmission of information between chips within computers.

Even before developments such as these, advances in communications technology led to the idea that we are in the midst of an information revolution which is rapidly changing us from an industrial to a post-industrial society. This transformation was first heralded by Daniel Bell in *The Coming of Post-Industrial Society* (1973) and has been subsequently extolled in works such as Alvin Toffler's *The Third Wave* (1980) and Yoneji Masuda's *The Information Society as Post-Industrial Society* (1981). However, it has also been described as a "myth" and may well give rise to less euphoric expectations when we understand more about its underlying dynamics. For post-industrial society is a product of an ongoing interaction between two sets of forces: one economic, the other technological. If we look only at the first phase of this interaction, there is a tendency to be optimistic about the future. If we look at the second phase, however, a number of serious concerns begin to surface.

The economic aspect of post-industrial society consists of a dramatic increase in the percentage of the work-force engaged in information-related activities. Until 1956 the number of blue-collar (industrial) workers exceeded the number of white-collar (information) workers in the United States; but in that year the latter surpassed the former for the first time. Since then the percentage of workers engaged in information-related activities has risen to just over 50 per cent in the United States. In Canada approximately 40 per cent of the work-force is engaged in information activities. (Warskett, 1981: 181) This development has been seen by Bell and others as a very positive development. But we need to ask ourselves why it is occurring.

According to G. Warskett, the rise of large corporations is primarily responsible for the development of an information-based economy. In the nineteenth century, there were numerous small businesses competing in each industry. For example, there used to be 200 automobile manufacturers in the United States; now there are only four. These small businesses had few information requirements beyond the need for market prices. They could rely on the price mechanism or the law of supply and demand to co-ordinate economic activity. They could tell from prices alone whether to increase or decrease their production of goods or services. (Warskett, 1981: 182-4)

By the early twentieth century, however, a vastly different set of information needs had emerged. The giant corporations which had come to characterize the capitalist system needed to be able to monitor and control their economic environment. Because of the heavy investment required to begin production, they had to be able to secure and sustain markets for a long period of time. To meet their greatly expanded need for information about the economy, the private corporations began to develop their own intelligence operations. They built up small armies of information workers, including sales and market researchers, research and development engineers, cost accountants, and advertising personnel. At the same time, the concern of the state to sustain aggregate demand and dampen the cyclical tendencies of the economy resulted in the growth of public bureaucracies. (Warskett, 1981: 185-90)

Both of these developments created jobs for information workers and thus provided a major thrust behind the growth of an information-based economy. However, as Warskett points out, information activities are inherently *unproductive*. They do not in and of themselves create goods or services. Thus they constitute a drag upon the economy. A few years ago, J. W. Halina estimated that 47 per cent of the Canadian Gross National Product is of an information nature. He also calculated that in the mid-1930s, $1 in information activity was associated with $6 of final product. But by the mid-1970s, this ratio had dropped to under $1/$3 and was still falling. From this he concluded that the economy is actually throttling down under its information overhead. There is, therefore, a major incentive to try to reduce information costs, especially as energy and other resources are depleted and become more expensive. (Halina, 1980: 266, 268, 276)

The need of the large corporations to reduce their information costs is considered by both Warskett and Halina to be a major factor behind the technological side of post-industrial society. This consists of the development of integrated information networks as a result of the linkage of computers with new telecommunications technologies such as cable, satellites, and fiber optics. These information networks are sometimes described as polymodal in the sense that all modes of telecommunications (data, voice, and video) have been reduced to a common denominator. By reducing the costs of accessing, processing, and distributing data, they hold the potential for greatly reduced information costs. Ironically, however, they may do so in part by reversing the very development that gave rise to the idea of a post-industrial society in the first place; namely, the steady increase in the number of information workers.

In a report entitled *Working with Technology,* released on September 29, 1986, the Economic Council of Canada sought to dispel fears that high technology is eliminating jobs. It argued that workers become more efficient in companies that adopt new technologies such as computers. As a result, the companies increase sales and hire more staff in non-automated areas. It is still not clear, however, whether computers have this effect on the work-force as a whole. Not all of the file clerks displaced by computers in public bureaucracies can be shifted to other jobs. Nor are new positions readily available for those who lose their jobs because of the introduction of such things as computerized banking and electronic mail.

The interaction between these economic and technological developments will affect all of society. But where is it leading us? And how much control can we exercise over it? In this chapter, responses to these questions will be approached with the aid of a double polarity derived from an article by the late Michel Benamou. In "Notes on the Technological Imagination" (1980), Benamou devised what he called a "subjective square" for classifying discourse about technology in general. His basic categories can also be applied to the debate about communications technology, though a few modifications would appear to be in order. As in previous chapters, the four positions to be discussed will be related to two basic questions. The first of these questions concerns the dynamics of technology; the second concerns its general effects.

The first question can be stated as follows. Does communications technology advance according to its own internal dynamic? Is it driven by an underlying logic that cannot be affected to any significant degree by what man does? According to determinists (or, more accurately, predeterminists), communications technology unfolds as if it has a will of its own. It is autonomous and its pattern of development is inevitable, so that man can exercise little control over it. According to indeterminists, on the other hand, there is nothing inevitable about the course of communications technology. It can be directed and controlled by man; it is really up to man how technology is used.

The second question is simply whether new communications technologies are having a positive or negative effect overall. To be more specific, are they liberating the individual and unifying society? Are they helping to free man from dependence on the physical environment and integrate him into a global community? Or are they are enslaving the individual and leading to social isolation? Are they destroying human values, undermining human relationships, and facilitating various forms of suppression?

Superimposing the basic responses to these two lines of questioning gives rise to the positions set forth in Figure 6:

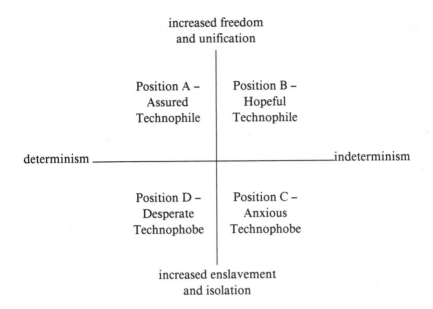

Figure 6

Several alterations have been made to Benamou's labels. The term 'assured technophile' (for Position A) has been used in place of 'happy technophile;' 'hopeful technophile' (for Position B) has replaced 'anxious technophile;' and 'anxious technophobe' (for Position C) has replaced 'hopeful technophobe.' Benamou's term 'desperate technophobe' (for Position D) has, however, been retained.

Position A — The Assured Technophile

The assured technophile believes not only that technology has the potential to increase human freedom but also that its course of development is inevitable. He sees in technology the salvation of man, provided that man just lets it take its course. The assured technophile is thus not only profoundly optimistic but also extremely conservative.

During the latter part of his career, the Canadian media guru, Marshall McLuhan (1911-1980) was essentially an assured technophile. In *The Mechanical Bride* (1951), he suggested that advertising had induced modern society into a "collective trance." But in later works such as *The Gutenberg Galaxy* (1962), *Understanding Media* (1964), and *War and Peace in the Global Village* (1968), he argued that the electronic revolution in communication had modified human sensibilities and improved human relations. It had led to the "retribalization of man," by which he meant that it had reintegrated the human senses into the perfect symmetry that had characterized the oral culture of early "tribal" man. Television in particular was thought to have been the crucial medium in the retribalization process. (Czitrom, 1982: 165-82)

The influence of McLuhan was apparent in works such as *The War in Man: Media and Machines* (1970) by Frederick D. Wilhelmsen and Jane Bret. The thesis of this little known, but quite interesting, study is that there are fundamental differences between machine technology and electronic technology and that each of these thus has profoundly different effects on man and society. Although machines begin as an extension of the human body, they become progressively more independent of man as they are perfected. Initially the machine is run and directed by man; before long it is merely tended and nursed by him. Indeed, its improvement is measured by the extent to which it makes human guidance unnecessary. Electronic technology, however, involves a radically different relationship with man. It engages man because it depends upon his personal involvement.

According to Wilhelmsen and Bret, machine technology fragments men into solitary units based on the most efficient division of labour. But electronic technology brings them back together by obliterating the restrictions of space and time. It reintegrates the individual into humanity or, as McLuhan put it, leads to the "retribalization" of man. At present, a war is supposedly taking place between mechanical and electronic technology. This is producing severe tension in the psyche of Western man. But as machine technology is steadily replaced by electronic technology, this tension will disappear and a harmonious social order will emerge.

Another example of an assured technophile is Daniel Boorstin in *The Republic of Technology* (1978). Boorstin subscribes to the belief fostered by the Scientific Revolution and Enlightenment that technology gives man increased control over the physical world. As evidence of the concrete benefits of technology, he cites man's increased standard of living, his greater longevity and reduced susceptibility to epidemics, his reduced hours of labour and safer working conditions, and his increased ease of travel. Beyond this, moreover, Boorstin suggests that technology has the less tangible effect of bringing men closer together by making their daily experiences more and more the same. In this way it helps to overcome chauvinism, persecution, and bigotry as well as the worst excesses of nationalism. The "republic of technology" is Boorstin's vision of a new global community with a set of shared concerns.

At the same time, however, Boorstin argues that we cannot control the direction of technology. In this regard, he introduces a distinction between political and technological change. Political revolutions, he argues, involve a conscious, purposeful, organized effort to redress perceived grievances and re-make society. While they sometimes get out of hand, they are nonetheless a deliberate attempt to guide events so as to achieve a vision of reform. They always have a "Why" and are roughly predictable and even reversible. Technological revolutions, however, do not have a "Why" and are neither predictable nor reversible. They lead to unintended and unpredictable consequences and cannot be stopped, deflected, or reversed. The reason for this, according to Boorstin, lies in our inability to predict what new discoveries will be made about the physical world.

According to Boorstin, technology does not respond to human needs as much as it invents them after the fact. This is another reason why we never know what consequences will unravel from it. He points to several communications examples to illustrate this point. There was, he says, no demand for the telephone that led to its invention and no understanding in advance of what it would mean for human communication. Similarly, those who experimented with radio had no idea of the kind of broadcasting that would emerge. A similar case could no doubt be made for the printing press and a number of other communications technologies.

Position B — The Hopeful Technophile

The hopeful technophile rejects the assumption that improvements in communications technology will *necessarily* make for a better world. But he is generally optimistic about the prospects for mankind. Examples of hopeful technophiles include Daniel Bell, Ithiel de Sola Pool, and Joshua Meyrowitz.

For Bell, post-industrial society is characterized by the liberation of the worker from the assembly line and the enhanced opportunity for different cultural expressions and life-styles. However, his approach is non-deterministic. He sees no guarantee that communications technology will necessarily achieve its potential for goodness. "Technology does not determine social structure," he wrote in the *Harvard Business Review* in 1979; "it simply widens all kinds of possibilities. Technology is embedded in a social support system, and each social structure has a choice as to how it will be used." Whether technology contributes to freedom or oppression depends on the society in which it is developed. "One can take the same technology and show how different support systems use them in very different ways." (Bell, 1983: 45)

Bell acknowledges that new communications technologies might be abused. But the major threat is thought to lie "in the expansion of regulatory agencies whose rising costs and bureaucratic regulations and delays inhibit innovation and change in a society. In the United States, at least, it is not Big Brother, but Slothful Brother, that becomes the problem." (Bell, 1983: 48) This theme has been developed at greater length by Ithiel de Sola Pool in *Technologies of Freedom* (1983).

Like Bell, Pool believes that new communications technologies could greatly increase freedom of expression. He also assumes that this result is not inevitable. Because of what he calls "convergence of modes," Pool fears that the constitutional protection for the American print media might be overridden by the kinds of controls to which the common carriers and broadcast media are subject. "Technology will not be to blame," Pool writes,

> if Americans fail to encompass this [communications] system within the political tradition of free speech. On the contrary, electronic technology is conducive to freedom. The degree of diversity and plenitude of access that mature electronic technology allows far exceeds what is enjoyed today. Computerized information networks of the twenty-first century need not be any less free for all to use without let or hindrance than was the printing press. Only political errors might make them so. (Pool, 1983: 231)

A third recent apologist for the liberating effects of electronic media is Joshua Meyrowitz, an associate professor of communication at the University of New Hampshire. In *No Sense of Place: The Impact of Electronic Media on Social Behavior* (1985), Meyrowitz attempts to resuscitate the reputation of television. To put this in context, it should be noted that the Canadian public's assessment of television has become increasingly negative over the last three decades. In 1956, 66 per cent of Canadians thought that the influence of television on family life was good; by 1966, only 48 per cent thought so; and by 1976 this figure had declined to 41 per cent. This trend has continued since then. In a Gallup poll conducted in May 1985, a mere 27 per cent rated television's influence on family life as good, compared to 51 per cent who considered it not good. Over half of those who were critical of television cited its violent content as their main reason. Other reasons given were its mindless content and interference with family life. (*The Ottawa Citizen,* July 29, 1985, A1)

Meyrowitz undertakes to integrate two bodies of literature. The first is what he calls "medium theory," which is the study of the impact of a given medium of communication *as a medium.* This is in contrast to the "effects school," which studies the effects of message content and treats different media as if they were neutral delivery systems. (The two most important medium theorists are considered to be Innis and McLuhan.) The second body of literature is what is called "situation theory," which is the study of how behaviour is shaped by social situations. The main contributor in this regard has been Erving Goffman, author of *Strategic Interaction* (1969) and *Frame Analysis* (1974) among other works. According to Meyrowitz, these two literatures have had opposite shortcomings. On the one hand, the medium theorists have failed to consider the effects of different media on everyday behaviour, especially face-to-face behaviour. On the other hand, the situationists have failed to treat situations dynamically and have focused almost exclusively on face-to-face interaction. By fusing the two, therefore, Meyrowitz hopes to show how different mass media have changed patterns of social behaviour over time.

The starting point for this analysis is the concept of a social situation. As we proceed through life, we move from one "situation" to another.

These are easier to illustrate than to define. Listening to a lecture is a social situation; so too is going to a party, attending a funeral, having a job interview, getting married, visiting the doctor, and so on. Unlike purely private situations, social situations shape and modify our behaviour. They do so, according to Meyrowitz, because each involves (1) a set of *roles* to be played by the participants; (2) a set of culture-bound *rules* governing those roles; and (3) an *agenda* or normal sequence of events within a situation. We are constantly forced to alter our behaviour as we move from one social situation to another. For what is considered to be appropriate behaviour in one situation is often totally inappropriate in a different situation. Socialization is essentially the process of learning the situational definitions of one's culture.

Our ability to separate one situation from another often serves as a psychological shock absorber. For example, once off duty, a doctor can temporarily leave behind his concern about a dying patient. Failure to do so would deprive him of an opportunity to revitalize his own energy and undermine his performance while on duty. But what is it that defines the boundaries of a social situation? According to Meyrowitz, it not simply the physical setting of the situation but the pattern of information flow. In particular, a situation is defined in terms of those who have access to the flow of information. For example, if television is added to a court-room, persons outside would have access to the proceedings inside. The situation of a trial being conducted would thus not be confined to the court-room itself. (Given the legal terminology used, persons within the court-room might not be part of the entire situation.)

According to Meyrowitz, access to information determines group identity, socialization, and hierarchy. Group membership arises out the information that certain persons share in common; becoming part of a group consists of gaining access to that information according to established practices; and holding a position of authority within a group depends on having greater access to information in comparison with other members of the group. This is why those in power try to protect and control information and knowledge. It is also why new media are such a potentially explosive force for change. Their introduction can shatter existing patterns of group identity, socialization, and hierarchy. By altering the pattern of information flow, a new medium changes the boundaries of situations themselves.

In addition to the concept of a social situation, Meyrowitz also borrows Goffman's description of social life as a kind of drama in which each person plays various roles on different stages. He suggests that in the same way that we distinguish between the frontstage and backstage actions of the participants in a play, we can also distinguish between the "front region" and "back region" behaviour of everyday life. Front region behaviour occurs when we perform a relatively ideal conception of a role in a given social situation in accordance with conventional expectations; back region behaviour occurs in isolation from our "audience" when we simply relax after a "performance" or learn and rehearse a certain role behind the scenes. In the "back region," we often develop strategies for behaving in the "front region."

It frequently happens that the boundaries of a social situation break down. Someone acts inappropriately (*e.g.* a doctor asks a patient for advice) or information "leaks" from one situation to another (*e.g.* an intercom is accidentally left on). However, these disruptions are usually temporary; the old boundaries are usually restored before too long. But what happens, Meyrowitz asks, if something causes a permanent breakdown? Two possibilities are examined in this regard. On the one hand, there are cases where two previously distinct situations are merged (*e.g.* a professor drops in on a student party). In such cases, it becomes necessary to develop what Meyrowitz calls "middle region" behaviour; that is, a mixture of "front region" and "back region" behaviour. On the other hand, there are cases where a situation is divided, as when teenagers move away from home. In such cases, there tends to develop both a "deep back" region, where behaviour is freer, coarser, and more idiosyncratic, and a "forefront" region, where behaviour is even more pristine and polished.

With the aid of these distinctions, Meyrowitz proceeds to compare the different effects of the print and broadcast media, especially books and television. He argues that print media have a "front region" bias; they deal with formal, front region messages. They present crafted, stylized messages, an idealized image of events. Moreover, because a relatively high degree of skill is necessary to encode and decode their messages, access is closely related to age, education, and even wealth. Print media thus foster separate information systems and elitism. The electronic media, by contrast, have a "back region" bias. They blur the distinction between public and private behaviour and invade the privacy of groups and hierarchies. When we watch part of a union meeting, political conference, or hostage taking on television, we often see union leaders, politicians, and the police engaging in "back region" behaviour. Because of this, it is much easier to decode and encode electronic media messages. There are fewer restrictions based on age, education, or social status, especially in terms of decoding expressive or non-verbal messages.

The emergence of electronic media is thought to have had two general effects. First, it has democratized access to information and thereby broken down discrete information systems. Lay persons and even children can decode non-verbal electronic messages just as effectively as "experts" since everyone has access to the same information. Secondly, it has had a levelling effect on communications competence. The ability to communicate on television is not closely related to group identity, socialization, or authority. A child can communicate on television as effectively as a military commander. As a result, we treat those in high places as if they were our peers.

Meyrowitz suggests that the democratization of access to the media has blurred the distinction between childhood and adulthood, contributed to the feminist movement, and made it more difficult for politicians to manipulate public opinion. Children have been exposed through television to the same harsh realities as adults. Women have come to see (albeit indirectly) that there is no reason why they cannot fulfill roles previously reserved for men. Politicians have been forced to communicate in situations in which the public also has non-verbal clues as to their sincerity. Television has made it more difficult for politicians to say one thing to one audience and something else to another (though many still try).

While this brief summary does not do justice to Meyrowitz's analysis, it does suggest a number of weaknesses in his position. By taking books as his main example of a print medium, he ignores the way in which newspapers and magazines break down discrete information systems through the popularization of knowledge. Moreover, while it is perhaps true that children can decode non-verbal messages as easily as adults, it is questionable how far this enables them to understand a political debate or a public affairs program. Our ability to understand electronic messages depends not only on what is said but on our capacity to put it into context. This in turn depends to a considerable degree on our print media experience.

It is also questionable whether Meyrowitz's analysis takes sufficient account of the development of computerized information systems. Computers are electronic in appearance, but in terms of the skill level required to use them, they are closer to traditional print media. They create discrete information systems once again and eliminate non-verbal behaviour from human interaction. Moreover, while the costs of personal computers and computer software are falling rapidly, they are still quite expensive compared to television for the average person. The costs of accessing computerized information systems are also far from negligible.

Position C — The Anxious Technophobe

The development of computers has led to a phenomenal growth of public and private databases containing information about individual citizens. In most cases, this has been collected without their awareness and has been used without their consent. There are obviously many legitimate uses for such information banks, but the potential for abuse remains. As Professor David Flaherty has pointed out, "one of the prime risks facing any person is that data about him or her will be collected and used in decision making but are in fact erroneous or poorly substantiated." (Flaherty, 1985)

In the fall of 1985, for example, Ontario landlords announced that they were setting up a central computer bank containing personal information on tenants. Among the information to be included were tenants' social insurance numbers, driver's licence numbers, and complaints lodged by previous landlords. The stated purpose of the data bank was to allow landlords to spot potentially troublesome tenants in advance. However, given that it was the idea of the Landlords Against Rent Control, a group representing Ontario landlords, tenants groups naturally suspected that it might be used to create a blacklist of tenants who lobby for rent controls. (Kennedy, 1985: A1) Given the growing evidence of computerized blacklists (*e.g.* Burnham, 1983), their suspicion was by no means groundless.

Another major concern of anxious technophobes is the impact of new communications technology on work and the work-force. In May of 1984, the Ontario government set up a task force on employment and new technology co-chaired by Bob White, director of the United Auto Workers, and William Boggs, chairman of de Havilland Aircraft of Canada Ltd. In a report submitted in October of 1985, the task force concluded that there is no evidence that new technology will reduce employment in Ontario in the next decade. It argued that there is a false perception that technological change is a major factor behind overall unemployment problems. But this viewpoint is not shared by all of those who have investigated the information revolution. Halina acknowledges that computers may create as many as 50,000 jobs in hardware and software industries in Canada. But he estimates that they may also displace as many as 500,000 white-collar workers. (Halina, 1981: 281)

Apart from the question of employment, there is the matter of job satisfaction. While computers have freed many workers from the drudgery of pushing paper, they have provided a new form of slavery for others. Apart from the growing evidence of a variety of health problems related to the sustained use of VDTs, there is a new form of stress in many jobs arising from the use of computers to monitor workers. Telephone operators, airline ticket agents, data-entry operators, and other workers using computers or electronic equipment are being watched over by the very instruments that supposedly help to set the worker free. For the last six years, for example, data-entry operators at OHIP offices across Ontario have been electronically monitored to see that they meet a quota of 11,400 keystrokes an hour (approximately 60 words a minute). As one operator noted: "It's a mind game. You're always conscious of the computer ticking. It's like Big Brother is watching." (Defalco, 1985: A1)

The anxious technophobe also raises a number of other concerns. Technophiles often argue that telidon-type systems will lead to a higher level of participatory democracy, whereas anxious technophobes question whether this will be genuine participation. They also point to the dangers of extra-legal and terrorist activities involving computers and satellites. The

October 1986 issue of *Mother Jones* suggested that a terrorist could start a nuclear war by jamming military satellites. While this is highly unlikely, the possibility certainly exists for disgruntled hackers to disrupt transmissions on civilian satellites. (Rogers and Risinger, 1986: 56)

Position D — The Desperate Technophobe

A good example of a desperate technophobe is the French social philospher, Jacques Ellul. In *The Technological Society* (1954), Ellul argued that Western societies are governed by an omnivorous force which he called *la technique.* This concept, which is best left untranslated since it is not equivalent to technology in the normal sense, is explained in a variety of ways. But it can be defined most simply as the modern obsession with absolute efficiency. It is the compulsion to adopt the most efficient way of doing things regardless of other consequences. This compulsion is, of course, closely related to the development of technology; indeed, it forms a symbiotic relationship with it. We adopt technology to increase efficiency; technology in turn strengthens the desire for efficiency generally.

The point which Ellul stresses about *la technique* is that it is not regarded merely as one value among many; rather it has become the prime value of modern society, superseding all other values. If, for example, efficiency comes in conflict with justice, or individuality or enjoyment, it is the latter that almost invariably give way. It is for this reason that technology proceeds as if it has a will of its own. Whenever a new technology appears that promises greater efficiency, there is no question that it will be implemented, regardless of the possible costs in terms of employment, job satisfaction, and so forth. The report by the Ontario Task Force on employment and technology exemplified this attitude when it said that external factors such as trade policy and competitiveness "really leave little choice between adopting [technology] or not adopting it; it has to be done." (Canadian Press, 1985: A5)

The problem is not simply that the collective social commitment to efficiency tramples over other values. It is also that, paradoxically, it often leads to inefficiency. The reason for this is that narrow, short-term criteria are usually used to assess efficiency. For example, it may be more efficient for many industries to replace some of their workers with computerized robots. But then society must cope with the inefficiency of higher unemployment, including the need for a larger bureaucracy to handle social welfare and larger police forces to deal with crime. In the case of the production of news, Ellul argued that *la technique* has given rise to a desire for steady increases in the volume, speed, and circulation of information distributed. The assumption is that democracy will function better if more people know more things more quickly. But according to Ellul, the tremendous volume of information to which the citizen is exposed has weakened rather than enhanced democracy. The unrelenting flood of news to which we are exposed has led to the effacement of human memory and a failure to perceive the real problems of society.

Ellul had in mind the traditional news media. But there is no doubt he would have been alarmed by the growth of computerized information networks, which are generating information at an exponentially increasing rate. Moreover, he is not alone in believing that our ability to assimilate and use this information is not keeping pace. There is a growing concern about "information overload." It is interesting to recall that back in the 1930s, sociologists Robert Merton and Paul Lazarsfeld discovered that when they exposed experimental animals to very high levels of information content over a long period of time, the animals became increasingly apathetic, lost their appetite and sexual drive, and eventually died. (Pelton, 1983: 61) We may not have reached quite so desperate a plight, but there are no doubt times when we can empathize with the animals in question. The problem, of course, is that information is not equivalent to understanding. And ironically, too much information can actually impede the growth of understanding. Often we would gladly know a little less if we could understand a little more.

Those who are concerned about information overload point out how it can become a means of control. By bombarding people with an excess of extraneous information, governments could supposedly deter effective political action. It remains to be seen, however, whether the computer will become our friend or foe in this and other respects. Information overload is not a function of the sheer amount of information; rather it refers to the individual's being overwhelmed by information. The computer could conceivably become an effective filtering or screening device, enabling us to receive only as much information as we need and can absorb. It could help us not only to process and analyze information but also to control the rate of information intake.

References

Bell, Daniel
    1973 *The Coming of Post-Industrial Society: A Venture in Social Forecasting.* New York: Basic Books.
    1983 "Communication Technology — For Better or Worse?" In Jerry L. Salvaggio (ed.), *Telecommunications: Issues and Choices for Society.* New York: Longman.

Bellamy, Edward
    1976 *Looking Backward 2000-1887.* Cambridge, Mass.: Belknap Press. Edited with an introduction by John L. Thomas.

Benamou, Michel
    1980 "Notes on the Technological Imagination." In Teresa de Lauretis, Andreas Huyssen, and Kathleen Woodward (eds.), *The Technological Imagination: Theories and Fictions.* Madison, Wisconsin: Coda Press.

Burnham, David
    1983 *The Rise of the Computer State.* New York: Random House.

Canadian Press, The
    1985 "New technology won't reduce jobs, govt. report says." *The Ottawa Citizen* (October 9): A5

Czitrom, Daniel J.
    1982 *Media and the American Mind: From Morse to McLuhan.* Chapel Hill: University of North Carolina Press.

Delfalco, Jane
    1985 "Computer watchdogs persecuting workers, causing illness: unions." *The Ottawa Citizen* (September 27): A1, A17.

Dupuy, Jean-Pierre
    1980 "Myths of the Information Society." In Kathleen Woodward (ed.), *The Myths of Information: Technology and Postindustrial Culture.* Madison, Wisconsin: Coda Press.

Eisenstein, Elizabeth L.
    1979 *The Printing Press as an Agent of Change: Communications and Cultural Transformations in Early-Modern Europe.* 2 vols., New York: Cambridge University Press.

Faulkner, Peter (ed.)
    1973 *William Morris: The Critical Heritage.* London: Routledge and Kegan Paul.

Flaherty, David H.
  1985 "Protection of privacy is basic to maintaining our freedom."
    The Ottawa Citizen (September 18): A10.
Halina, J. W.
  1980 "Communications and the Economy: A North American Per-
    spective." *International Social Science Journal* 32: 264-82.
Kennedy, Mark
  1985 "Landlords to keep files on tenants." *The Ottawa Citizen*
    (November 4): AI, A13.
Madden, John
  1982 "Simple Notes on a Complex Future." In David Godfrey and
    Douglas Parkhill (eds.), *Gutenberg Two: The New Electronics
    and Social Change.* Toronto: Porcepic.
Mandeville, Thomas
  1983 "The Spatial Effects of Information Technology." *Futures* 15
    (no. 1): 65-72.
Masuda, Yoneji
  1981 *The Information Society as Post-Industrial Society.* Tokyo: In-
    stitute for the Information Society.
Meyrowitz, Joshua
  1985 *No Sense of Place: The Impact of Electronic Media on Social
    Behavior.* New York: Oxford University Press.
Pelton, Joseph N.
  1983 "Life in the Information Society." In Jerry L. Salvaggio (ed.),
    Telecommunications: Issues and Choices for Society. New York:
    Longman.
Pool, Ithiel de Sola
  1983 *Technologies of Freedom.* Cambridge, Mass.: Belknap Press.
Rogers, Michael and Brad Risinger
  1986 "Uplinks and high jinks." *Newsweek* (September 29): 56-57.
Smith, Gerald W. and Jerry D. Debenham
  1983 "Mass Producing Intelligence for a Rational World." *Futures 15
    (no. 1): 33-46.*
Telecommission Directing Committee
  1971 *A Report on Telecommunications in Canada.* Ottawa: Informa-
    tion Canada.
Toffler, Alvin
  1980 *The Third Wave.* New York: Alfred A. Knopf.
Wagar, Warren
  1961 *H. G. Wells and the World State.* New Haven: Yale University
    Press.

Warskett, George
  1981 "The Information Economy in Late Capitalism." In Liora
       Salter (ed.), *Communication Studies in Canada.* Toronto:
       Butterworths.
Wells, H. G.
  1905 *A Modern Utopia.* London: Chapman and Hall.
Williams, Frederick
  1982 *The Communications Revolution.* Beverly Hills: Sage
       Publications.

Chapter 7

What Should Be the Basis of Canadian Communications and Cultural Policy?

On Saturday, August 16, 1986, *The Ottawa Citizen* published an essay entitled "Bogeyman: the U.S. 'threat' to our culture." It was written by Marion Daniel Bailey, who had retired from the American government in 1984 and was currently working as a consultant in Ottawa. Intended as a contribution to the debate over free trade and culture, it provoked an intemperate response. For Bailey argued that the fear that Canadian culture "is being swallowed by the massive, dark and yawning jaws of U.S. culture" is based upon a misconception of culture. American media products, he asserted, "have no influence on the basic fabric of the culture of Canada or of any other country, just as Canadian or other electronic and tape transmissions have no influence on the American culture." (p. B3)

A few weeks later, *The Ottawa Citizen* published several letters responding to Bailey's essay. "Congratulations to *The Citizen* on increasing the size of your daily joke to the half-page allotted to Marion Daniel Bailey," wrote one angry reader. "Protests about cultural imperialism will probably go on so long as people like Mr. Bailey demonstrate that they do not know what all the fuss is about." "Canadian culture is at risk in free-trade talks," began another, "and we don't need Marion Daniel Bailey, an ex-patriate American, however lofty his credentials, to define what Canadian culture is, or should be." (*The Ottawa Citizen,* September 8, 1986: A9)

Several months earlier, journalist Robert Fulford lamented on a segment of the CBC radio program "Morningside" that the issue of free trade was deflecting attention from other important aspects of cultural policy. But the free trade controversy no doubt helped to make many Canadians more aware of the problem of preserving a distinct national identity. Items on cultural policy began to find their way onto the front pages of newspapers. Radio programs such as "Morningside" devoted substantial time to its discussion. Even the Canadian Senate became concerned; on December 4, 1985, it held a special debate on cultural sovereignty, which ran until 2:00 a.m. the next morning. "No matter what kind of economic partnership Canada and the United States eventually enter into," journalist Carol Goar wrote ten days later, "the next two or three years will be one of the most stimulating periods of soul-searching this country has ever

165

been through." (Goar, 1985: B2) Reprinted with permission — The Toronto Star Syndicate.

The free-trade controversy began about five months after the election of the Progressive Conservatives led by Brian Mulroney in September of 1984. "Free trade is terrific until the elephant twitches," Mulroney had said during the 1983 leadership campaign. "And if it ever rolls over you're a dead man. We will have none of it." (Turner, 1986: H3) After being elected Prime Minister, however, Mulroney reversed his position and began to argue that Canada's economic future depended upon free trade with the United States. External Affairs Minister Joe Clark was given overall responsibility for free-trade talks, and Simon Reisman was hired to serve as Canada's chief negotiator.

Initially, the protection of Canadian culture was not seen by the government as a major problem raised by the concept of free trade. Indeed, when fears were first expressed that Canada's cultural heritage might be compromised by a free trade deal, they were impatiently dismissed by Trade Minister Jim Kelleher. Instead of alleviating public concern, however, government statements tended to increase suspicion and uneasiness. Although Mulroney declared that Canada's "cultural identity" was not up for negotiation, he did not rule out the possibility that certain cultural programs and policies might be. Moreover, his External Affairs Minister seemed to confirm that this would be the case.

During a speech in New York in November of 1985, Clark stated that "direct financial support" from the government for the so-called cultural industries would not be "on the table." But he neglected to say anything about the various indirect subsidies and protective measures that are used to bolster culture in Canada. The implication was that he might be prepared to use these to bargain for greater access for Canadian cultural products to the American market. The argument that Canada should discuss cultural matters with the United States with an eye to increased access to its market was reiterated by Clark at a meeting of cultural leaders organized by the government later the same month.

The cultural leaders who met with Clark were not impressed by this line of reasoning. As one representative said afterwards: "Joe Clark's concern has been trying to get access to the American market. Our concern is getting access to our own market." "Everyone is interested in expanding into the U.S. but only after we've repatriated our own culture." (Cleroux, 1985: A4) "Free trade in cultural products?" TV Ontario chairman Bernard Ostry asked a couple of months later. " 'Our' cultural industries already belong to the other side, with few exceptions. Only those that are unequivocably our own could reasonably be put on the table. Otherwise, the issue will be ludicrous: whether to accept foreign domination from within or from outside." (Ostry, 1986: A7)

This viewpoint was shared by a group of cultural industry leaders who decided about this time to form a "cultural communications industries strategy committee" to "make certain that the interests of cultural industries were properly represented in any free-trade negotiations." (Young, 1986: C8) The committee stated that it was not opposed to free trade as an option for *other* industries in Canada. But it was against free trade in the cultural sphere. It also rejected the idea that free trade might give Canada's cultural industries access to the huge United States market.

Several other developments cast doubt on the government's commitment to a strong and consistent set of cultural policies. In the spring of 1986, for example, despite strenuous opposition from the cultural community, the giant American corporation Gulf and Western was allowed to take over the publishing house Prentice-Hall of Canada, albeit with a few minor concessions. During the summer, the Canadian book publishing industry suffered an additional blow when a ten per cent tariff was hastily imposed on books imported from the United States in partial retaliation for an American tariff on Canadian cedar shakes and shingles. The main effect of the book tariff was to reduce the revenues of a number of Canadian companies involved in the book trade without inflicting any appreciable damage on the United States.

The recent free-trade controversy is not the only reason that the basis of Canadian cultural policy needs to be carefully considered. The exposure to American media products has always made Canadian culture vulnerable to absorption by the United States. The free-trade debate has merely served to point out that some Canadian politicians and bureaucrats still have an inadequate grasp of the essential role of the state in fostering Canadian culture. To some extent, indeed, there seems to have been a declining awareness of the fact that culture, like transportation or education, cannot exist in Canada without a state-supported infrastructure. Some Americans have argued, in effect, that the creation of this infrastructure is an indirect tariff on trade. This is equivalent to arguing that the building of roads or schools is a form of trade tariff.

Even without free-trade negotiations, it would still be imperative to re-examine the basis of cultural policy making in Canada. For there are many longstanding inconsistencies and irrational practices in Canadian cultural policy. For example, although the CBC was created specifically to provide Canadians with homegrown programs, it still spends millions of taxpayers' dollars every year buying expensive American programs that would in most cases be available on other networks. Despite the existence of a special fund and tax provisions to stimulate the production of Canadian films, there are no policies to ensure the distribution of such films to Canadian audiences. And as already mentioned, the recent tariff on books imported from the United States weakens the financial basis of Canadian publishers who use revenues derived from the sale of foreign books to publish Canadian ones.

What these examples make clear is that cultural policy is closely related to communications policy. For both are intimately bound up with the production and flow of information and ideas. This is not to say that the two are identical. There are some aspects of cultural policy, such as learning about our heritage in the schools, that are not directly related to communications policy. Similarly, there are some areas of communications policy, such as the technical management of the radio spectrum, that do not touch directly upon culture. In the Canadian context, nonetheless, cultural policy and communications policy are inextricably interwoven. It is impossible to think for long about the one without being forced to think about the other.

The close relationship between cultural and communications policy has not always been reflected in Canadian institutional arrangements. For the first decade or so after the creation of the federal Department of Communications by the Trudeau government in 1969, arts and culture remained part of the portfolio of the Secretary of State. The Department of Communications concentrated on the development of faster and more efficient delivery systems without worrying too much about their impact on Canadian culture. As George Galt observed, "much attention was paid to wires, cables, transmitters, and receivers, but little thought was given to the messages they might carry." (Galt, 1983: 18) Not until 1980 was responsibility for "cultural industries" such as film and book publishing transferred from the Secretary of State to the Department of Communications.

How we conceive of the relationship between culture and communication depends in part on our understanding of communication. The message-making concept of communication that dominated early Department of Communications thinking led naturally to the view that culture is a product that prospers according to how well it is disseminated. If American culture thrives globally, it is because it successfully exploits the space-biased media of our age. From this perspective, the challenge for Canadian culture is to keep itself on the leading edge of new communications technologies such as cable and satellites. If, on the other hand, we identify communication less with mere message making and more with honest exchanges of ideas, then the role of communication in stimulating culture is likely to be approached more in terms of institutional arrangements than technology.

The relationship that we see between communication and culture also depends, however, on how we conceive of culture. In this regard, the situation is no less complicated than in the case of the concept of communication. In *Culture: A Critical Review of Concepts and Definitions* (1952), Alfred L. Kroeber and Clyde Kluckhohn analyzed no fewer than 160 English definitions of culture. According to Howard Brotz, the term 'culture' originated in German thought in the eighteenth century to replace the phrase "way of life." (Brotz, 1980: 42) The first English-language definition was offered by the British anthropologist Edward B. Tylor in 1871; he defined culture as "that complex whole which includes knowledge, belief, art, morals, law, custom and any other capabilities and habits acquired by man as a member of society." (Rocher, 1985: 456) Since then there have been many refinements and variations of this definition. In general, however, anthropologists have regarded culture as encompassing all of the various ways of thinking, feeling, and behaving that the members of a society share in common. It was on the basis of this definition of culture that Bailey argued that "cultures are not easily overthrown (governments are often more quickly revolutionized) because they represent the sturdy psychic infrastructure of the life-long criteria, persuasions and practices of a people." (Bailey, 1986: B3)

The anthropological definition of culture is not irrelevant to media studies, but it is not the definition that has underlain most of the discussion of the media and culture in the United States. In addressing the question of the impact of the mass media on culture, most American researchers have identified culture with the various arts and some forms of entertainment. Or to put the matter more formally, culture consists of artistic and literary interpretations of the beliefs, values, and purposes of society. From this perspective, the cultural content of newer media such as paperbacks and television is considered by many to have debased the cultural coinage of modern society by catering to the needs and capacities of the lowest common denominator. For others, however, the mass media have raised cultural standards overall by making the arts and letters available to the public to an unprecedented degree.

In an innovative article entitled "The Great Debate on Cultural Democracy" (1961), Bernard Berelson constructed a representative discussion of the impact of the mass media on culture between Academicus (an elitist critic), Practicus (a media practitioner), and Empiricus (a social science researcher). His imaginary debate still makes for interesting reading, but it is worth noting that Berelson himself thought that it was time for Americans to shift their attention to other considerations about the media and culture. One such consideration, about which Americans had not been particularly concerned to that point in time, was obviously the impact of their own media products on other cultures. To study this topic adequately, however, we need to consider at least one additional way of understanding culture.

In *Einstein's Space and Van Gogh's Sky* (1982), Lawrence LeShan and Henry Margenau write that "of those attempts at the organization of reality made by its artists, each culture selects some as 'successful' and rejects others. What the culture selects then helps shape that culture." (p. 184) Modifying this idea slightly, we might say that what a society chooses to recognize from among the available literary and artistic constructions of reality does not merely contribute to its culture, but does, in the final analysis, *constitute* its culture. From this standpoint, the important thing about culture is that it is created by the *joint* action of a society and its intellectual and artistic community.

In other words, to become part of a society's culture, an interpretation of reality (*e.g.* a painting, a novel, a play, a musical composition, a sculpture, a film, a radio or television drama) must be recognized as having meaning for that society. It is not enough simply for it to be produced. It must be given a certain status by the society to whose experiences it supposedly relates. Many attempts to find meaning, value, or order in the life of a society fall by the wayside as irrelevant. Only a few — the paintings of the Group of Seven, the radio drama "Jake and the Kid", the television series "La famille Plouffe", the film "Mon oncle Antoine", the comedy of Wayne and Shuster, the historical writings of Pierre Berton, the early songs of Gordon Lightfoot, and so on — strike a chord within a country's consciousness and become part of its culture.

Two Canadian scholars have suggested that culture consists of "a shared symbolic blueprint which guides action on an ideal course and gives life meaning." (Roberts and Clifton, 1982: 89) The most conscious influences on this blueprint emanate from the realm of art, including music, literature, and dance. But certain non-artistic activities also help to give a society a sense of meaning or purpose and can thus be considered part of its culture. Comedy, for instance, constitutes culture when it is based upon certain values shared by a society. This approach to culture still excludes many kinds of thought and behaviour. The inferiority complex from which Canadians are often alleged to suffer would not be considered part of Canadian culture. On the other hand, the devotion to ice hockey might be regarded as a cultural form insofar as it helps Canadians relate to their harsh northern environment.

Culture does not encompass the entire pattern of thought and behaviour within a society. Nor does it even include all attempts within a society to find meaning, value, or a sense of order. Rather it consists of those efforts to find purpose and organization that are selected by a society as meaningful and relevant to its experience. Thus, as LeShan and Margenau note, a painter who imitated Rembrandt would not produce something to which a modern society could relate, no matter how good his work was. We might admire Rembrandt's art as part of another culture, but that does not make it part of our culture, no matter how many of his paintings we hang in our galleries.

From this perspective, what is dangerous about the endless flood of American media products into Canada is not so much that it will change our way of life or corrupt our cultural values. Rather the threat lies in the way that it deprives Canadians of the opportunity to create their own culture. As we have said, Canadian culture is created not simply by those who produce its interpretations of reality, but also by those who purchase the art, buy the books, listen to the music, and watch the television programs in which these interpretations are expressed. To the extent that Canadians spend their time and money consuming foreign cultural products, they lose the opportunity to participate in the creation of their own culture. The choices that Canadians make among American cultural products have little or no effect on American culture. That culture is determined first and foremost by the choices that Americans make.

At present, about three-quarters of all television programs viewed by English-speaking Canadians are American. In the case of drama, about 98 per cent are American. The number of feature films made by Canadians has increased substantially during the last decade, but many of these are produced with an American audience in mind. In any event, film distribution remains largely in American hands, so that over 95 per cent of the films shown in Canada are American. In the recording field, the situation is only moderately better; about 85 per cent of the records and tapes made in Canada are based on imported master tapes. In the case of books, about 75 per cent of book sales in Canada are of foreign books, while over 80 per cent of the publishing industry is in foreign hands. By 1981 there were some 5000 Canadian periodicals and magazines with a total one-issue circulation of 71 million. But despite these figures, more than 75 per cent of the magazines sold on Canadian news-stands are still American.

It is easier to describe the problem facing Canadian culture than it is to propose a solution. The government does not have unlimited resources at its disposal to stimulate cultural growth. Some kinds of action that might appear promising on paper would not be politically feasible, while others might lead to retaliation by the United States. In what follows, therefore, we shall look at the main policy approaches that are available to the government with an eye to narrowing the field to those which are the most appropriate in the Canadian context.

Policy formulation involves a series of interrelated tasks. The first thing that must be done is to establish a set of general objectives. Sometimes, after a policy has been in place for many years, the original purpose behind it is forgotten. It continues to operate, but without necessarily accomplishing what it was intended to do. Only by reconsidering the ends which it is supposed to serve can its appropriateness be ascertained. In addition to setting objectives, it is also necessary to establish priorities in the event of conflicts among the various ends being pursued. The communications system is meant to serve not only cultural endeavours but also political, economic, and social activities. But at times these may make competing demands upon it. A desire on the part of the market-place for more advertising space or time, for example, might conflict with the requirements for properly presenting certain cultural products. Working out priorities seldom consists of making one objective entirely secondary to another. In most cases, it involves an attempt to find ways of accommodating all objectives to a reasonable degree.

Having specified the ends to be served by a policy, the next task is to examine empirical research and theoretical perspectives pertaining to their accomplishment. Policy formulation does not exist in isolation from historical and social science studies. On the contrary, it uses them as a partial basis for deciding between various policy options. To take a simple hypothetical example, the architects of a new urban transportation policy might propose as objectives better service and reduced costs for taxpayers. These goals might conceivably be pursued on the basis of a scientific study concluding that reduced fares would result in increased traffic and that the gains resulting from additional passengers would be greater than the losses caused by fare reduction.

Finally, there is the task of working out specific means to achieve the goals which have been set. Steven Globerman has provided a useful catalogue of the main tools available to governments in the formulation of policies. These range from direct intervention in the form of public ownership (*e.g.* the CBC, TV Ontario, Radio-Québec) or joint public-private ownership (*e.g.* Telesat Canada) to indirect techniques such as negotiation and moral persuasion. Between these extremes are various other possible instruments, such as grants and subsidies, tax exemptions, loans or loan guarantees, and regulation. In general, the more direct the instrument is, the more effective it is likely to be. At the same time, however, the most direct mechanisms are also the most politically dangerous, which is why governments often prefer regulation and exhortation. (Globerman, 1983: 7-8)

A policy model integrates certain objectives, empirical and theoretical assumptions, and preferred tools into a consistent way of dealing with particular policy issues. In "Culture and the State" (1984), Thelma McCormack has identified four cultural policy models: the market model, the welfare model, the nationalist model, and the post-nationalist model. For the most part, these can be applied to communications policy or, at least, to the area of communications policy that overlaps cultural policy. They can also be analyzed in terms of the double polarity format used in the other chapters of this book. What follows, therefore, is an adaptation of McCormack's categories using the double polarity schema. This will help to illuminate the four models in question by clarifying the main points of agreement and disagreement. As with the previous issues which we have discussed, there are several questions which give rise to a polarity of viewpoints about cultural/communications policy. Again, however, only two of these have been selected for the purposes of analysis.

The first question to be considered is whether Canadian national identity is still problematic. Is there a distinct Canadian identity and can we now take it for granted? Or is it still something that we must consciously strive to achieve? Is it as secure as Mr. Bailey would have us believe? Or is it threatened by alien forces whether from within or outside of Canadian society? The second question is whether the emphasis in cultural policy should be on the *production* of cultural goods or on *access* to them. Obviously, each of these concerns should be addressed by cultural policy makers. But in working out a strategy for stimulating cultural growth in Canada, which should receive the most attention? Should we seek to increase the production of Canada's cultural industries and let audiences take care of themselves? Or should we devote our energies to making cultural products more readily available and assume that this will stimulate cultural production?

With the aid of these questions, McCormack's models can be distributed in four quadrants as indicated in Figure 7:

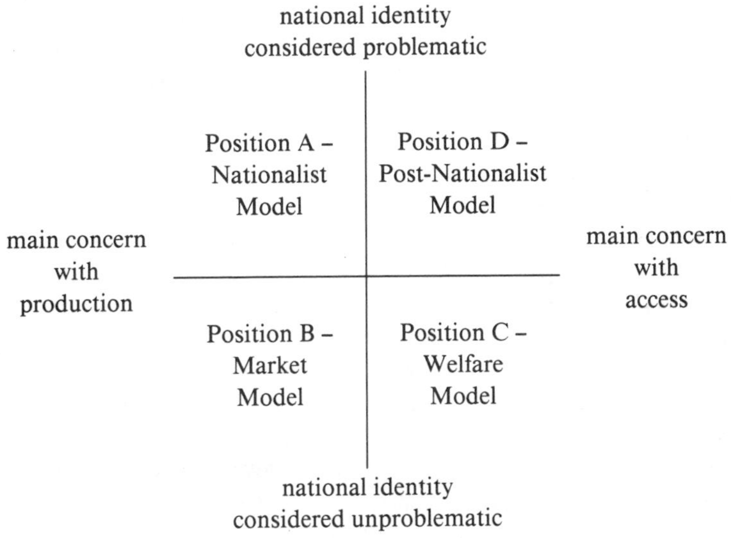

Figure 7

Position A — The Nationalist Model

The nationalist model maintains that Canadian identity is a fragile entity because Canadians are subjected to so many cultural productions reflecting other cultures. It argues that the state must provide a variety of support mechanisms for Canadian cultural products if these are to have a chance to develop. It generally favours mechanisms that keep the government at "arm's length" from the cultural community so that it will have the freedom necessary for maximum creativity. But it also assumes that the state has the right to ensure that its support for culture is used responsibly. What this means, in effect, is that state-supported cultural activities should contribute to the development of the national identity. Otherwise the state has no obligation to continue its support.

The nationalist model of cultural/communications policy underlay the creation of the CBC in 1936 and the establishment of the National Film Board in 1939. But it received its clearest articulation in the report which was tabled in the House of Commons by the Royal Commission on National Development in the Arts, Letters, and Sciences in the spring of 1951. During the Liberal Convention in 1948 to choose a successor to Mackenzie King, the Canadian University Liberal Federation had suggested an enquiry into the cultural resources of the country. The Convention rejected their proposal, but the new Prime Minister, Louis St. Laurent, was persuaded by Brooke Claxton, J. W. Pickersgill, and Lester B. Pearson to establish a royal commission to examine the state of the arts in Canada. In April of 1949, Vincent Massey, who had served as Canadian High Commissioner in London during the Second World War, was appointed chairman of the commission. The other members were Hilda Neatby, a professor of history at the University of Saskatchewan, Georges Henri Levesque of Laval University, Norman A. M. Mackenzie, President of the University of British Columbia, and Arthur Surveyor, a Montreal engineer.

It is important to recall the rather bleak cultural state of the nation as the Massey Commission began its deliberations. There was still no national library or art gallery in Canada. There were only two good museums, the National Museum in Ottawa and the Royal Ontario Museum in Toronto. Canadian universities, which were dependent on private endowments and provincial grants, were in serious financial difficulties. There were no scholarships for students and no research grants for faculty in the humanities and social sciences. Except for a few places like the CBC and NFB, writers, performers, and musicians still had a difficult time finding outlets for their work. Movie houses were controlled by American distributing companies, book publishing was dominated by American interests, and radio stations played mostly American music.

The Massey Commission expressed deep concern about the American domination of Canada's cultural life at a time when few other Canadians seemed to be troubled by it. It acknowledged that the United States had given intellectual and cultural aid to Canada (Canadian scholars, artists, and writers had received considerable support over the years from the Carnegie, Rockefeller, and Guggenheim foundations.) But it argued that Canada's dependence on the cultural resources of the United States had not only eroded its national identity but also frustrated its creative powers.

Until Canadians took steps of their own to stimulate the arts and culture, they would not achieve their full potential.

The Massey Commission concluded that only by means of bold measures would it be possible for Canada to escape from its cultural poverty. It also recognized that these measures would require much more money than could ever come from private Canadian sources. If Canada was to develop a strong and healthy culture of its own, it would have to draw upon the resources of the state. In addition to recommending that the federal government provide financial aid for universities, the Massey Commission proposed that a new body called the Canada Council be created to encourage and promote the cultural interests of the nation. The federal government acted almost immediately on the first of these recommendations. But the second recommendation was ignored until the eve of the federal election of 1957 when St. Laurent, worried about the electoral prospects of the Liberal party, finally approved the creation of the Canada Council. Since then it has awarded thousands of scholarships in the humanities and social sciences and distributed millions of dollars worth of grants to individuals and voluntary associations in the arts and letters.

Between 1957/58 and 1978/79, government expenditures on culture increased 1600 per cent, while increasing only 600 per cent on goods and services. To keep this in perspective, however, two points should be noted. First, the growth in government expenditures on culture outstripped increases in other areas at least in part because there was so much ground to make up. Secondly, expenditures on culture in 1978/79 still constituted only 2.2 per cent of total federal expenditures (only 0.7 per cent if funding for the CBC is excluded). By contrast, 35 per cent of federal monies went to health and welfare, while 11 per cent went to economic development. (Globerman, 1983: 9)

Government support mechanisms for culture have taken a variety of forms. One of the principal means has consisted of tax regulations favouring Canadian cultural products. Since 1974, persons investing in certified Canadian films have been able to claim a Capital Cost Allowance of 100 per cent and even to deduct 50 per cent of the interest on money borrowed to finance their investment. The passage of Bill C-58 in 1975 (now *An Act to Amend the Income Tax Act,* 1974-75-76, c-106) has allowed advertisers to deduct the cost of placing commercials on programs broadcast by Canadian television stations, but not on those shown by American ones. Legislation has also helped to prevent the saturation of the Canadian magazine market by special "Canadian" editions of United States publications such as *Time* and *Reader's Digest.* Canadian advertisers are only allowed to deduct the costs of ads placed in Canadian-owned magazines that produce Canadian material. (Canadian-owned has meant, in effect, 75 per cent Canadian ownership.) This forced the departure of *Time Canada,* enabled

MacLean's to become a weekly Canadian newsmagazine, and encouraged *Reader's Digest* to add more Canadian content.

Under certain conditions, the government has also been willing to provide funds directly to besieged cultural industries. In March of 1980, for example, the Department of Communications created the Canadian Book Publishing Development Program. Its stated purpose was "to render the Canadian book publishing industry financially viable, aware of its cultural roles, capable of acting independently to ensure optimal development of Canadian writers and publishing and effectively distributing the widest possible range of books by Canadian authors in Canada and abroad." To accomplish these grandiose aims, it was given an initial three-year budget of $20 million. During the first year of its operation, it saved a number of Canadian book companies that were on the verge of collapse. However, it was not able to prevent the demise of Virgo Press in 1981 and Clarke, Irwin in 1983.

Despite measures such as these, the overall state of Canada's cultural industries is still far from satisfactory from a nationalist standpoint. The nationalist approach, therefore, would be to institute even stronger government measures to stimulate cultural production. One recent proposal in this regard was made by the Task Force on Film created by Communications Minister Marcel Masse in the fall of 1985. In the report which it submitted in mid-December of the same year, the Task Force recommended that all movies and videos in Canada be distributed by Canadian-owned and controlled companies that would pay "fair market price" for them. This would end the domination of film distribution in Canada by the Hollywood studios. The Task Force said that by controlling the film pipeline, Canadian distributors would have more money to invest in Canadian production, while Canadians would still have access to American movies and video cassettes.

However, the government did not take any immediate action on this proposal. On the contrary, it indicated a distinct lack of sympathy for an aggressively nationalistic approach to culture. The nationalist model of cultural policy is by no means dead. But it has certainly come in for increasing criticism in recent years. According to some critics, it does not take sufficient account of what the market economy can achieve in terms of the production of cultural goods. According to others, the time has come to shift our emphasis from the problem of production to the question of access. Whether these critiques are warranted remains to be seen. But it is clear that the nationalist must refine his case if he is to prevent the further erosion of state support for culture.

Position B — The Market Model

The basic assumption of the market model is that culture should be supported by means of private enterprise as far as possible. The state should intervene with subsidies, regulations, and institutional mechanisms only where there is clear evidence of a failure on the part of the market to provide a reasonable opportunity for culture to flourish. Advocates of this position usually acknowledge that the arts are "meritorious goods" in that they deserve to be fostered even if the market fails to provide for them. But it is stressed that public support for the arts should supplement rather than displace market-place incentives for the production of cultural goods. In other words, nothing should be done to discourage the market from operating to its full capacity.

Market economists such as W. J. Baumol and W. G. Bowen maintain that government support can sometimes be counter-productive. They argue, in particular, that contributions to the arts from the private sector tend to decrease as government subsidies increase. They do not call for the complete elimination of subsidies. But the best subsidy is considered to be one that: "a) does not deviate too far from the market mechanism; b) does not interfere with the possibility of present market failures becoming future market successes; and c) does not compete unfairly with the infant industries in the arts." (McCormack, 1984: 271)

The market model underlies cultural policy in the United States. Although special funds such as the National Endowment for the Arts have been created, most funding for the arts comes from private and corporate philanthropy. Public support for the arts and culture is kept to a minimum. But is this an appropriate approach for countries such as Canada? Would it not return us to the cultural poverty that existed on the eve of the Massey Commission?

Thelma McCormack has suggested that movement away from the nationalist model towards the market model began in Canada with the Federal Cultural Policy Review Committee. Set up in 1981 under the chairmanship of Louis Applebaum and Jacques Hébert, this committee advocated, among other things, that much of the CBC's in-house production be turned over to private production companies. Taken overall, however, the Applebaum-Hébert committee still subscribed to the core assumptions of the nationalist model. It believed in extensive state support for culture and maintained that this should be aimed at fostering an indigenous Canadian culture.

One Canadian policy analyst who has argued for the market model is Steven Globerman. In *Cultural Regulation in Canada* (1983), Globerman deplores the lack of guiding principles for evaluating government intervention into cultural activities in Canada. He adopts the federal government's definition of culture as "the creative and expressive activities generally referred to as the performing, visual and creative arts and those functions related to their preservation and dissemination." (pp. 4-5) He assumes that the government can, quite legitimately, seek to improve the welfare of Canadians by giving support to such activities. But he sets out to "provide a

structure within which hitherto rhetorical arguments for cultural intervention can be made subject to critical examination and hitherto un-
scrutinized government policies in the cultural sector can be critically
evaluated." (Globerman, 1983: 4)

It is not enough, Globerman says, to justify government support for
culture by simply referring to the threat of American cultural imperialism
or the need to preserve Canada's cultural identity. Two conditions should
be met before governments intervene to promote culture. First, it should be
clearly demonstrated that the market is incapable of providing cultural
goods either in sufficient quantity or of adequate quality. Secondly, it
should be demonstrated that the costs of intervention do not outweigh the
costs of the problem. In other words, it is not enough simply to offer proof
of market failure; it must also be shown that government action to rectify
the situation is cost effective.

Most policy analysts would agree with Globerman that the economic
implications of government support for culture need to be carefully evaluated. But this does not mean that cultural goals must be limited to those
that private enterprise chooses to seek. We can set whatever cultural goals
that we wish and then ask to what extent private enterprise would be able to
achieve them. In Canada, this would still probably mean in most cases that
a degree of state support would be necessary to achieve the goals which
have been proposed.

There has been a tendency in recent years for the market model to
sneak in by the back door. In "Selling Canada with culture, not hockey
pucks," for example, Peter Swann, former director of the Royal Ontario
Museum in Toronto, has argued that we should support culture in order to
boost tourism and that the tourist industry should contribute to cultural
institutions. (*The Ottawa Citizen,* February 15, 1986) But once we begin to
justify cultural expenditures in this way, we are likely to lose sight very
quickly of what culture is and why it is worth supporting for its own sake.

Perhaps the main flaw of the market model is that it cannot be safely
tested. The only way to judge what the market would be capable of
achieving on its own would be to dismantle all of the existing support
mechanisms for culture. But should this experiment prove that market
failure does exist, it would be more difficult afterwards to do anything
about it. It could be argued that the only test that needs to be conducted has
already taken place. Except for a few institutions such as the CBC, cultural
production was controlled by the market-place on the eve of the Massey
Commission. The result, as we have seen, was extensive market failure.

Position C — The Welfare Model

The welfare model would appear to be more applicable to countries
like England and France where national identity is taken for granted. It is

based on the assumption that art is a public resource which everyone has a right to share. Because of regional, ethnic, and class barriers, however, some groups do not have adequate access to cultural productions. Government policy should thus be aimed at making cultural products available to all levels of society.

According to one study, only 20 per cent of Canadians attend at least one live performing arts concert in any given year. (Globerman, 1983: 38) If this is correct, there are probably at least three reasons for it. Most performing arts events are too expensive for many Canadians; they are presented in too formal an environment; and they are, in some cases, difficult for the average person to appreciate. To make the performing arts more accessible, therefore, three things might be done. Ticket prices could be subsidized; there could be more emphasis on things like concerts in the park; and greater efforts could be made to educate people about the intricacies of ballet, opera, and so forth. As described by McCormack, the welfare model sees education as the principle means of breaking down class structures that restrict access to culture.

It is at least worth considering whether Canadian culture might flourish more readily if there was more emphasis on providing access to its products. Traditionally, Canadian cultural policy has concentrated on the creation of distinctively Canadian cultural products to compete with those produced in the United States. But it could be argued that by shifting their emphasis to the question of access, policy makers might actually do more to stimulate cultural production than by assisting it directly. This would require imaginative as well as aggressive measures, but it might remove the stigma from the cultural community of being dependent on government handouts. It would also force the reconsideration of policies such as pay television, which siphons off valuable resources in broadcasting for the benefit of the more affluent.

Position D — The Post-Nationalist Model

In presenting his case for the market model, Steven Globerman challenged adherants to the nationalist model to show that cultural intervention actually increases national consciousness. He questioned the nationalist premise that "indigenous cultural output and Canada's national identity are necessarily positively related." (Globerman, 1983: 31) In so doing he was striking at the Achilles heel of cultural nationalism. For it is difficult, if not impossible, to prove that increased spending on culture actually increases national consciousness. The reason for this is not simply that national consciousness cannot be quantified in the way that we can add up expenditures on culture. It is also that Canadians have had great difficulty elucidating the distinctive characteristics of their identity.

The unique identity of Canada, it is often suggested, lies in the extent to which Canadians have embraced the pluralistic ideal of multiculturalism. Unlike the United States, which is said to have been a kind of cultural melting pot, Canada has tried to preserve a cultural mosaic. It is usually acknowledged that this was not always the case. During the nineteenth century, English-speaking Canadians subscribed to what has been called the Loyalist myth; that is, they saw themselves as differing from Americans by virtue of being staunchly British. Between Confederation and the First World War, a number of English-speaking Canadians tried to develop a more indigenous conception of Canada's national identity. They proposed that Canada's northern environment had fostered the development of superior physical, mental, and cultural attributes, including such virtues as hardiness, self-reliance, and individualism. But this new myth of a great northern race, with its assimilative and even racist overtones, was largely discredited by the end of the First World War. It did not take account of significant climatic variations within Canada and was shown by anthropological studies to be without scientific foundation.

After the First World War, however, a different notion of national identity began to emerge. This was the idea of the social or cultural mosaic. The term mosaic was apparently first used in 1922 by Victoria Hayward in *Romantic Canada* to describe the West. Then a few years later Kate Foster wrote a study of the foreign-born in Canada and called it *Our Canadian Mosaic*. She suggested that the existence of a cultural mosaic is not only aesthetically pleasing, but also socially rewarding for Canadians. Gradually the idea took hold, providing a paradoxical but inspirational conception of national identity. It came about, not because the immigrants who flooded into Canada between 1896 and 1914 were actively encouraged to retain their customs, characteristics, and beliefs, but rather because many of them had refused to conform to the existing English-Canadian mould. Nonetheless, it was eventually reflected in many of Canada's social and cultural policies.

In *The Vertical Mosaic* (1965), John Porter showed that the cultural mosaic should be regarded more as an ideal pursued by many Canadians than as an accurate description of Canadian society. But even as an ideal, the concept of the cultural mosaic has had its validity challenged in recent years. It is, according to some Canadians, a distortion of reality to distinguish between the American melting pot and the Canadian mosaic. In "Multiculturalism in Canada: A Muddle" (1980), for example, Howard Brotz maintains that Canadians are of one mind about their fundamental way of life. All ethnic groups in Canada are said to accept the desirability of the bourgeois-democratic way of life with its tolerance of different religions and primary interest in improving the standard of living of the individual and his family.

In "Exploring the Ideology of Multiculturalism" (1982), moreover, Lance W. Roberts and Rodney A. Clifton have argued that "the traditional vision of a Canadian 'mosaic' composed of viable ethnic groups and communities is not credible." (p. 91) Canadian multiculturalism policy assumes that "a variety of cultures can exist without separate social structures." (p. 89) But according to Roberts and Clifton, the structural assimilation of most ethnic groups in Canada makes their eventual cultural assimilation inevitable. The policy of multiculturalism does not permit different cultures to preserve their heritage. It merely promotes symbolic ethnicity; that is, "a love for and pride in a tradition that can be felt without having to be incorporated in everyday behaviour." (p. 90) In other words, different ethnic groups retain a link with their past, but are free to share the benefits of modern society.

These attacks on the policy of multiculturalism also strike at the nationalist model of cultural policy. But this does not entail that we are forced to choose between either the market or the welfare model. It only means that we need to strengthen the case for significant government support for culture. One way of doing this has already been suggested. This consists of altering our definition of culture to refer to the representations of reality that a society has selected as having meaning for itself. When this is done, cultural policy does not have to be defended on the grounds that it somehow stimulates common national characteristics which distinguish Canadians from Americans. It is enough to show that government support is essential for there to be adequate opportunities for Canadians to create and relate to meaningful indigenous interpretations of their own experience.

A second way of transcending the traditional nationalist model is to shift our focus from culture back to communication. This is perhaps the most promising way of working out a new nationalist — or post-nationalist — model that avoids the pitfalls of earlier ones. Put most simply, we do not need to defend support mechanisms for culture on the grounds that they contribute to the development of a distinctively Canadian culture. We can provide a perfectly good defence in terms of their being essential for a reasonable degree of communication among Canadians.

If Canadians possess sufficient means to communicate among themselves, there can be little doubt that they will create a vibrant and original culture. If we strengthen communication, Canadian culture will take care of itself. But at the same time, we need to remember that culture is not the only thing served by communication. Our political, economic, and social systems also depend on Canadian control of the message-making facilities within our country. Nor is culture an adequate focal point for working out a sound communications policy. For communication, as we have seen, also depends on many other things, including a strong journalistic tradition, a large number of media voices, and an appropriate balance between free enterprise and the right of a community to determine its destiny.

References

Audley, Paul
   1983 *Canada's Cultural Industries: Broadcasting, Publishing, Records and Film.* Toronto: Lorimer.
Bailey, Marion Daniel
   1986 "Bogeyman: the U.S. 'threat' to our culture." *The Ottawa Citizen,* (August 16): B3.
Baumol, W. J. and W. G. Bowen
   1976 "Arguments for Public Support of the Performing Arts." In Mark Blaug (ed.), *The Economics of the Arts.* London: Martin Robertson.
Breton, Raymond
   1980 *Cultural Boundaries and the Cohesion of Canada.* Montreal: The Institute for Research on Public Policy.
Brotz, Howard
   1980 "Multiculturalism in Canada: A Muddle." *Canadian Public Policy — Analyse de Politiques* 6 (no. 1): 42-46.
Burnet, Jean
   1978 "The Policy of Multiculturalism Within a Bilingual Framework: A Stock Taking." *Canadian Ethnic Studies* 10: 107-13.
Cleroux, Richard
   1985 "Do not sell out culture, free-trade meeting told." *The Globe and Mail,* Toronto (November 27): A4.
Cook, Ramsay
   1984 "Imagining a North American Garden: Some Parallels and Differences in Canadian and American Culture." *Canadian Literature* 103 (Winter): 10-23.
Crean, Susan M.
   1973 *Who's Afraid of Canadian Culture?* Don Mills: York University.
Federal Cultural Policy Review Committee (Applebaum-Hébert)
   1982 *Report.* Ottawa: Supply and Services.
Galt, George
   1983 "Unscrambling the Future," *Saturday Night* (October), 15*f.*
Globerman, Steven
   1983 *Cultural Regulation in Canada.* Montreal: The Institute for Research on Public Policy.

Goar, Carol
  1985 "In Ottawa, free trade debate revives interest in our identity."
       The Toronto Star (December 14): B2
Handler, Richard
  1984 "On Sociocultural Discontinuity: Nationalism and Cultural
       Objectification in Quebec." *Current Anthropology* 25 (no. 1):
       55-71.
  1985 "Canadian Content and the Nationalism of Applebaum-
       Hébert." *Canadian Public Policy — Analyse de Politiques* 11
       (no. 4): 677-83.
Helwig, David (ed.)
  1980 *Love and Money: The Politics of Culture.* Oberon.
Kroker, A.
  1982 "Cultural Imagination and the National Questions." *Canadian
       Journal of Political and Social Theory* 6 (Winter-spring) 5-11.
Le Shan, Lawrence and Henry Margenau
  1982 *Einstein's Space and Van Gogh's Sky: Physical Reality and
       Beyond.* New York: Macmillan.
McCormack, Thelma
  1984 "Culture and the State." *Canadian Public Policy — Analyse de
       Politiques* 10 (no. 3): 267-77.
Netzer, Dick
  1978 *The Subsidized Muse.* London: Cambridge University Press.
Ostry, Bernard
  1978 *The Cultural Connection: An Essay on Culture and Government
       Policy in Canada.* Toronto: McClelland and Stewart.
  1986 "To have its own culture, Canada must tend its garden." *The
       Globe and Mail,* Toronto, January 23, 1986: A7.
Peter, Karl
  1981 "The Myth of Multiculturalism and Other Political Fables." In
       J. Dahlie and T. Fernando (eds.), *Ethnicity, Power, and Politics
       in Canada.* Toronto: Methuen.
Roberts, Lance W. and Rodney A. Clifton
  1982 "Exploring the Ideology of Multiculturalism." *Canadian Public
       Policy — Analyse de Politiques* 8 (no. 1): 88-94.
Rocher, Guy
  1985 "Culture" In Volume I of *The Canadian Encyclopedia.* Edmon-
       ton: Hurtig.
Swann, Peter
  1986 "Selling Canada with culture, not hockey pucks." *The Ottawa
       Citizen* (February 15): B3.
Turner, Dan
  1986 "Even PMs can change their minds." *The Ottawa Citizen,* (June
       14): H3.

University of Toronto *et al.*
   1984 *Cultures and Collision: The Interaction of Canadian and U.S. Television Broadcast Policies.* New York: Praeger.
Young, Kathryn
   1986 "Group of cultural leaders quietly planning strategy on free trade talks." *The Ottawa Citizen* (Feburary 15): C8.

Index